DESIRE FOR DEVELOPMENT

DESIRE FOR DEVELOPMENT
Whiteness, Gender, and the Helping Imperative

Barbara Heron

Wilfrid Laurier University Press

[WLU]

This book has been published with the help of a grant from the Canadian Federation for the Humanities and Social Sciences, through the Aid to Scholarly Publications Programme, using funds provided by the Social Sciences and Humanities Research Council of Canada. We acknowledge the financial support of the Government of Canada through the Book Publishing Industry Development Program for our publishing activities.

Library and Archives Canada Cataloguing in Publication

Heron, Barbara, 1949–
  Desire for development : whiteness, gender, and the helping imperative / Barbara Heron.

Includes bibliographical references and index.
ISBN 978-1-55458-001-9

  1. Women, White—Developing countries. 2. Women, White—Race identity. 3. Women in development—Developing countries. 4. Power (Social sciences). 5. Economic development—Social aspects. 6. Imperialism. I. Title.

HD82.H434 2007   305.48'9622   C2007-903510-8

Cover design by P.J. Woodland. Text design by Catharine Bonas-Taylor.

In memory of my parents

CONTENTS

ACKNOWLEDGEMENTS

This book would not have been possible without the support of a number of people. Although it draws from my years as a development worker in Zambia, the book's beginning is really traceable to my encounter with Sherene Razack at the Ontario Institute for Studies in Education, University of Toronto, where I did my doctoral studies. I am deeply indebted to Sherene, who became my thesis supervisor. Her critical thinking on race and subjectivity challenged me to conceptualize my part in the development enterprise in new and unsettling terms. Sherene's wisdom, courage, and brilliance continue to inspire me, and her friendship to warm me. Kari Dehli and George Dei, who were members of my thesis committee, have also been enormously important in the development of the original dissertation from which this manuscript has been created. Perhaps only I know how deep are the imprints of all three of these extraordinary scholars on the work, but I do know, and I thank them.

I have been sustained through revisions and the whole publishing process by fast friendships. Sheryl Nestel has been a pillar of strength, to whom I have turned often for advice and encouragement. I have also been buoyed by the confidence directed toward me by Donna Jeffery, Dawn Sutherland, Jane Ku, and Amina Jamal. Tina Martin, her husband Ted Vanderklugt, and their children Brendan and Kyla have made their home my home, and, as through the thesis years, they have supported me with their love. Norma Knuckle's friendship and understanding of development issues has kept me grounded as I worked on this project. Sydia Nduna and Jane Ferguson, based in Geneva and working in the international field, have given me fresh perspectives on international issues and support from afar. Lynn Ann Lauriault and Ann Sutherland, my friends from CUSO-Zambia days, have also kept me mindful of the importance of persevering with the book manuscript. At the School of Social Work, York University, where I work, close friends and colleagues Renita Wong, Amy Rossiter, Grant MacDonald, and Narda Razack have offered intellectual stimulation and shored up my determination to persevere.

My brother, Keith Heron, has evinced confidence in this undertaking all along, and I am more grateful for his support than he can possibly know. My parents would have loved to have seen the thesis become a book. The memory of them has nurtured me through this process.

Research grants have enabled me to do more work to ensure that the manuscript is current. A Social Sciences and Humanities Council of Canada internal York University grant supported me to carry out additional interviews with recently returned development workers in the spring of 2005, and two Atkinson research grants from York University helped me to ascertain changes in the development worker context. Mary Newberry provided needed assistance with the process of editing my thesis into a book. I especially want to express my appreciation to Jacqueline Larson, the former acquisitions editor at Wilfrid Laurier University Press, for her unflagging faith in my project. She has played a crucial role in bringing this book into the world. Lisa Quinn, who replaced Jacqueline, has also helped enormously.

Finally, I need to thank all the women who agreed to be interviewed by me. I could not have written this book without their generous sharing of their development worker experiences in Africa. I saw much of myself in them, and still do. Their words gave theory meaning for me, and became the very stuff of my understanding.

CHAPTER 1
CHALLENGING THE DEVELOPMENT WORK(ER) NARRATIVE

There is a 1989 Canadian film called *The Midday Sun*. It is based on incidents that occurred when a young, white Canadian woman went to live in an unnamed African country as a development worker in the 1970s. In the film, the Canadian woman's domestic employee, an African man, is wrongly charged with theft following a break-in at her home. Married, the father of three children, and the main income-earner in his family, he is sentenced to ten years in prison for a crime he did not commit. Soon after, and for reasons indirectly connected with the theft, the development worker is forced by local authorities to leave the country. On the eve of her departure, she reflects that she could never belong in "their" society, but neither is she any more at home in her own. In a post-screening interview, Lulu Keating, the director whose personal story the film narrates, stated that she had wanted to make a movie about "the most profoundly life-changing experience a person can have." She went on to explain that it is the *Canadian woman* whose life was so profoundly changed.

Since my telling of this story provides only a brief précis, Keating's interpretation of her development work experiences may seem surprising in that she appears to entirely overlook the far more transformative, and devastating, impact of a Canadian woman's sojourn on the lives of an African man, his wife, and their children. It is noteworthy that Keating had held on to this perspective for several years through writing, fundraising for, and directing her film. Yet I would suggest that for many viewers watching as I did *The Midday Sun* on Canadian television one Saturday afternoon in the winter of 1995, the explanation Keating gave in the interview following the film made sense: what *really mattered* to the white Canadian audience was what happened to the Canadian woman. Further, I suspect that Keating's story would especially resonate with Canadian development workers.[1] I say this because I, too, was a development worker. For eleven years (from 1981 to 1992) I lived in Zambia, initially as a volunteer and then as the coordinator of a Canadian non-governmental organization's development program. I recognize the director's reading of this episode in the development worker's life and in her own; it calls to me personally while evoking recollections of similar reactions on the part of Canadians I knew over the years in southern Africa.

Why begin a book about Canadian women's desire to contribute to international development with an "old" film about something that happened over thirty years ago and with reminiscences from the 1980s and 1990s? The answer, in the first instance, is that the brief synopsis of Keating's film encompasses elements of a standard development worker narrative that continues to be reiterated across time and location. Development work still is, as it has been from its inception, axiomatically assumed to be altruistic. It is touted as a "life-changing" experience for *us*, and its constitutive effect on Canadian and other Northern development workers' identities is considered indisputably laudable.[2] The enduringness of these understandings about what it is to do development work is an effect of discourse circulating in Canada about the "Third World"/"developing countries,"[3] "development," and what "we" are doing to or with "them" over "there." Keating's film and commentary operate in and contribute to this discourse in a typical manner. Hence the resonance of her narrative for Canadians who recognize her perspective as a familiar, even shared, one.

The "Third World" or "developing countries" are presented in Canada as places of "suffering, starvation and bloodshed"[4] via persistent magazine and newspaper articles, television programs and news clips, as well as direct-mail and TV fundraising drives by many development organizations. The "Third World" seems to be on the outside of globalization processes.[5] As Pieterse points out, the media age in which we live has the effect of increasing and escalating the Othering that has inhered in various kinds of representations over time, in part because the images received in the North come without historical analysis. They appear, rather, as manifestations of culture, and as such are illustrative of the meaning of Othering in postmodernist theory, where the "Other," or difference from the unmarked norm, is conceptualized as produced through discourses that establish opposition, hierarchy, and exclusion.[6]

Altogether, these images have the effect of (re-)establishing the idea that the South in general and Africa in particular are in need of Northern—in our case, Canadian—interventions. This discourse normalizes our centring of ourselves in relation to other people's needs, not by recognizing how we are implicated in global economic processes of globalization that underlie these needs, but by erasing the agency of local peoples who are Othered in these processes, and by presenting "our" (read white middle-class Northern) knowledge, values, and ways of doing things as at once preferable and right, since the North, especially Canada, appears orderly, clean, and well managed in comparison. In this way our "development gaze," in the words of Longreen, is constructed and directed.[7]

The "Third World" is also familiar to us through literary representations that have produced for us cultural "knowledge" of other parts of the world. In his work on Orientalism, Said has charted this vis-à-vis the Middle East,[8] but such knowledges have been constructed from the colonial era and earlier in respect to all non-European parts of the world and disseminated through literature.[9] The result is the circulation of recurrent tropes in Western discourse that are easily drawn on and, as a consequence, freely reproduced in popular culture. Travel literature is a particular vehicle for this operation, since, as Blanton points out, it functions to introduce "us" to the Other.[10] This equally affords us a way of knowing ourselves.[11] The proliferation of travel brochures and certain clothing catalogues that feature imports contribute to this discursive process by conveying "the desire for the exotic, a disdain for 'natives,' a search for the 'authentic Other,' and a need to merge with 'native' culture and not be seen as a visitor."[12]

However, the homogeneity implied by the concept of "Third World" has been ruptured by the events of September 11, 2001, and its aftermath, and this needs to be acknowledged here. Returning to Said,[13] it is apparent that despite the wider applicability of his theorizing, there are features of Orientalist discourse that are unique to the "Orient" or "Near East"—today known as the Middle East—which have set apart this area of the world from the time of the colonial era and earlier. "Arabs" have thus been construed in Orientalist discourse as "evil, totalitarian, and terroristic,"[14] epithets that seem to have been imbued with new currency and depth of meaning in Western/Northern discourse since the attacks on the World Trade Center in 2001. I would suggest that this recent denigration/demonization of "Arabs" and "Islam"—for Said, the two are always connected—can be usefully understood through

Pieterse's discussion of stereotyping.[15] His argument is that there are two main varieties of stereotypes: "outcasts" and "competitors."[16] The former are really excluded from all that matters, whereas the latter are inherently threatening, for they compete in various ways with those who generate the stereotypes. Pieterse points out that when a group of people undergo a change from "outcasts" to "competitors," this process is accompanied by a marked increase in pejorative stereotyping. It could be argued that, as "terroristic" stereotypes of Islam and the powerful impact of Middle Eastern oil reserves have begun to impact Northern countries in unprecedented ways, the place of the modern-day "Orient" has shifted not only in respect to the Northern/Western imagination but also in material terms, producing a corresponding alteration in the import of Orientalist stereotypes. One effect is to render the "Third World,"' to which the "Orient" only ever ambiguously belonged and from which it has now been thoroughly discursively displaced, as a locus of relative safety and security for Northern subjects and our longings. In fact, the peril now attributed to "Arabs"/"Islam" may render the "Third World" and its peoples as reassuring outcasts despite localized political conflicts and even genocide, as in Rwanda. Such outcasts are seen as deserving of, and available for, Northern beneficence.

Notwithstanding which, when ethnic/racialized Southerners reside within the nations of the North, as they increasingly do, their outcast status is perceived as less than reassuring up close and personal, so to speak. Thus, the effects of official multiculturalism policies work to fix them in a place where they are not quite citizens, but rather permanent "Third World–looking people" and, as such, objects of government to be "welcomed, abused, defended, made accountable, analysed and measured."[17] In these representational processes the differences between Northerners and Southerners are markedly racialized, although, in keeping with the claims of multiculturalsim, explanations for "difference" are usually proffered in cultural terms and race is denied. Elite discourse, from politicians and other leaders, both sanctions and frames these responses on the part of "ordinary citizens"—that is, members of the dominant group.[18] The actualization of such discursive and objectifying practices in development/aid interventions is thereby also normalized and operationalized in the work of development agencies, bilateral aid projects, and so on. In this process, the unspoken subtext is that what really counts and must be preserved are our standards, our perspectives, our national fantasies, our imaginings of the Other, and, when we do development work, *our* experiences "there."

Embedded in the discourse inviting us to know the world and our place in it in these ways is the message that Northern countries have a special role to play in alleviating the woes of the poor global Others. In the case of Canada, this has become one of the most significant narratives of the res publica, a kind of national calling, that coalesces in both aid/development commitments and peacekeeping activities. As S. Razack comments: "A Canadian today knows herself or himself as someone who comes from the nicest place on earth, as someone from a peacekeeping nation, and as a modest, self-deprecating individual who is able to gently teach Third World Others about civility."[19]

An example of the constancy of this kind of global interventionist discourse is furnished by an article that appeared in one of Canada's leading daily newspapers on May 25, 2000—five years from the time *The Midday Sun* aired on Canadian television, more than ten years after the film was made, and at least twenty years following Keating's own development work venture in Africa. This article was written by Stephen Lewis, formerly Canadian ambassador to the United Nations and at the time the UN secretary general's special envoy for HIV/AIDS in Africa. At the time Lewis was a member of the International Panel of Eminent Persons set up by the United Nations to review the 1994 genocide in Rwanda. Among other points made in his discussion regarding the current situation in Africa, Lewis stated the following:

> If you can ever take a few months, half a year, a year, even more to work in a developing country, I promise you nothing, but *nothing*, will be *so gratifying in your entire lifetime*.
>
> One of the things that excites and astounds me is that when I travel, no matter how distressing the circumstances—refugee camps, camps for internally displaced people, conflict, floods, famines—I see everywhere young foreign persons, aged roughly 23 to 38. Remarkably enough, the majority are young *women* working in the most difficult conditions to calm lives, to help lives, to save lives, especially the women and children who are always the most vulnerable.
>
> It's like a new renaissance of commitment, a rejuvenated peace corps. *They love it* and it's invaluable.[20]

Here again is a story where "developing countries" appear to be in a state of unmanageable disarray, and where what seems to matter is not just the assistance that is given, but the helping imperative and the effect that "helping" the passive Other will have on our own life experiences. However, this rendition raises a number of additional questions: What is it that women like myself "love" about doing such work in "develop-ing countries"? What makes it so gratifying to us? And why is this work so much a sphere for women?[21] Although Lewis is mainly describing what is known in international aid circles as refugee and relief work, his comments invoke a larger issue: white/Northern women's desire for other people's development. This book addresses these questions.

Situating the Theoretical Framework

In a general sense, this is a book about whiteness and development, the connections between them, and the ways in which they rely on the con-struction of a racialized Other. It is also about the production of white feminine subjectivities and the experiences of Canadian women who are drawn to development work. The conclusions that are presented here call into question the accepted notion of development (and the helping imperative to which it gives expression) as unproblematically "good," and suggest that the ever-increasing influx of Canadians and other Northerners into the spaces of the South ought to be given seri-ous reconsideration. I draw from race theory, including space and white-ness studies, post-colonialism and colonial studies, post-structuralism, feminism, and development theory, to trace the operation of global rela-tionships of power at the micro level in the development enterprise. In so doing, I demonstrate that ongoing processes of bourgeois identity formation cannot be comprehended without grasping the imperative that a white middle-class bourgeois subject thinks of her/himself as moral, and to be perceived as such. The concept of "bourgeois" references the discursive construction of a simultaneously mythical and normative iden-tity pertaining to and shaping Northern white middle-class subjects and, as such, always connotes whiteness. Properly speaking, such personages are male, although the term "bourgeois subjects" is used here at times to more generally encompass white middle-class women as well as men. I prefer to employ the term bourgeois rather than "white" because the former inherently connotes class as well as race and gender—and an implicit heteronormativity—and this in turn implies that there is a con-stitutive relationship between all these in the production of whiteness. However, at times I use white in order to stress the salience of race in rela-tion to the other aspects of bourgeois identity at a given moment.

   This is a subjectivity that now views racism with a normative disap-probation bordering on repugnance. Notwithstanding this, deeply racial-ized, interrelated constructs of thought have circulated from the era of empire, and today remain integral to the discursive production of bourgeois identity. I term these constructs "colonial continuities." My focus is on certain colonial continuities that have been modified over time in respect to their particular expression and yet are recognizable for their similarity to their original colonial manifestations and effects. These include an integrated global awareness or "planetary consciousness," that is, a world view that infers relations of comparison with the Other on a global scale, comparison in which the Other always comes off as somehow lacking or not quite up to an unmarked standard. Operating alongside this sense of comparison and simultaneously authorized by it are a sense of entitlement and an obligation to intervene for the "betterment" of the Other wherever he or she resides.[22] Race, while no longer overtly articulated, remains essential to the meaning and functioning of these continuities of thought. This can be discerned in Canadian and other Northern discursive framing of the spaces of development as "exotic" places inhabited by people who are "different" (from us) in peculiar, even fantastical, ways—places which "we" from this part of the world are free to access and alter. These normative perceptions structure to varying degrees the identities of white middle-class Canadians and other Northerners. Further, since we have an intrinsic need to think of ourselves in an all-of-a-piece fashion as moral, and to be seen by others this way, the racialization inhabiting some of our most commonplace understandings of global realities may threaten even while silently affirming the moral cohesion of bourgeois subjects' unitary views of self.

The operation of colonial continuities can also be detected in constructions of gender, which position white middle-class women as simultaneously subjects and non-subjects who may enhance their hold on bourgeois subjectivity through the performance of "goodness." This exerts a special pressure on middle-class white women to stake a claim to the moral high ground. Because it is ostensibly about "helping" Others, development work particularly fulfills this imperative for female members of the dominant group in Canada and other Northern countries. Direct experiences of intersecting relations of power in the racialized spaces of development—the "Third World"—have a transformative effect on feminine subjects' claims to "true" bourgeois identity. All of this is bound up in the depth of bourgeois femininity's desire for development.

The "desire" that is theorized here is not the desire of psychoanalysis, which may be at the level of the unconscious, as discussed by Seshadri-Crooks in relation to race, or the sexual, as elaborated by Young in respect to colonialism.[23] Although it can be conceived as "that which remains always *unthought* at the heart of thought"[24] following Foucault, desire can be viewed as discursively constituted through processes exterior to the subject, which the subject embraces and invests in.[25] My interest is in the larger forces that produce a bourgeois or white subjectivity with a particular desire for development, and the stake that white middle-class women have in this particular helping imperative. Nevertheless, it is noteworthy that Seshadri-Crooks, working from psychoanalytic and critical race theories, contends that desire is really about a longing for whiteness, which holds the promise of wholeness. This has resonance with some of the conclusions that I will also present, but I do not make a psychoanalytic argument. Rather, I proceed from colonial studies, which have demarcated the historical constitution of a normative—one could even say, mythical—bourgeois subjectivity to identify ongoing features of this very subjectivity, that is, colonial continuities.

Although my usage of the term colonial continuities dates from my doctoral work, it is a concept that has been referred to by Gregory in his book *The Colonial Present: Afghanistan – Palestine – Iraq*.[26] Indeed, the notion of continuities from colonial times to the present is foundational to much, but not necessarily all, post-colonial theorizing. I use post-colonial to mean, in the words of Ashcroft, Griffiths, and Tiffin, "the totality of practices, in all their rich diversity, which characterise the societies of the post-colonial world from the moment of colonisation to the present day."[27] As these authors go on to note, "colonialism *continues* in neo-colonial mode" (emphasis mine). With the seminal work in post-colonial studies being Said's *Orientalism*,[28] the emphasis has tended to be on issues of culture and representation and the enabling discourses of Western/Northern domination.[29] While it is recognized that these discourses have been in play since colonial times, the specific continuities under consideration here have received little attention. This is so despite the fact that, as was once characteristic of the colonizers, concerns for the well-being of those who are subjugated are today mobilized in development discourse.[30] I would suggest, however, that the post-colonial constructs interrogated here have a significance beyond the development field. As with discourse circulating between the colonies and the metropole in the era of empire, the discussions surrounding Northern development interventions are essential to the current representational practices noted above—that is, to affirming the story of the North's putative superiority. Following Stoler and McClintock, who demonstrate how this operated in the colonial era, I posit that such Northern-dominated discursive processes work toward the securing of bourgeois identity formation in the global arena.[31] Consequently, there is much more at stake in understanding the colonial continuities in the Northern development impulse than might at first seem apparent.

Lopez argues that with the exception of Dyer's 1995 "*ur*-text," *White*, there has been little attention paid by post-colonial studies to issues of whiteness, and vice versa.[32] He adds that it is "both significant and curious that European colonial whiteness—arguably whiteness at its apex, in its most ascendant and global powerful form—has not loomed large in these analyses."[33] This is ironic in view of the recognition that whiteness exerts a force that is both global and colonizing in its effects.[34] Exceptions are to be found in the work of feminist writers who theorize the relationship of "goodness" and the social construction of gender and whiteness—"good" being equated with white womanhood—in the colonial era, specifically in the work of Ware, Supriya, and Davy.[35] Dyer brings a discussion of Christianity's influence to bear on this same relationship. Attending to the intersections of race, class, and gender and drawing on critical studies of colonialism as I track colonial continuities, I build on their analyses and thereby further efforts to fill this lacuna.

Feminist writers have also addressed the ethics of whiteness. Frye argues that knowing the right thing to do constitutes the agency of white middle-class Christian-raised Americans, but that the ethical code is differentiated by gender, so that when a woman from the dominant group attempts to animate the agency normally reserved for men she does so on the basis of her own moral code, which is not that of the conventional "good" woman.[36] Frye makes the point that the moral basis of thought and action is "doubly important" to a gender-transgressing woman because it is the basis for "Be-ing, for Presence, for Ability," as well as agency.[37] Frye also remarks that for middle-class white Christian-raised Americans, "Right makes Might," a quote that she attributes to Carolyn Shafer.[38] I want to bring historical depth to this latter point and in the process demonstrate that it pertains to bourgeois subjects more generally, not just Americans. In contrast, my argument is that, in effect, "Right makes *white*," in the sense that whiteness is constituted through doing what is "right." Tracing the historical origins of this white middle-class ethics also leads me to a somewhat different conclusion about white middle-class women's investments in preserving a moral narrative. This is a distinction that has important implications for resisting whiteness.

How to resist whiteness is a recurring theme of whiteness studies. Alcoff raises the ethical question of what white people should do. Her conclusion is that we need to develop a "double consciousness," by which she means "an everpresent acknowledgment of the historical legacy of white identity constructions in the persistent structures of inequality and exploitation, as well as a newly awakened memory of the many white traitors to white privilege who have struggled to contribute to the building of an inclusive human community."[39] My project contributes to the first aspect that Alcoff identifies: the acknowledgement of the historical legacy of white identity. However, I do not make claims about "white traitors" because I see the possibilities of refusing whiteness as more complex than this. The notion that one can be a "traitor" to one's white race is particularly associated with Ignatiev,[40] and is one of the main responses in the literature. Other writers advocate the abolishment of whiteness or its re-articulation.[41] The key issue revolves around movement toward change that is broader than the individual positioned in dominance, that is, to social and political change. While this is ultimately the goal, it seems to me that, following Giroux,[42] the most hopeful approach is the re-articulation of whiteness by means of individual transformation. Like Andersen, Frankenberg, Bishop, and Davies,[43] I am cautious about the resiliency of whiteness, and the difficulty of transforming it. My hesitancy arises both from my understanding of the enduring tenacity and constitutive strength of colonial continuities, which this book explores, and from my theoretical analysis of subjectivity and power, which draws on Foucault.

Foucault has stated that "the individual is not to be conceived as a sort of elementary nucleus, a primitive atom, a multiple and inert material on which power comes to fasten or against which it happens to strike."[44] Rather, in Foucault's schema, subjects are constituted through discourses that *subject* individuals to discursively available positions—hence the concept of "subject positions."[45] In this conceptualization, power is something that circulates, and all individuals and groups are, positioned in relations of power and are in effect, its vehicles. As Foucault's quote states, power is not some "thing" that acts on a person, although there is a process of auto-colonization involved—the acceptance of subjugation—via what Foucault has called technologies of self, which are the ways in which individuals comply (or not) with discursively established standards of conduct.[46] In the latter lies the actualization of agency. This view of subjectivity is important to my project because it enables a non-essentialist and historically grounded understanding of whiteness that takes into account multiple and shifting subject positions, the effects of discourse, and the possibility of refusing dominance. In working with the concept of bourgeois subjectivity from the era of empire and beyond, I seek to unpack its overlapping subject positions and their implications for twenty-first-century white middle-class femininity's desire for development. The significance of discourse to the production of this desire has already been indicated above. Thinking of subjects as being discursively constituted anew on a constant basis makes evident the challenges of resisting one's positioning in dominance. Refusing whiteness, for example, becomes more complicated than deciding to refrain from exercising privilege because such a choice does not, in and of itself, dislodge internalized dominance. Nor can such a subjectivity be easily, or once and for all, refused. It can, however, be deconstructed and continually challenged.

Foucault's conceptualization of power leads to a level of microanalysis: "One must rather conduct an *ascending* analysis of power, starting, that is, from its infinitesimal mechanisms, which each have their own history, their own trajectory, their own techniques and tactics, and then see how these mechanisms of power have been—and continue to be— invested, colonised, utlised, involuted, transformed, displaced, extended etc., by ever-more general mechanisms and by forms of global domination."[47] I attend to the micro level of development worker experiences because, put simply, it seems to me that in the analysis of how North–South relations of domination are kept in play, "the devil is in the detail." I am interested in a particular facet of these relations—in the individuals who, like myself, enact the processes of Northern interventions called "development." What calls us, how we make meaning of our experiences, why we are likely to participate again in development work despite any personal criticisms of the aid industry: these are issues that bear elucidation.

To trace micro processes in operation, I attend to the self-constitutive stories that remain salient for women like myself who have worked in the development context in sub-Saharan Africa. As Woodward asserts, a story or stories provide coherence and help us to make sense of ourselves.[48] As such, they are important for the exploration of identity. The humanist idea of "a core or essence to which other qualities are added later,"[49] in other words, an identity, comprises an accepted part of how most modern subjects, including Canadians and those of us who become development workers, understand ourselves. In this conception, "I" is "the center from which a person look[s] out upon, and act[s] upon, the world."[50] Through personal accounting for action and self-description, unitary subjects work to compose non-contradictory identities both publicly and privately. In so doing, they draw on cultur-ally available discourses.[51] In this accounting and self-description, then, storylines or narratives are central,[52] and comprise a technology of self (in Foucauldian terms), since they are the means by which we internal-ize to ourselves, and comply with, the meanings that circulate in dis-course. It is this narrative aspect of identity—or subject—formation from which I work in exploring how Canadian development workers negoti-ate and understand their/our positioning in power relations in the devel-opment context. My focus is not on the life story per se, but on how white middle-class women retrospectively make sense of the develop-ment experience, and particularly the relations of power in which they/we were positioned "there." While I recognize that each new telling is dif-ferent, and that stories are in fact emergent,[53] I view stories told at a given moment as significant for what they reveal about how global dom-ination is perpetuated.

Critiquing Development

Young has pointed out that the concept of development does not con-fine itself to economic change, but focuses as well on social transforma-tion, so that potentially "the whole fabric of social life is subject to control."[54] This can be seen as an extension of Mohanty's critique in respect to Western feminist interventions that homogenized knowledge about "Third World women" so as to render them objects for develop-ment.[55] However, as Escobar argues, and Young's remarks corroborate, this is a critique with enormous relevance for mainstream development.[56] Central here is what Sardar refers to as "the power to define,"[57] and it is this curtailing of epistemological spaces to which some critics of devel-opment particularly object: the loss, absence, or overall negation of the right to define development in one's own terms. There is no getting out of the binary on which the concept of development rests, with its inher-ent contradiction between assumptions that the "natives" will eventually "catch up" and the impossibility of their ever doing so.[58] These con-cerns are echoed by African development theorists who are grounded in shared values and recognition of the validity of indigenous knowledges. The centrality of the latter to African conceptions and critiques of devel-opment cannot be overstated. Dei proposes an African definition of development rooted in the values and moral order of society: "Such new thinking ... would have as its primary goal to enrich the social, spiritual and the non-material circumstances of people and allow them to develop and utilize their full potential."[59] Implied here, as Nyerere explained as far back as 1974, is that "roads, buildings, the increases of the crop output, and other things of this nature, are not development; they are *tools* of development."[60] If African definitions of development reflect shared cultural values, they equally depend on African ways of knowing, so that it is not surprising that these conceptions of development are seen as needing to originate from and rest with Africans.

The very development policies and programs that as a consequence are so strongly critiqued are actualized through the endeavours of Northern development workers. A 1995 study compiled under the direction of the African Research, Education and Development Association (AFREDA), based in Dar-es-Salaam, Tanzania, investigated the perspectives of staff in a total of 170 African non-governmental organizations and groups in five different African countries regarding their "partnership" relations with Northern donors. The report of this research, called *Perspectives from the South: A Study on Partnership*, makes some relevant and critical points in respect to African organizations' experiences with Northern development workers, termed in this instance "volunteers."[61] Here are some of the comments made by authors Muchunguzi and Milne:

> Doubts were expressed about the quality of some of the volunteers sent to work in South. Indeed, considerable frustration was expressed at the continued practice of using Northern "experts," over local people who possessed comparable academic and professional experience. Especially upsetting was the fact that most of the Northerners coming to the South lacked basic understanding of and respect for, local cultures and customs.[62]

In fairness, it should be mentioned that the harsher critiques appear to have been levied at students doing field placements or practica with African organizations as part of Northern universities' international development programs. Nevertheless, the concerns raised cannot be seen as limited to, or in some way excluding, any one group from within the category of development worker. This report goes on to state that, from the perspective of Southern development agency personnel, Northern organizations privilege the views of Northerners over those of African "partners"; this was considered an especially egregious issue in partnership relations. It is noteworthy that the displeasure expressed with Northern development workers turns in large part on their disregard for the two key issues mentioned in the discussion of African definitions of development: indigenous knowledges and cultural values. The point is that these aspects, which very much comprise cornerstones of the African development process *in African terms*, disproportionately bear the brunt of the incremental penetration of Northern development personnel into African countries and their governments, organizations, and social relations.

It is perhaps not surprising in light of the foregoing that recently there has been an articulation of "critical alternative development," which, rather than focusing on larger power structures, is concerned about issues of cultural imperialism and forms of sustainability that would support cultural values and the preservation of indigenous knowledges.[63] Calls for Northern would-be development workers to interrogate their desire for development may be seen as one aspect of this approach. Rahnema refers to the "masks of love" to which development workers become "addicted," meaning that the love they claim to feel is for abstract target groups (such as Mohanty's homogenized "Third World women") rather than real people with their own particularities, perceptions, and agency.[64] Like Elabor-Idemudia and Porter,[65] Rahnema urges Northern development workers to question themselves and their impulse to intervene. The urgency of this exhortation becomes more apparent when the proliferating presence of various kinds of development/aid workers is recognized. In 1991 Wangoola stated that there were more (white) development workers in Africa than at any time in history: "They operate in nooks where they had never been before."[66] Today there are thousands of organizations involved in development work, to the extent that there are likely more expatriate development workers operating in Africa at this point than there were ever colonialists in the era of empire.[67] Cook's conclusion is that, taken on a global scale, Northern development workers need to be considered as a separate, significant group of transnationals who are transmitters of Northern knowledge, values, and identities.[68]

A body of research on the international aid experience is beginning to appear from the perspective of the Northern individuals who are the conveyors of aid or development. This research includes Baaz's study of paternalism in foreign donor relationships in Tanzania and Goudge's Nicaraguan-based study of racism in aid and development work.[69] Kothari and White have also written about racism in development work, and Simpson has examined Othering in "voluntour" experiences of young Britons taking a "gap year."[70] As well, Cook has completed a poststructuralist analysis of expatriate development workers in Pakistan, which is partially presented in her article "What to Wear? Western Women and Imperialism in Gilgit, Pakistan," and which will be more fully articulated in her forthcoming book, *Gender, Identity and Development in Pakistan*,[71] and Watts has explored how VSO (British Volunteer Service Overseas) development workers look at their relationships with their Cambodian counterparts.[72] Mindry has examined gendered representations of virtue in relations between aid workers, both foreign and nationals, working with local women's organizations in Durban, South Africa.[73] In 1997 Kidder reprised her 1977 article synthesizing interviews with 139 expatriates in a city in southern India in 1970, where she found that the enhanced status of foreigners correlated with their dislike of, and disrespect toward, Indian "culture."[74] In the helping profession more generally, N. Razack has studied the experiences of faculty and students from Canadian schools of social work involved in international exchanges, particularly around student practica, and Parfitt has investigated how the personal values of expatriate nurses working in many different "developing countries" affect their cross-cultural encounters. S. Razack's work on Canada's international peacekeeping role in Somalia traces the emphasis in Canada on what "our" peacekeepers "had to endure there."[75]

My research has been on how white middle-class Canadian women development workers negotiate and understand our positions in relations of power in sub-Saharan Africa.[76] This book is based on my research, and attempts to respond to calls for Northern development workers to interrogate their/our own investments in development work. Since white middle-class women make up the majority of development workers today, those are the narratives on which I focus. It bears mentioning that the key features of these narratives are strikingly similar to those cited in the related studies mentioned above, and are of a piece with the précis of Keating's film at the beginning of this chapter.

The Empirical Basis for the Book

Although there are enormous regional differences between different parts of Africa, owing to some extent to their varying experiences under colonization, nevertheless there are also important similarities that make it reasonable to compare development worker experiences across regions. Some parallels and commonalities are cultural and epistemic, as mentioned previously. Others are a consequence of the homogenizing effects of imperialism:

> Imperialism is ... the common historical force that makes it possible
> to consider an area as large and diverse as the African continent as
> having general features that transcend the boundaries of nation, cul-
> ture, and geography. This collective African experience—being con-
> quered by the colonizing powers; being culturally and materially
> subjected to a nineteenth-century European racial hierarchy and its
> gender politics; being indoctrinated into all-male European admin-
> istrative systems; and facing the continuous flow of material and
> human resources from Africa to Europe—has persistently affected all
> aspects of social, cultural, political, and economic life in postcolonial
> African states.[77]

Beyond this, development work in sub-Saharan Africa is a site especially suited to an exploration of the operation of colonial continuities
and the moral imperative in processes of white feminine identity formation since this is a context where the contradictions and complexities of
Northern development workers' positions in relations of power are
played out with particular starkness. For the legacy of Africa as the "dark
continent" is evident today in media portrayals, such as Lewis unwit-
tingly perpetuates, of Africa as a modern-day trope for all that is not
"developed," indeed, for much that is "savage," a view that mainly over-
writes but at times still coexists with an earlier romantic notion of Africans
as heroic and beautiful, both of which are repeatedly represented in
film.[78] A third image, that has seemed to be irrevocably consolidated by
media coverage of the Ethiopian famine and the resulting Band Aid
Concert in 1985, is that of the passive, helpless African.[79] Africa occu-
pies a corresponding position in respect to the latter in Northern development discourse, where it is increasingly construed as a "hopeless"
case: a continent in (supposedly self-produced) "crisis." As Grovogui
points out,[80] skepticism about Africa's overall capability in comparison
to other parts of the world has come to pervade papers developed by
international institutions such as the World Bank and International
Monetary Fund, the policy statements of Northern governments, and
research and articles by academic "experts."

It is indisputable that very difficult economic and social conditions
do now obtain throughout almost all of sub-Saharan Africa. However,
the description of these conditions via ahistorical statistical information has the effect of obscuring how the situations being depicted are
rooted in colonial processes of wealth extraction and are perpetuated
through political-economic arrangements that many African development theorists, along with critical writers from the North, have named

as "neo-colonialism." The terms of world trade, acquired national debts of crippling proportions, and externally imposed fiscal policies known collectively as "structural adjustment" (spearheaded by the World Bank and the International Monetary Fund) have been instrumental in compromising the autonomy of post-colonial states and keeping them in a dependent relationship with the former colonizing powers, thereby continuing exploitative relations that have been operating for the last five hundred years.[81] In the case of sub-Saharan Africa, the consequences of these economic processes have been particularly harmful. The region also has the highest prevalence of HIV/AIDS in the world,[82] a fact that has only recently begun to be recognized as linked to the deepening impoverishment of the continent. The response to statistics attesting to declining standards of living in this part of the world is almost invariably to make the case for ever more Northern intervention. This is the context where Canadian and other Northern development workers come to "help."

What happens on the part of Canadian women development workers when they/we seek to ameliorate other people's lives in "developing countries," when living out the distances between the rhetoric and the reality of the Northern development project in the South, and between their/our own moral commitments and complicated positionings in relations of power vis-à-vis the "Third World" Other? To explore these questions, in 1996 I carried out lengthy, open-ended interviews with seventeen middle-class white women who had been sent by a variety of Canadian NGOs[83] to do development work in sub-Saharan Africa on long-term contracts (usually two years or more). One of these women then interviewed me. In 2005 I interviewed another ten women[84] who had more recently been development workers in Africa in order to determine whether social and economic changes in African countries in the previous ten years or so would have an impact on their development worker narratives. For both groups the interview process attempted to uncover a chronology of our development worker experiences, from the time of decision to go overseas through to the process of readjustment on return to Canada.

As noted earlier, there is a standard development worker narrative that is fairly impervious to change, and this is reflected in the stories told by both sets of participants. The main differences overall in the accounts of the two groups have to do, first, with developing in-depth relationships with African people, which seemed to happen less frequently among more recent development workers, a finding that has a parallel in Baaz's study of British, Norwegian, and Swedish development workers in Tanzania in the late 1990s.[85] This suggests that worsening socio-economic circumstances in African countries may adversely impact on the possibilities of developing closer relationships.[86] The second important difference concerned the amount of prior development worker experience. Where the original participants had mainly not done development work before, with the second group this correlation was inversed, so that most of them had been on short-term contracts as development workers prior to undertaking the longer commitment that was the focus of the interview. It seems that the sharpness of the experience lessens for participants after their initial overseas posting. For this reason, and because my analysis concerns the specificities of the stories that are told, I focus on the earlier group of interviews, my own included.[87] While twenty-eight is a more impressive number, working from so many recollections would entail a different kind of approach to the data. However, I do make reference to the newer interviews as appropriate.

In examining the stories that women who are former development workers tell ourselves about our past involvement in the development enterprise, I am seeking not the potential gaps in personal recollection, but what individuals choose to disclose of their/our desires and investments, and the obverse of what is revealed: that which is not named. While tracking emerging themes in the personal narratives of development workers, I attend to the discursive practices, knowledge bases, narrative strategies, positionings of self, and narrative shifts in the stories participants tell. In this way, while operating within an ethnographic framework,[88] I can trace shifting subject positions as well as other themes related to what participants see, and how they/we negotiate power relations and enact resistance. It should be noted that in quoting participants, all indications of added emphasis occur in the original unless otherwise stated.

In analyzing the interviews, I usually refer to the stories of participants in my research in terms of "we," "us," and "our" rather than "they," "them," and "their." I am conscious that at times the effect may be to overly homogenize differences among participants, to inadvertently suggest a greater degree of consensus than exists, or to make it appear that I am speaking for all who participated in this study. However, my concern is to place myself within the analysis and to signal that I see myself implicated in the issues I raise in respect to relations of domination. Similarly, in writing about white middle-class women, or Canadian women development workers, I use the first-person plural so as to include myself within the nexus of these subject positions. I am acutely aware of the dangers of positioning myself as simultaneously ethnographer and participant. The dual roles are not easily negotiated, and the inherent oppositions between them are not dispensed with through this imperfect method of conflation. As Ware and Back point out, in researching whiteness there is an added peril for the ethnographer of assuming a kind of moral high ground as the person with the greater, or "true," anti-racist analysis. These authors warn that research subjects can be "patronizingly consigned to the backwoods of bad-sense whiteness."[89] In addition to including myself in the analysis, I attempt to address the latter concern by showing the complexity of participants' stories, and acknowledging at this point that my own narratives are, despite some personal inflections born of my own history and trajectory in the development enterprise, fundamentally similar to those of other participants. While I cannot avoid imposing my frame of analysis, given that I am the person who is commenting on the stories presented here, at the same time I am aware that my subject position limits and is reflected in what I understand. As A. Ferguson so eloquently puts it, there is a "horizon of ignorance" that necessarily limits and may even distort my interpretations.[90] Thus, a person of colour with a critical race analysis would no doubt read some things differently from me, and with greater insight. Nevertheless, I contend that the intimate knowledge of the subject position of white middle-class woman development worker that I bring to bear on the analysis of the stories women have shared with me is of value to my project.

I prefer to examine accounts rendered in the past tense, although I realize that doing so has significant implications for this study. My intention is to avoid emotionally charged responses of the kind espoused by Goulet, and Goulet and Wilber,[91] and, to a considerably lesser extent, by Northern development workers in the recent studies by Cook and Baaz.[92] Development theorists who are also practitioners, such as Edwards and Moser,[93] demonstrate, too, that once we are involved in the overseas development experience, it becomes difficult to challenge the logic and imperative of the Northern development project. Development becomes, as J. Ferguson has said, its own standard of measurement, and the issue becomes how to get it right.[94] For these reasons I chose to interview women who are no longer caught up in the urgency (for Northerners) of the Southern development context. It seems to me as well that this way of entering the terrain of the development experience is more fair to the women who agreed to participate in the study, since it affords them/us an opportunity to reflect back rather than to describe the exigencies of the immediate present, as would have been the case had the interviews taken place overseas.

The decision *not* to carry out interviews with Africans was also consciously made, partially in connection with the point just discussed, but also because I did not want to pit the words of African people who work with Canadian development workers against the views of the latter, as if to prove my points. However, as a result, direct comments from African peoples regarding the questions under investigation here are missing, except when reported via the narratives of the participants. I sometimes use the word "Other(s)" to refer to African(s) mentioned in participants' narratives because this is reflective of how African individuals appear in the stories that are told. This may have the effect, at times, of seeming to repeat the very essentialism that was noted in the discussion of development critiques. Even more troubling is that African people almost disappear from the story of development worker experiences, in much the same way as the domestic worker becomes a mere backdrop for the "more important" changes that occurred for the Canadian woman in the vignette from Keating's film at the beginning of this chapter. This is a hazard of deconstructing dominance: at the moment it is challenged, it reclaims centre stage and makes its issues the ones that count. Yet if not challenged, relations of domination will continue. This has been debated within whiteness studies, and in the end I agree with Warren on two counts: first, as Warren has said, "if we uncover how race gets made and how the social, cultural meaningfulness of whiteness maintains its power ... then we can struggle to change it";[95] and, second, this is my ethical responsibility as a white person. This book is a contribution to these ends.

Overview of the Book

The book provides a specific kind of reading of development worker narratives, including my own. It has turned out differently from what I originally imagined. When first I conceptualized the outline of the original research findings, I saw a prevailing theme of resistance in our narratives: resistance to some of the colonial continuities that had emerged—although I also perceived in the operation of these continuities the making of selves. However, I thought of our resistance moves, and the ways in which they became compromised or subverted, as a kind of "dance of resistance," which resonated with Visweswaran's point that there is neither total resistance nor complete capitulation.[96] It seemed to me that although participants struggled against the unmarked gaze of our own planetary consciousness, as we told our stories we were careful to frame our altruism in respectful ways, we worked to develop reciprocal relations with African peoples, we were conscious and uncomfortable about our dominant positionings in power relations—the status conferred by whiteness—and frustrated by the limitations that our gender imposed; we dealt with both as best we could, we worked hard at our jobs and were modest about what we had achieved, and we were so committed to our time as development workers that it was difficult to let go of an emotional identification with "Africa" on return to Canada. It had in actuality been a "life-changing experience" for virtually all of us, as Keating's film suggests. Moreover, we developed a first-hand critique of the development enterprise when we were overseas, and several of us continued to be thoughtfully critical of volunteer-sending, and our own roles as development workers. A number of us are still involved in development work in various capacities. This completes the sketch of what is probably the standard ex-development-worker narrative.

While I acknowledge that this is a valid account, what I ask is how would repeating the usual reading be helpful? And, perhaps more important, what do such readings accomplish or keep in place? The standard narratives circulating about doing development work are essential to the dominance inhering in the development enterprise as it is now constituted, and these readings perpetuate rather than work to rupture Northern control of development processes. Treating our narratives in this normative fashion does not tell those of us who continue to seek a meaningful alternative practice within the development enterprise much that we do not already know. On the other hand, while the reading I am putting forward is not the whole story, I strongly contend that it *is* a crucial part of the development worker story, *and* one that is inadequately articulated. This interpretation of our accounts offers potentially oppositional, although not always comfortable, understandings of our relationship to the development enterprise and our actions as development workers. And I believe that everyone who participated in this study is committed to development practices that comprise alternatives to many of the prevailing models.

In the face of the overdetermined operation of global relations of power at the micro level in the spaces of development, our resistance moves seemed to produce not just accommodation but uncertainty and even frustration for us, rather than more substantial change. It was not so much that our enactments of resistance (that is, our alternative practices and our negotiations of power relations) were mixed with countermoves, as that they were not very effective or oppositional. Our limited enactments and conceptualizations of resistance are not surprising, given the intensity and complexity of the development worker experience, and the way it is discursively framed for us *before* we go overseas. Here I am referring to the narratives available to us through discourse, and our own racially inscribed discursive repertoires that, replete with colonial continuities, configure the meanings we make of our development worker experiences.[97] As a consequence, it is only after a period of disengagement from the experience itself that we begin to be able to ask more foundational questions about our participation in development work.

In any case, as I pursued colonial continuities through the chronological arc of our development worker stories, what began to predominate was an enduring, continuing feminine narrative of self as both moral and more fully a (white) bourgeois subject. Although this is in some respects a severe reading, it is, I think, of value to those white women like myself who struggle, as Patti (one of the participants) so effectively expresses it, for "a place of integrity" in relation to the problematic project of development.

In the next chapter I address the origins of the development worker phenomenon. I argue that, viewed from a historical perspective, there is a logic to both the existence of the position of development worker and the commonsensical embracing of this identity by white middle-class subjects. The strong affinity that white women feel for the development project begins to be more comprehensible as well. While I emphasize that my approach is not deterministic, nevertheless historicized imperial relations shape the world and our subjectivities, so that if we do not understand how we are implicated in the perpetuation of global domination, we are bound to help reproduce it. I then turn to the interviews with women like—and including—myself who have been development workers on long-term contracts in sub-Saharan Africa. In our decisions to go overseas can be read the themes of morality, planetary consciousness, and a sense of entitlement and obligation to intervene elsewhere. Chapter 3 looks at how our social relations, inscribed with Othering and desire, are played out in the spaces of development. In Chapter 4, our negotiation of the privileges of whiteness and development worker status, moves to protect innocence, and our gendered positionings are traced. The latter afford insights into the making of white middle-class subjectivities, which are further elucidated by our experiences on returning home.

Through the various aspects analyzed in each chapter run the themes of racialized domination and resistance. The decision to go overseas can be seen as an attempt to resist imperialism and the terms in which our own subjectivities are constituted. Indeed, our relations with African peoples are complicated by moves toward and away from granting mutual subjectivity, and white development worker status is alternately, sometimes simultaneously, embraced, and repudiated and disavowed. Similarly, the constitution of bourgeois subjectivities with their attendant effects is not unproblematically accomplished in the development context: participants raise and foreclose questions about these processes. Although resistance is discussed along the way, in Chapter 5, as I examine the significance of the moral self for bourgeois subjects, I come back to a discussion of the possibilities of resistance to perpetuating racialized domination. In the conclusion, Chapter 6, I reflect on the investments of white women development workers like myself in our desire for development, and in what we see and do not want to see of our responsibility for domination. Perhaps most important, this book offers a way of understanding our development worker commitments and conduct that provides some explanation to African and other Southern development theorists for our growing presence in the South, as well as our behaviour when we are "there."

CHAPTER 2
WHERE DO DEVELOPMENT WORKERS *REALLY* COME FROM?

How has the subject position of development worker come to be, and how are race and gender implicated in it? The advent of the phenomenon called development worker is historically traceable, and not simply in terms of the predictable analogy between development workers and missionaries/colonialists. The origins of the Western bourgeois self in the era of empire—a white male subjectivity constructed through the intersecting relations of race, gender, and sexuality in the ongoing formation of a class identity—and the overall Enlightenment legacy of the individual afford an understanding of how *something like* the position of development worker was in fact implicated from the outset of the post-colonial period, and offer insight into the raced, classed, and ambivalently gendered nature of this subject position. This chapter explores these antecedents and traces their presence in participants' motivations for becoming development workers.

The discussion with participants was at its least expansive when it came to the point of talking about *why* we wanted to do development work, although several questions were raised concerning the choice to go. The following exchange with someone whom I have called Lorraine exemplifies the brevity with which participants delved into the moment of choice, and reflects, as well, many of the recurrent themes in participants' narratives that will be discussed.

> Lorraine: You know you see things in the news, I mean I was studying journalism and you think, "God, there's so much strife in the world you know, isn't there something someone can do?" So I guess that's sort of where it all came from.
>
> Interviewer: What, what did it have to do with you though? Like—

Lorraine: What do you mean?

Interviewer: —if you see that there is strife in the world.

Lorraine: Well I'm a human, I'm part of the world community, and
I just, uh (in mock-serious voice), "I cannot stand idly by …"
(voice trails off, laughing). You know, that, just a sense of if you
know better and there's something you can do then you, you
should do it. So, I don't know what, where one gets that sense,
whether it's in your upbringing or a certain amount of awareness. So I guess that's what it had to do with me, a, a conscience
thing, make myself feel better by doing something for someone
somewhere.

Lorraine exhibits an apparent self-consciousness about admitting to
wanting to "do good" through development work, and this was not
restricted to her responses alone. Participants not only tended to founder
on recalling minutiae of the decision or what led up to it, but also seemed
to feel particularly awkward in talking about why we/they thought this
was what one should be doing. I read into this terseness some hesitation
about how a response might position the participant, given the issues I
had explained I was researching.

Lorraine's comments incorporate several other moves that are also
representative of what other participants said. How the "Third World"
is portrayed—"issues in the news"—demonstrates a global awareness, or
what is called here planetary consciousness. This generates a sense of obligation, since as Lorraine argues, "I'm part of the world community."
However, this is not a recognition of being implicated in relations of
domination, for Lorraine then pleads, "Isn't there something someone
can do?" which is quickly converted into a moral imperative to act, "I cannot stand idly by," in which the language of entitlement and comparative superiority predominates: "if you know better and there's something
you can do then you, you should do it." Next follows an intimation of
selfishness, "make myself feel better by doing something for someone
somewhere," in the latter part of which statement can be read an indication of desire for the Other. These are the major themes that were
operative when participants talked about why we wanted to go overseas
as development workers, and they were espoused by both groups of
interviewees. The infiltration of colonial continuities into the imperative
to do development work sounds the keynote for my analysis of participants', including Lorraine's, explanations for wanting to do international development work, which comprises the focus of this chapter.

Bourgeois Subject Formation: The Era of Empire

To understand the production of colonial continuities inhering in development work I will examine the production of this subject position by first sketching the emergence of bourgeois subjectivity in the era of empire. Next I will take up the continuing discursive production of some racialized aspects of this subjectivity that connect to today's development workers. The effects of gender in constituting the appropriateness of development work for white middle-class women in particular will then be considered. Ann Laura Stoler and Anne McClintock have both undertaken important explorations of the production of bourgeois subjectivity.[1] Stoler examines the Dutch experiences with colonization, while McClintock concentrates on the British empire, and I base much of my analysis on their work. I am cautious about the simplification inherent in providing a brief synopsis of such complex, historical processes via Stoler's and McClintock's carefully researched studies. Wherever appropriate I take care to augment their points with comments from other authors. However, the very premise of colonial continuities that is being argued here can only be established by tracing some of the contours of bourgeois subjectivity that took shape in the colonial era.

To set the context for the synthesis of Stoler's and McClintock's work, it should be pointed out that capitalism, which has been evolving over a period of centuries, has been predicated not only on the conquest of foreign territories, the advent of the nation state, and the nineteenth-century Industrial Revolution, but also on the creation of the bourgeoisie as a class in numerous countries in Europe and, eventually, North America.[2] The actual period of class emergence in an economic sense extended from 1780 to 1832, so that by the mid-1800s the middle class could be said to be properly in existence in England and elsewhere.[3] There were differences in the processes of class formation, in relations with ruling groups, and in the historical events that in some respects facilitated and in other respects impeded the establishment of the bourgeoisie, but there were also important commonalities among the middle classes from one country to another. It is noteworthy that this class, which became so influential over time, amounted to only 10 to 15 per cent of the population during the Victorian era.[4]

Tracing the intersections of race, gender, and sexuality, primarily but not exclusively during the latter half of the nineteenth century,[5] Stoler and McClintock reveal the ways in which the structuring of the bourgeois self took shape in the era of empire.[6] Although Stoler argues that there was no coherent class identity prior to the nineteenth century, Pratt demonstrates that by the end of the 1700s some of the crucial features of the incipient landscape of bourgeois subjectivity were already present: it was raced, gendered, and superior, with a planetary consciousness that assumed the right to intervene in any part of the world.[7] The latter is a frame of thinking that pre-existed the emergence of the bourgeoisie as a class and already formed a part of European identity during the era of maritime exploration, but it underwent a sea change beginning in 1735, when an emphasis on circumnavigation and mapping gave way to interior exploration under the exegesis of applying new theories of natural history. Through such activities the emerging bourgeois subject understood himself as passive (merely a recorder for science, for example) in his global interactions: not seeking to dominate, but only to explore, to record, to trade, and so on.[8] Pratt explains that such justifications for these undertakings comprise "anti-conquest strategies": "the strategies of representation whereby European bourgeois subjects seek to secure their innocence in the same moment as they assert European hegemony."[9] However, as McClintock shows, to know in this context was (and is) to control. A key aspect of these undertakings was to Christianize.[10]

During this time the concept of the individual took firm hold. The Enlightenment's legacy of rationality and human progress coalesced to some extent in the work of Descartes, with his views of the rational, conscious thinking subject, and Locke's notion of the sovereign subject, particularly articulated in his influential 1690 *Essay Concerning Human Understanding*, which expounded the idea that a person has an identity that stays the same throughout life.[11] Thus, as the middle classes subsequently began to form and to claim and fashion an identity, the stage was set to scrutinize the appropriateness of the classed behaviour of each and every bourgeois subject. As Said summarizes: "We can locate a coherent, fully mobilized system of ideas near the end of the eighteenth century, and there follows the set of integral developments such as … the consolidation of power in the bourgeoisie. This is also the period in which … the importance of subjectivity to historical time takes firm hold."[12] How these foundational elements were shaped, expanded on, and incorporated in the continuing bourgeois ascension during the era of empire will be seen below.

While bourgeois life had its material basis in owning property and earning a living,[13] during the nineteenth century the demarcation of middle-class identity was tenuous and shifting, and colonialism was not "a secure bourgeois project." Rather, it imported and created middle-class sensibilities, in the process of which bourgeois meaning was invented through a discursive dialectic circulating between colony and metropole. The focus of the middle class was necessarily on the affirmation of difference between itself and everyone else: on the one hand, the aristocracy, and on the other, "that which was uncivilized, lower class, and non-European."[14] Consequently, as both Stoler and McClintock agree, the creation of the middle class was a *relational* undertaking that relied on the presence of a changing set of Others: the working classes, the colonized, women, gypsies, Jews, the Irish, and criminals.[15] In this project race was the "organizing grammar,"[16] and theories of racial difference were applied to explain/justify class distinctions.[17] The universal humanism of the Enlightenment with its assumptions of sameness shifted in the mid-1850s to the trope of "the same but different," shored up by theories of scientific racism that were in part a manifestation of economic interest (justifying slavery), but also a response to ideas of evolution and other empirical thinking.[18]

The bourgeois identity that was produced was, as both Stoler and McClintock point out, more than a function of class: it was male and fundamentally tied to notions of being "European" and "white." The demonstration of "cultural competencies"—in other words, the knowledge, values, and sensibilities by which bourgeois subjects disciplined themselves—enabled the distinction to be made between those who were "truly white" and those merely "held to be white."[19] Cultural competencies included, in addition to owning property, rootedness, an orderly family life, rationality, and self-mastery;[20] and, from the domestic sphere, monogamy, thrift, order, accumulation, classification, quantification, and regulation.[21] The culturally competent person also exhibited, from the early eighteenth century on, a certain sensibility termed "sympathy," which regulated passions and manifested in benevolence and acts of charity toward those less fortunate or less advanced.[22] The foregoing defined many of the key aspects of how to live, including the appropriate—and essential—(hetero)sexual practices for bourgeois membership.

The process of drawing the distinctions that could secure a middle-class identity placed the bourgeois subject in deeply imbricated relations with the very Others he wished not to be like. In the metropole, these relations took place within the bourgeois home where the continuous affirmation of class difference was crucial to justifying and maintaining exploitative labour relations between maid and mistress (and master).[23] Outside the home, in both a local and global sense, social constructions of space were mobilized to delineate the distinctions between the bourgeois subject and various groups of Others.[24] However, social relations across racialized, spatial difference, even while affirming bourgeois subjectivity, also potentially threatened it: through the corruption/diversion of cultural competencies, the loss of racial purity, the possibility of degeneration, and, as Stoler and Cooper note, the instability of "difference."[25] Since bourgeois identity formation was constructed through notions of how to live and the education of appropriate desire, in short, *moral* regulation, it followed that the various groups of Others were seen to lack these very attributes and understandings, and could not be considered fit to govern themselves. They required moral regulation specific to their deficiencies; that is, Others needed to be civilized, through governance, education, and learning how to live and what to desire *in bourgeois terms* since this represented the highest achievement of civilization. In the process the Other could become "white but not quite" (in the words of Bhabha, quoted in McClintock),[26] and the bourgeois subject could be reassured of his "inherent" superiority. Played out in respect to empire (and the working classes at home), the civilizing mission of colonialism was foundational to the bourgeois self, a "natural" outgrowth of a relationally configured subjectivity of global dimensions. Today, it remains among what McClintock has called "the tenacious legacies of imperialism"—particularly as expressed through the development enterprise.[27] In the words of Stoler and Cooper: "Just as colonial regimes let culture do much of the work of race in establishing distinctions, the notion of the civilizing mission gave way after World War II to the notion of development, embodying in a subtler way the hierarchy that civilizing entailed."[28]

In the notion of bourgeois cultural competencies the themes of how to live and the education of desire met, forming and being formed by the social constructions of gender, sexuality, and race. Ideals of propriety were fundamentally gendered.[29] The burden of ensuring that cultural competencies would be transmitted and appropriately attained was located in the domestic sphere and assigned to bourgeois women, but could not be left to their discretion.[30] Here the contradictory positioning of white middle-class women is apparent. Not fully bourgeois subjects, since this was the arena of white middle-class men,[31] such women found themselves "ambiguously complicit as both colonizers and colonized, privileged and restricted, acted upon and acting."[32] Although middle-class women were seen as "custodians of morality, of their vulnerable men, and of national character,"[33] their sexuality was suspect, in part due to the growing influence of Freud, whose theories referenced the already-existing view of women as the simultaneous embodiment of good and evil.[34] Women as a category were considered to inhabit, along with all racialized Others, what McClintock calls "anachronistic space": a "permanently anterior time within the geographic space of modern empire" where human beings are "atavistic, irrational, bereft of human agency."[35] Stoler echoes this perspective, stating that women were seen as possessing passion instead of reason. The pre-eminence of these conceptions, together with the perceived necessity to breed virile empire-builders, was instrumental in regulating bourgeois women's sexuality.[36] Motherhood became a "class obligation and duty of empire"[37] since, in Christianity, motherhood offered women a path to virtue and goodness.[38] The domestic sphere then comprised a focal point for bourgeois control, to the extent that the "cult of domesticity ... became central to British imperial identity."[39] Within the domestic realm, bourgeois women were able to transcend their suspect passions and sexuality through the assiduous cultivation and intergenerational transference of middle-class sensibilities and morals, to the extent that the moral became the purview and domain of respectable white womanhood. In part, this was a reflection of the public/private sphere split that was foundational to bourgeois life: a middle-class man was a public person, whereas proper middle-class femininity belonged in the privacy of the home.[40] Davidoff and Hall capture this dichotomy in a popular image of the day: "a rose-covered cottage in a garden where Womanhood waited and from which Manhood ventured abroad: to work, to war and to the Empire."[41]

As women struggled in the era of empire to gain a position in the public sphere, they expanded their role in areas where gender was not as strongly a prohibiting factor; that is, where middle-class women's nurturing goodness might render their involvement more acceptable, and where their respectability would not be compromised. Hence, bourgeois women joined in benevolent activities associated with the church and other philanthropic work to "help" the deserving poor of the working classes and, later, enslaved peoples.[42] Initially under the control of men, philanthropic associations later on tended to be segregated by gender.[43] Through this work the very attributes of service and self-sacrifice ascribed to nineteenth-century bourgeois women translated into the generation of a domestic mission in respect to the "fallen" women and families of the working classes,[44] and perpetuated the (self-) regulation of "proper" feminine and masculine standards.[45] In the process, participation in public areas of activity began to be considered as not just appropriate, but obligatory for bourgeois women if they were to be seen as truly "good."[46]

For some women, missionary work fulfilled this requirement. During colonial exploration, however, colonized land was presented as both feminine and savage, calling for a heroic male conqueror.[47] In the process of colonization the perceived savagery of the land and its inhabitants, compounded by the bourgeois focus on domesticity, circumscribed the possibilities for most middle-class women to participate directly in the civilizing mission of empire. Although the perception of (sexualized) threat to white womanhood in the colonies was more contrived than real,[48] it was enabled by the creation in nineteenth-century discourse of a racially erotic, primitive, colonized Other.[49] Thus, the land of the colonized was, in the words of McEwan, "No Place for a White Woman"[50]— unless she was under the protection of a husband. As a consequence, initially the missionary field was predominated by men for whom proper middle-class women could only be helpmates. However, over time this perception changed, and the cloak of Christianity was deemed an effective safeguard of respectability for bourgeois women who were willing to make personal sacrifices in the service of their religion's beliefs. Consequently, recruitment of missionaries started to focus on single British women in the last thirty years of the nineteenth century, and led to there being over a thousand more women than men serving as foreign missionaries by 1899.[51]

In Canada, itself first a colony and then a settler society, bourgeois notions of suspect feminine sexuality and prescribed moral propriety circulated from the metropole, disciplining both women and men and establishing the meaning and necessity of class difference. The discourse on republicanism following from the Lower and Upper Canada Rebellions of 1837–38 incorporated gender concepts that were seen as preconditional to the very possibility of founding a republican nation. Such a nation would entail a public arena presided over by men whose virtue was the product of proper upbringing by a mother of morally unassailable conduct and support by a wife of equal calibre.[52] A social purity movement gained momentum in the 1800s, leading to women's benevolent activities becoming common. Although organized by men, the movement propagated and made use of the idea of "Lady Bountiful" as the epitome of all that was pure, chaste, good, and selfless. This figure was particularly expressed in the position of the white mother-teacher.[53] Gendered participation in the development of a home and school association in Toronto from 1916 to 1930 was another, related manifestation of the same processes.[54] The discursive norm of masculine/feminine spheres and middle-class behaviours was unevenly adhered to in every-day life, however. The demands of survival, not to speak of maintaining a middle-class standard of living, in a settler society meant that notions of class respectability were often quite loosely followed, despite efforts to the contrary on the part of government, church, and educational offi-cials.[55] Perry traces these complexities in respect to the settlement of British Columbia from 1849 to 1871,[56] and Bitterman examines them in relation to the Escheat Movement in Prince Edward Island in the 1830s.[57] Such inconsistencies notwithstanding, the prescribed class and gender behaviours were widely understood by the colonizers and func-tioned to marginalize Aboriginal communities and de-legitimize mixed race connections. As Perry notes, "Gender and race were a sharp edge of colonial politics, programs, and policies in mid-nineteenth-century British Columbia"—and the rest of Canada as well.[58] Thus, Coleman argues that the ideals of whiteness, masculinity, and Britishness coa-lesced into notions of white civility, which were foundational to early Canadian identity and which remain an organizing theme in national nar-ratives today.[59]

Colonial Continuities: Planetary Consciousness, Entitlement, and Obligation

The foregoing section highlights some of the main themes from Stoler's, McClintock's, and other writers' analyses of the generation of bourgeois subjectivity in the era of empire. There are several interrelated fea-tures—colonial continuities—that remain operational, which I regard as constitutive of white middle-class identity today. Underlying my argu-ment is a view of bourgeois subjectivity as a kind of mythical construct, which, although not absolutely homogeneous across geographical spaces, is constituted through, and also reproduces, historically derived common-alities that are productive of the identities of white middle-class subjects in the world today. As Fellows and Razack state: "We recognize the dan-gers inherent in transposing to North American soil the making of the European elite in the nineteenth century. Although the histories of Euro-pean and North American nations differ, a powerful argument can be made for their interconnectedness both in the nineteenth century and today. With European empires expanding to link vast sections of the globe, nineteenth-century imperialism laid the groundwork for today's global world."[60]

The work of discourse, in collusion with the operation of early twenty-first-century capitalism (or neo-colonialism), in which development work plays a small but crucial part, furthers processes of bourgeois identity formation begun in the era of empire. Both as individuals and as national subjects, white middle-class Canadians and other Northerners continue to construct through the prism of a planetary consciousness a sense of self in moral terms that expresses the entitlement and obligation bourgeois subjects feel to "help" Others. This globalized world view is shaped by spatial representations that have remained intact over time; namely, that the countries of the North—home to the former metropoles of empire and their white-settler dominions such as Canada—are places of greater civilization, of order, cleanliness, and a truly good quality of life, which has an evident material basis of comfort and security, while those of the South—the former colonies—languish in anachronistic space, where chaos often reigns, disorder and disease are rampant, and life seems (from our perspective) to be hardly worth living. Implicit here is the disciplinary organization of individuals established through spatial concepts.[61] Thus, Jacobs notes: "Imperial expansions established specific spatial arrangements in which the imaginative geographies of desire hardened into material spatialities of political connection, economic dependency, architectural imposition and landscape transformation."[62]

Building on and furthering foundational spatial constructions of metropole and colony, representations of North/South and "First World"/"Third World" also accomplish the affirmation of a racialized superiority on which bourgeois identity continues to rely, complete with the interrelated pulls of dread and desire, and fear of and fascination with racialized difference that have marked white engagement with the Other from the era of empire.[63] Today, in the words of Roman, "white fantasy is the untold allegory of our (white) desire to know the 'racialized other.'"[64] This desire to know the Other takes various forms: romanticizing, identifying with (being "at one with"), caring for, saving, being seduced by, and being transformed through this relationship.[65] Nevertheless, binary relations remain unchanged throughout: it is a question of "them" being known by "us," and being assessed by and understood through "our" standards.[66] In the notion of "our standards" can be detected the continuation of cultural competencies from the colonial era, the operation of which is particularly evident in Northern development projects. For the "superiority" of white middle-class subjects, which has continually to be affirmed, is intrinsically connected to what they/we know—and Others do not.[67]

Stoler and McClintock explain the ambiguous positioning of middle-class women in the colonial bourgeois-formation project: on the one hand, guardians of the race, boundary markers of empire, crucial to the upbringing of truly white bourgeois children; but, on the other hand, part of a large group of undifferentiated, racialized Others who were seen as operating outside of reason and whose sexuality was suspect. Today, to the extent that white middle-class women were, and are, situated close to the bourgeois centre, elements that are constitutive of male bourgeois subjectivity and its current connection to development work also pervade female bourgeois subjectivity.[68] A planetary consciousness, affirmation of self through comparative racialized discourse, and both entitlement and obligation to intervene globally pertain, although in somewhat gender-specific ways, to bourgeois women. The selflessness that affirmed appropriate femininity remains intact, reflected in stereotypes that depict women as good in the sense of being self-sacrificing and kind.[69] For white middle-class women, the comparison of Northern to Southern countries, and specifically the focus on gender relations and the status of women in the "Third World," not only reinforces a sense of our own "freedom" (derived from the supposed comparative "advancement" of our society, and our position in it vis-à-vis "Third World women"), but also compels us to act out our "goodness" by finding ways of joining the intervention processes that claim to better the lives of women elsewhere. On these grounds alone, it would seem that if connections exist between the subject position of development worker and male bourgeois subjects, there is likely to be an even stronger affinity between development work and white middle-class women, whether or not this may result in our assuming the position of development worker in an overseas context. As Roger notes: "Such [Northern white] women are seen to be fervently fighting for a variety of social causes that involves vulnerable others who are seen to be in need of their help."[70]

At the same time, in an apparent contradiction, there is often an assumption of shared experience or affinity on the part of white middle-class women in relation to "Third World" women by virtue of being women, as there was between middle-class women in the imperial metropoles toward indigenous women in the colonies.[71] What attracts white middle-class women to development work is, therefore, more complex and potentially more powerful in its effects than what comes to bear on male, bourgeois subjects. For the legacy of planetary consciousness takes on a special meaning if, in a kind of transnationalist feminist gesture, all women are thought of as the same; when, in the words Stephens uses, it is assumed that "a Western woman reader from an intellectual elite can identify with the suffering of a *bidi* roller in Calcutta."[72] Thus, the legacy of the good woman renders development work especially compelling for white middle-class women.

The subject position of development worker has not been unproblematically available to white middle-class women, however. In view of the connections I have been tracing between development work and the bourgeois subject, and given that full bourgeois subjectivity is the purview of males—white middle-class women being liminally positioned at the bourgeois nexus of race and class—it is evident that development was intended to be a white male middle-class project. As has already been discussed, little has changed since the colonial era in the depiction of the "Third World" in late-twentieth-century discourse. The former colonies remain implicitly presented as places for Northern "heroes." Moreover, the supposedly unrestrained and unrestrainable sexuality of the racialized Other combines with the lingering trope of rape to insinuate an enduring if unspoken threat to white womanhood in the countries of the South.[73] For although the passion of all women's sexuality remains suspect and therefore in need of regulation, as does the sexuality of the racialized Other, white middle-class women occupy, as we have from colonial times, the position of boundary markers of bourgeois "civilization." We are in this sense crucial members of our class, and must be protected from the sexual exigencies of the Other. Our usual, *appropriate* place in the development enterprise would, therefore, seem to be either confined to the Canadian context or restricted to that of accompanying the bourgeois hero who brings development to the South. Yet as Lewis has remarked, the majority of development and relief workers today are women.[74] This comprises a kind of gender transgression, which has become increasingly commonplace over the last twenty years or so, and which was not previously the case in the development field. Despite the normalcy nowadays of development workers being women, issues of safety in the spaces of "Third World" Others haunt our going, especially if we do so alone, and inscribe it as an experience somewhat beyond the pale of appropriate white middle-class womanhood: something at once heroic and simultaneously feminine and unfeminine.

I am proposing that the ongoing discursive validation of Northern, white, bourgeois superiority, planetary consciousness, and morality collaborate with modernity's enduring idea of progress as universally valued and the purview of the West/North to produce a sense of *entitlement and obligation* to intervene globally on the part of bourgeois subjects, to such an extent that these manifest as twin dimensions of the bourgeois self in the late twentieth century. This elucidates, for example, why middle-class Americans respond to media portrayals of global problems by feeling, as Said argues, that it is up to them to set right the wrongs of the world, and how it is that political leadership in Western Europe and Canada can at once contribute to and draw on white bourgeois notions of obligation by using "for their own good" as a policy justification in respect to immigrants and refugees.[75] These colonial continuities were not only foundational to the project of nineteenth-century bourgeois subjectivity, but have endured into the early twenty-first century where they interweave to produce, if not the actual subject position of development worker, certainly its possibility, along with some of the complexities and contradictions inherent in it. Thus, entitlement and obligation to intervene so as to ameliorate the Earth and the lives of its human inhabitants (continue to) need to be acted out worldwide, in the process (re-)constituting bourgeois subjectivities. While white middle-class subjects are virtually all inscribed by these processes, this does not occur in the same way or to the same extent in everyone. Nor is it necessary for each one of us to feel compelled to do development work. On the contrary, to perpetuate the circulation of this discourse, it is enough if the development enterprise goes on, and *a few* of us engage in it directly—as was the case with colonialism in the era of empire.

While this imperative for global intervention may appear, as some development critics contend, to be a direct descendant of empire's "civilizing mission,"[76] there is a more complex process implied here than an anachronism in disguise. If entitlement and obligation on a global scale are understood to comprise important, racialized, and self-affirming relational aspects of white middle-classness in the late twentieth century, it is possible to comprehend the deep and mutually reproductive connection between bourgeois subjectivity and the subject position of development worker. It is also possible to begin to account for the otherwise apparently inexplicable affinity Canadians feel for development work. Although white-settler Canadians are descendants of colonizers—or at least implicated in the colonial process in North America with its continuing imperial relations in respect to indigenous peoples—the Canadian national story is one of colonial and imperial innocence.[77] Our historical complicity notwithstanding, we lack the metropole antecedents of white middle-class subjects in countries such as Britain, and their bequeathed relationships to former colonies. Consequently, the prima facie sense conveyed in suggesting that development workers are the colonialists/missionaries of the late twentieth century is less commonsensical in the Canadian context than in the spaces of the former "mother countries." It is apparent from Canada's prominent place in the foreign aid panoply, however, that the Northern desire for development speaks to more than collective national memories of empire.[78] The analysis of the colonial continuities presented here offers a way of understanding what it is about other people's development that calls so powerfully to bourgeois subjects, particularly women.

Development Worker Motivations: Colonial Continuities in Play

Having theorized the emergence of the modern-day phenomenon called development workers, the discussion now returns to participants' personal narratives about their reasons for choosing this path. The quote from Lorraine presented at the beginning of the chapter continues to form the centrepiece for analysis of themes that are common among participants. These are grouped here under the colonial continuities of planetary consciousness, obligation, and entitlement (to intervene), all of which are operating in the complexity of reasons that middle-class white Canadian women decide to become development workers.

Planetary Consciousness: The View from Here

In Lorraine's responses, presented earlier, she initially mentions "issues in the news." This is perhaps an ambiguous phrase on its own, especially since in a demonstration of planetary consciousness she references "the world," which literally speaking includes Canada. However, the absence of a discursive move to specify Canada as part of this picture of global strife, coupled with the fact that she is talking about her decision to go to Africa, silently positions Canada as outside of, unaffected by, and not implicated in world strife—a familiar Canadian national narrative ("the best country in the world"). This is affirmed in a subsequent statement when Lorraine says:

> Well, look at the images we get of, of Africa ... There's a lot of problems there and that's all you see, so you get this notion of this continent in peril which I suppose it is, I mean relatively speaking.

It would seem that Africa's "peril" derives its meaning through implicit comparison with Canada's supposed safety and stability; a perspective available to, and reflective of, membership in Canadian white middle-classness.

Lorraine is not the only participant to acknowledge the Africa-in-crisis discourse, the same representation that African development writers critique. In Vickie's words: "You think of Africa as Ethiopia and *hopeless starvation*." Debbie talks about images of Africa this way:

> The sort of image that most Canadians probably have in their mind of this, of the cracked earth and skinny people and maybe distended bellies, the images from the mid-80s are all I had in my mind.

Although Vickie went to Southern Africa in the late 1980s, Debbie was in Eastern Africa in the mid-1990s. As noted earlier, the trope of starving Africans in a continent in crisis continues to circulate over time in Northern discourse, and to shape understandings of white middle-class Canadians, drawing some of us to development work. Currently such images would likely conflate with those of people dying from AIDS. The conclusion is that we must personally intervene since, as Lorraine continues: "But I, I guess after a while you know that's your, your image and you've got to go and *do* something."

Only Laura spoke explicitly from her subject position as a *white woman*, when she noted that the urgency to intervene elsewhere might be affected by gender:

> Laura: Um, but I think there's, there's enough circulating around that says, "Yes as a wom—, as a white woman in Africa, you are going to be very susceptible to a lot of risks," um so I suppose that might deter some people.
> Interviewer: Is that stuff that you would think of circulating around here in Canada?
> Laura: I think it is. Um—
> Interviewer: So like the images of Africa?
> Laura: Yes as a, as a dangerous … (sentence left incomplete).

Here Africa appears not as in danger, but as actively dangerous, especially to white womanhood. The continent in peril carries its own perils, which operate through often unnamed referents unavoidably conjured by the tropes so relentlessly at play in Northern discourse. Kris gives voice to some of these conceptions and the fears thereby generated:

> I had been afraid of Africa. I read in the, we had to read *On the Edge of the Primeval Forest* in high school, and I thought that all of Africa was like that. And it was like Albert Schweitzer and it was all full of these horrible diseases and jungles and things.

Implied in such discursive moves is the opposite image of Canada/the North, in this case as a place where white people are free from harm and "horrible" disease. Both constructions of space are of course fictive, but commanding in their effects and clearly serving the interest of the more powerful North.

Although only Laura explicitly names the perception of danger to white womanhood, both Lorraine and Wendy corroborate her point in acknowledging concerns about going alone to do development work: Lorraine would not have gone on her own, and Wendy would not do it alone again. And Linda, herself part of a couple placed in Southern Africa, similarly discusses the need she and her partner felt to be protective of a single woman development worker posted with them in a remote, rural area. Operating here in a subterranean fashion, unable to be explicitly named even by Laura, is an intensified version of the sexual threat to safety that shapes and regulates white middle-class women's lives in the North today as it has from the era of empire and beyond. There is, thus, gender transgression in white women's decisions to undertake development work in sub-Saharan Africa. This is a kind of resistance to these particular, if sometimes implicit, terms of our production as feminine, bourgeois subjects. Resistance in this sense is present, too, in participants' self-descriptions of our pre-development work selves as "confident," "strong," "intrepid," "adventurous," "optimistic," and (emotionally) "self-sufficient." We are evidently claiming a fuller bourgeois subjectivity in our own terms with these descriptors, a move that contradictorily coexists with our embracing of other, more traditional aspects of bourgeois femininity as we choose to engage in the "helping" gesture of development work.

These responses to my question about images of Africa come from just five participants, and yet they comprise almost the sum-total of comments pertaining directly to this topic. The more recent interviewees had even less to say about this than the original group, several of whom quite often simply said that they had no prior images of Africa or expectations about what it would be like. What is to be made of such assertions? One explanation is that participants may have felt self-consciousness about acknowledging altruistic motivations or reluctance at articulating negative images of Africa, which would respectively position us as "do-gooders" or "racist," calling into question the legitimacy of our moral selves. Or, some of us could have felt that while we were aware of such representations in discourse, *we* did not accept what the media conveyed but were rather keeping an open mind: a move of resistance. It can also be theorized that, embedded in imperial relations, the images of Africa ceaselessly circulating in Northern discourse are so normalized *and* internalized by white bourgeois subjects as to be largely imperceptible to us. Because the discursive portrayal of the South in general and of Africa specifically through a repertoire of repetitive, familiar tropes is constitutive of Northern white middle-class identities, much that we see, hear, and read appears to us unremarkable, building as it does on what we have previously been exposed to, and produced to accept. Similarly, white bourgeois awareness routinely if unconsciously incorporates a planetary outlook in which racial and geographic superiority merge. The logic of the existence and availability (to us) of something called development work then appears so taken for granted as to be unquestionable.

Obligation: Making a Contribution

At the same time, planetary consciousness can be detected manifesting as global obligation. This is comprised of both some awareness of human conditions around the world and a feeling of being undeserving of all that one has. Lorraine exemplifies the former when she goes on to explain that strife in the world affects her because "I'm a human, I'm part of the world community." The latter conviction is epitomized by Vickie, who says:

> I've always lived in affluent circumstances and I owe the world something in return—but do you? Well, I think I do. I mean that doesn't bother me. I think I do. I should do something to improve the state of the world.

In very important ways these are noble aspirations shaped by our efforts to live moral lives. Here are white bourgeois subjects seeking to situate themselves in the global context by claiming a common humanity, and wanting to redress injustice on a global scale. In this respect participants' decision to become development workers can and should be read as conscious resistance to social injustice.

Where resistance turns in on itself, though, becoming less pure, is in the elision of relations of power and racialized domination that belie the narrative of simply being human, and underwrite the material inequalities of the North–South economic binary. That the privileges accruing to each of us by virtue of being human are not only different in terms of, for example, standards of living in countries of the South, but that some of us are better off *because* others are and historically have been poor, and that this is structured by the intersections of race, class, and gender, is almost unrecognized. Margaret illustrates this when she says:

> I mean, *of course*, you know, we should have aid and development money. Cause we're rich over here, why shouldn't we share? You know, I think we should be sharing as much as we can until there's a more equitable balance, and, and maybe we have to start with some of these forgiveness of debt loads because we are crushing people.

Having acknowledged that "we are crushing people" with Northern debt loads, an unusually sophisticated analysis among the participants, Margaret stops short of identifying that the comparative richness of Northern countries such as Canada is predicated on the continuous impoverishment of other parts of the world originating in colonial times. Even more absent is any awareness that our identities as white Northern subjects are shaped by a discourse of racialized comparison with Others, especially in the countries of the South. In fact, race in any overt sense is unnamed in this and other explanations participants offer for our motivations for choosing to do development work. Carol was the one exception, acknowledging that the development process with its "Western way of doing things is paternalistic, and then because it happens to be cut along racial lines, it's racist." This awareness notwithstanding, Carol sought, by her own admission, to find justifications for becoming a development worker.

Patti shows the deepest critique of global relations in comparison to other participants:

> There's lots of reasons that people in the South could have to be very upset with us, and you know, and maybe some *mea culpa* for having so much economic resources at the expense of people who don't have that you know. Cause I do see some of that global connection, and am not sure how to live with that with integrity here or there, (laughs) but there at least I still go with it more in my face.

Having confronted a dimension of global guilt that eludes most of us in this study, namely, that Canadians' relative wealth is procured at "*the expense of* people who don't have" (emphasis mine), Patti's struggle for integrity results in her choosing to work in the South where she can "go with it more in my face." Again resistance, this time in the form of seeing past the prima facie presentation of the world as a place where some are rich and some are poor, and in terms of seeking a way of being in the world given that one comes from the privileges thereby accrued, leads to development work in the Southern context.

Returning to Lorraine, her conclusion is:

If you know better and there's something you can do then you, you should do it. So, I don't know what, where one gets that sense, whether it's in your upbringing or a certain amount of awareness. So I guess that's what it had to do with me, a, a conscience thing …

Here the more knowledgeable person is morally obligated to intervene; it is a matter of conscience. For as Lorraine had just previously said, one cannot "stand idly by." In this discourse Lorraine demonstrates both a moral imperative to act and a resolve to resist or change some of the inequities of the North–South relationship: an assertion of agency that at once fulfills and exceeds the paradigm of bourgeois femininity. Yet this is not the whole story. For in the same moment her reaction reproduces the position of white bourgeois subjects from the era of empire, invoking the moral justification of the civilizing mission replete with its panoptical gaze, and entitlement and obligation to intervene *elsewhere*.

Looking more closely at Lorraine's response, it is notable that a number of participants spoke with apparent modesty, as indeed does Lorraine, about wanting to "make a contribution," or as Joanne puts it, do "a little bit of good for some people." However, even the more humble idea of doing "a little bit of good for some people" seems somehow more straightforwardly attainable there than here. In fact, we inadvertently paint ourselves larger-than-life, or at least larger than our lives in Canada, when we perceive the Southern context as needing and amenable to our interventions. At the same time there is an unspoken corollary in our impetus to intervene, to the effect that when we act it will make a difference in what we think of as dire circumstances—else why intercede? Why not just do comparable work at home? Regardless of how we may frame the altruism of our choice to go overseas in our own thinking, this decision is predicated on the presumption that our presence will somehow help to redeem a desperate situation: one that Diane describes as needs "of a completely different magnitude and on a completely different scale" than what is to be found in Canada.

I mean suffering on such a large scale, ah, I mean then those feelings [of compassion, altruism] are just overwhelming. You know, *that* sort of takes over. You mentioned you know, "Why not stay in Canada? There's needs here." Well, sure (laughs) but, they're of a completely different um, magnitude and on a completely different scale. There's sort of a continuum of need, um, and I've just, I've always felt compelled to be working on the higher end of that (laughs) continuum

of need, you know, with, with people who um, don't have the means
or the opportunities necessarily to help themselves.

What can be seen to be operating here, in addition to Northern portrayals of "Third World"/African crisis and attendant assumptions of
Northern entitlement and obligation to intervene, is a definition of need
that enables a performance of self on a grand scale and in terms that are
unassailably moral. Choosing to work with whomever we consider the
poorest, or worst off, also calls on the bourgeois legacy of the good
woman, since fulfilling needs is something we are socially mandated to
do. Positing a global continuum of needs enables a narrative of goodness where the dictates of conscience are followed. The moral self is
secured as innocent of any hint of implication in domination, even as this
very relationship of power is enacted through the panoptical, judging,
and unmarked gaze of white bourgeois subjectivity. White middle-class
women who choose to do development work are thereby definitively
self-established as "good persons." Conversely, those we select for our
interventions are patently seen as worthy of our efforts, reflecting the
effect of personally internalizing Northern media portrayals of the
"Third World."

Our altruism is also contingent on positioning the Southern Other
as *available* to be changed, saved, improved, and so on, by us, thereby
ensuring our entitlement to do so. The validation of Northern knowledge and concomitant erasure of indigenous knowledges are decisive
here, as implied in Lorraine's statement: "if you know better and there's
something you can do, then you, you should do it." Joanne captures the
assumption that Northerners know best when she says: "I mean that's
what got you over there basically in the first place anyway—is what you
knew, is your degree and everything else got you over there, into your
assignments." More knowledgeable Northerners are obligated to act,
and "they" await our interventions. The epistemic violence[79] inhering in
such moves escapes our notice as the North's superiority is affirmed in
this discourse and the Other is rendered devoid of heterogeneity, agency,
and thereby subjectivity; a racializing move crucial to producing our
understanding of Africa's "crises."

The discursive moves that I have been tracing in Lorraine's compulsion to "do something," which are reflective of the views of most of
the participants, are often supported by one anti-conquest strategy in particular. Joanne's declaration that "we didn't go there to *change the culture*"
(emphasis in the original) is echoed time and again in various ways by
many participants. Here are some examples: "You can't expect everything

to change overnight" (Vickie); "It's going to take years and generations for people to get over the, you know, traditional ways of relating to each other" (Diane); and "I mean you can't, you can't change, you can't change things that much" (Jane). Thus, paradoxically, although we are doing development work to effect change, we feel unimplicated in altering people's "cultures," which appear impervious to our interventions. This delineates at once the need for, and a limit to, our rescue efforts. The apparent imperviousness of the Other's culture suggests that which is static and fixed,[80] while implicit comparison to an unmarked dynamic, progressive Canadian norm insinuates that "their" culture, or culture "there," is traditional in a pejorative, backward sense. That African culture is not susceptible to change through our interventions is a point of ambivalence, however: it affords us reassurance about the innocence of what we are undertaking to do, and at the same time imparts a hint of futility to our efforts before they even begin.

Larger-than-life in what we assume we can achieve and yet leaving no marks, how do we conceive our place in development work? Participants speak of reciprocity in the form of "mutual partnership" (Joanne), "exchange" and being a "bridge" (Patti), "learning" (Linda), and "bringing knowledge back to Canada" (Diane). In a more dynamic stance, Margaret perceives her position as "cheerleading": "being right at the grassroots level, working as a cheerleader, I guess that's my role, is to cheerlead." In this discourse of reciprocity and non-intrusiveness, domination has disappeared, taking with it unequal power relations operating both at the macro and micro levels; and racism has no place. Thus, without a critical historicized analysis of the operation of power through imperial relations, our ways of resisting domination produce and rest on its reinscription, the denial of which processes secures our moral selves. For participants coming from a strong Christian background, faith both simplifies and complicates altruistic motivations. The belief that this is "what God wants us to do" (Patti) is in a sense beyond contestation. Yet it allows the same elision of power relations, even when inequality is acknowledged.

Entitlement: Making a Choice

Not only do participants feel morally obligated to intervene, and through planetary consciousness see the world as our field of action; not only do we position Others as amenable to our intercessions; but we take for granted that we can go to, live in, and be active in other people's countries—and lives—*if we choose* to do development work. In a sense, our altruism becomes our passport to the South, and we think this is as it should be. The development option, the *fact* of the development enterprise, is unremarkable to us. Travel costs are covered, work permits are provided, accommodation is arranged, and salaries are paid to us so that and because we want to be development workers, to "do good." The classed nature of this entitlement does not occur to us. Debbie's comments illustrate the normalcy of the development option for white middle-class Northerners:

> I was working here at the time, and I seasonally sort of get laid off in September—wanted more overseas experience. I had been overseas working before, and I thought, I thought I was worthy of someone paying for my flight you know, and giving me some medical coverage and just the backup, I wanted the backup when I was overseas and stuff. And I knew the history of the country, and I wanted to support the rebuilding of the nation. But I, I knew a lot about it and I was quite curious to see how a new nation emerges, you know?

Debbie adds later in the interview: "I sort of feel like being in Canada for a while. But if I get really restless and annoyed with the economy, I'll probably go away again." In Debbie's comments the sense of entitlement inherent in the decision to do development work overseas is normalized as a choice available to her. It is her option, to exercise or not. Here the Other, although still vitally implied, has receded from view, replaced by a field of potential action warranted by altruism, and underwritten by a middle-class sense of self-worth and material expectations.

That development is a choice at participants' disposal to make is further sanctioned by the invisibility (to us) of the fact that it is a one-way street. Of the participants in this study, only two (Carol and Patti) mentioned this as a concern. Carol summarizes:

> I think it's exceedingly valuable for people to travel and go overseas and live overseas, um, I think it would be just as valuable for a [Southern African][81] and the fact of the matter is that that's not an easy option.

Such a recognition, however, did not dissuade these participants from engaging in development work. More commonly, we responded as Margaret did: "But if somebody said to you, 'Do you want to go up to Algonquin Park for a weekend and you know, whatever?'—Yeah, why not? You know, why not? Why not *seize life*?" The importance of our own experiences and the quality of our own lives take precedence over altruistic concern for Others. Development appears thus as a means to a fuller life experience for bourgeois subjects. Again, the discursive positioning of countries and peoples of the South as serving our learning and personal growth leaves our desires unmarked and masks deeper moral issues in respect to the choice we are making.

Participants' internalization of the perspective that the choice is ours, that is, of an attitude of entitlement, reasserts itself when we describe the decision to *leave* our overseas postings and return to Canada. The point is, however, that development work's embedment in domination is rendered invisible to white middle-class Canadians in part because of its morally legitimated normalcy. Although there is, no doubt, selflessness in our motives, they likewise express the relations of domination that shape them and that we cannot, or will not, see.

Lorraine ends her comments about her decision to do development work by saying that she wanted to "make myself feel better by doing something for someone somewhere." Lorraine's frank admission that she was making herself feel better, that there was something in this for her, is echoed by a number of participants who volunteered that they were perhaps selfish in wanting to go overseas. Linda offers a candid self-critique when she says:

> We really *did* go with pretty selfish motives in that sense that, you know we were really interested in experiencing what *we* would learn and hopefully, you know we could pass on something to them, when we were there.

Although attempting to be honest about their motivations, both Lorraine and Linda are also effecting a kind of double-move, whereby acknowledging selfish motives enables the foreclosure of further self-scrutiny, securing the moral self. This is illustrated more clearly by Carol, who says:

> I didn't go for altruistic reasons, I didn't go because I thought I can make a difference, I can help—and in fact those reasons were reasons that I didn't want to have. Because I was concerned that I would go with the idea that *I had something to give*, that I was the bestower of something. Because I think that's not particularly respectful.

Carol's attempt to distance herself from the more overtly altruistic, helping/saving motivations expressed by many participants actually serves at this point to place her further up on the moral high ground in her accounting to herself. Carol, however, works her way through a number of justificatory moves, which are significant because they speak to an apparently lingering unease with the ethics of her decision to go overseas, especially in light of the racism she recognizes as inhabiting development work. She is the participant who is most at pains to establish a rationale for going overseas as a development worker. Having declared that because of her earlier travel experiences in Africa, where she felt what she describes as "freedom," Carol exclaims: "I had an *urge*, I *had* to go!" She goes on to say:

> I think I did what I could to justify going because I wanted to go, anyway. So what I told myself was, "Well, the [Southern African] government, which happens to made up of all Black [Southern Africans], except for one who happens to be a white [Southern African], are building a lot of schools and they can't staff the schools with [Southern Africans] so they're asking for foreign teachers. So I'm not going as some kind of missionary who believes she knows what's right, I'm going because I've been requested." And that was my way of justifying it. And then I sort of justified it by saying, "Well if I can produce two teachers and put myself and one other expat out of a job, then I could justify being there." And then I *further* justified it by saying, um, "And besides, I'm not going to teach, I'm going to learn. And if I can bring *back* sensitivity and so forth to my own culture and change as a person, then um, then that's for the best. So I'm not going to leave any marks on [Southern Africa], I'm going to have [Southern Africa] leave marks on me." But right from, uh, so these were the reasons I told myself why it was okay for me to go. But there's, but it's not okay because it is such an unbalanced relationship. And until it becomes a balanced relationship I think that anybody who does go ought to realize what's going on—what's *really* going on.

This is a multi-layered justification for participating in what remains acknowledged as an "unbalanced relationship." Carol produces a number of rationales for her decision to do development work. Although each of her reasons appears to have some validity, at the same time she seems only tenuously convinced by the accounting she renders of herself. Apparently, she reached a point of some accommodation, because she did go overseas as a development worker. An explanation may lie in the latter part of Carol's dialogue, where the contradiction between asserting that the experience she has had is valuable and yet wrong is contained by arguing that people who "go" "ought to realize what's going on." This opens a way out of the moral impasse that appears inherent for Carol in "going" at all: if one is aware of the inequities, one may still participate. A moral narrative of self is thus shakily preserved.

For a number of participants there were other plainly self-interested reasons for deciding to do development work. Such motives are cast in terms of enriching one's life and learning about/developing oneself. Of these, travel figures prominently. In Erica's case, the urge to do development work was also about travel: "[It] was a chance to see, like what does go on in these poor countries where people end up being refugees, *and* I get to travel. It was the two, for sure. And I would say they were about equal." In this statement altruism and self-interest coexist, with the former remaining undisturbed by the self-centring move of the latter. Again a sense of entitlement underwrites the acceptance of foreign travel as a benefit of doing good through development work, and the commodification of Otherness[82] remains imperceptible to a white middle-class subject. Especially troubling in respect to the latter is that the political-economic conditions productive of refugees are presented as a point of attraction.

Previous travel in the South also influenced a number of participants. As was evidenced by Carol above, these experiences fired their interest in development work. Laura explains:

> I was away for almost a year and I was in many, many different places, and I always sort of thought throughout that trip and, and after I got back that, it was, it was one thing to be passing through places and seeing them as a traveller, but it would be really different to, to actually have to live in a place and, and not just move on to the next country when things got uncomfortable or you got bored or whatever else.

Elsewhere on the same spectrum is Kris, who emphatically says:

> I, I couldn't begin to explain to you how sure I was that I had to do this. I mean I had seen poverty, (laughs) I had, I had already been there. This was not an abstract thing—the "Third World"—I had been there. I had been in Africa, I'd been in Latin America. I knew absolutely, the kinds of situations that I thought that I had to be involved in, in changing.

Here white middle-class access to travel, as well as the culturally sanctioned normalcy of its benefits, operates in collusion with racialized and ongoing legacies of obligation and entitlement to strengthen development work's appeal for white bourgeois subjects. Although few participants owned up as unequivocally as Erica to the lure of travel in shaping motivations, it became self-evident as the interviews progressed that travel formed a valued part of the overseas experience for the majority of participants.

In addition, opportunities for adventure, excitement, and the experience of something different, "living in a different culture" as Yvonne and Laura put it, are quite unselfconsciously accepted as part of development's appeal to white middle-class subjects. Bev frankly says: "I don't know what I had to offer *them*, but it was interesting for *me* to go and see ... (pause) It was something to do, it was, it was something exciting and *available*." Although Bev is apparently aware of her multiple motivations, she is not overly ambivalent about the choice she is making. Here the admission of not knowing what she has to offer curiously acts to legitimate Bev's confession that it was interesting for her to "go and see." Bev's self-presentation as a moral person is therefore not threatened by what amounts to a declaration of self-centredness.

In a reflection that articulates what is more profoundly at stake in our self-interested motivations, Carol takes Bev's admission a step further, identifying that her investment in going overseas to live was really about personal growth. She echoes as well Laura's previous comments about wanting to know what it would be like to have to stay and not simply move on "when things got uncomfortable for you or you got bored or whatever else." Carol says:

> Now I realize I, that what was making me go was an attempt to figure out what kind of *life* it was that I wanted. What I was trying to do was, to re-evaluate what it was I wanted to be and what I wanted to do. And I wanted to put myself in a situation in which I had none of the support systems that I had had all the way through. I mean I was always good in school, and I always knew how to get good grades, I always had friends, I always—et cetera, et cetera, et cetera. I had, um, never had a challenge that felt like a real challenge. I wanted to see what kind of person I would be in a situation in which all the sorts of things that are *valued* for *us* are not necessarily valued in a different place. But I didn't *know* that at the time.

Carol is, in a sense, consuming the world in her quest for her self, trying to find out "what kind of person" she would be amid Others, somewhere else. She negotiates the domination expressed in her self-absorbed longing by means of a detailed justification, a key to which is her intention not "to leave any marks on [Southern Africa]" but rather to have "[Southern Africa] leave marks on me." Several other participants, like Patti, put the same idea more prosaically, as a matter of "what we wanted to do with our lives," but the same enactments of dominance inhere. In a move evocative of the effects of travel literature, the Other is presented as crucial in helping us to know and/or attain our real selves. This quest for self is, of course, equally an actualization of class privilege.

Implicit here is our desire for the racial Other, which has as much to do with our constructions of self as with exoticized attraction to difference. Both are legacies of bourgeois subject formation from the era of empire, although the latter has been constructed in somewhat changed terms by the discourse of multiculturalism and the marketing of foreign travel destinations. Our yearning for "authentic" (read exoticized, racialized) difference is very much productive of our desire for development and bound up in our enthusiastic reactions to the commonplaceness of the opportunity to do development work. Longing for relationship with the Other and experiences of Otherness are implicit in participants' acknowledgement of wanting adventure, the experience of living in another culture, of "something different." However, the encounter with the Other that is sought—that seems to count—can only be obtained by going to the spaces of the Other. The same Othered people on our home ground do not satisfy our need for these engagements with difference. For some participants, the desire for development has its beginnings in childhood, in yearning to go to Africa or another part of the world. As Norma says, "I always wanted to go to Africa." To some extent this is a craving for a fictional space, but it cannot be separated from a longing for a fictional/fantasy Other. For as Yvonne explains:

> When I was a young girl, sitting in church, I dreamed of being a missionary. I went through a religious phase where I was, where I was going to go to Africa and save the Africans, and bring *them* Christianity.

Although it is not often explicitly stated, "they" are always implied in our narratives of intervening, of saving or helping, because without "them" these narratives would have no meaning. In this way Othering and the Other are necessary to our stories of manifesting and attaining goodness through development work.

The overwhelming importance of relationships with Others in participants' development work narratives becomes apparent as the stories of our experiences in the sites of development unfold. At this pre-departure stage, it is presaged by Linda, who puts it simply: "Your real interest in being there was to meet the African people." And Wendy concurs: "I mean that's why we went, right? Or that's why I went." Yet participants frequently omitted discussing our interest in seeking relations with Others as a central reason for doing development work. Perhaps this can be attributed to both our uncertainty about such relations and the depth of white middle-class desire for the Other. This desired relationship is not unproblematic. Although carefully and consistently positioned as passive, available, and non-individuated, the Other nevertheless possesses the latent capacity to destabilize that which (s)he is needed to produce and secure. Close contact is therefore a risky business, at once potentially comforting and discomforting. Participants evince an incipient awareness of this. As Wendy asks:

> I mean how do you form relationships with people and work with them and live with them when your whole context for your—every-thing that has made you who you are—is entirely different?

Concluding Remarks

What I have traced thus far is how a plethora of forces derived from the era of empire, constitutive of bourgeois identity-making and evidently imperceptible to white middle-class feminine subjects, are operative in, and productive of, what we take as our natural, "altruistic" desire for development. Northern discourse, planetary consciousness, entitlement, and obligation to intervene, all organized around racialized comparisons and assumed class privilege, commingle in participants' predominant social justice explanations of why we want(ed) to do development work, establishing and protecting the moral self even while warranting participation in domination. While theoretically not surprising, the depth of our initial desire for development is more thoroughly comprehensible through the narratives participants provide.

I have offered a somewhat close reading of participants' stories about how we became development workers because it is essential that the contradictions and complications inhering in our imperative to undertake development work be traced in depth at the outset. Although the focus here is on the explanations offered by the earlier group of interviewees, the rationales given are not substantially different from those of the more recent development workers. For this is a compelling calling, the ethical complications of which cannot be understood either ahistorically or without grasping the effects of interlocking relations of race, gender, and class. Minus continuities from the era of empire, including the operation of racialized comparison in the construction of white bourgeois identities, the impetus of our moral need to intervene elsewhere in the world loses its force. For example, the economic situation in Eastern Europe following the collapse of the Soviet Union did not elicit from white middle-class Northerners a similar compulsion to act despite the diversion of foreign aid money from the Southern arena to Eastern Europe at that time. The fact that the development option is fundamentally raced and classed nevertheless appears invisible to most participants, who, failing to recognize who gets to know what in Canadian society, and whose knowledge counts, simply state that it is our knowledge that is important in getting us overseas.

Goldberg has suggested that in the modern world the social subject is "split between a conception singularly self-interested and free, on the one hand, and altruistic and egalitarian, on the other."[83] This splitting is abundantly clear in the way participants explain our motivations for doing development work. Altruism and self-interest coexist frequently and often effortlessly in accounts participants give. Only occasionally does a participant show signs in her development accounts of being disturbed by holding these apparently opposing views. Resistance moves are plagued by the same contradictory dualism, so that not only is the resistance present in our motivations revealed to be less than total, as Visweswaran points out,[84] but its foundations tend to generate its undoing. Racial and class omissions undermine our understanding of the global injustice we seek to resist.

Gender seems notably absent from participants' narratives, with very few exceptions. This is not to be wondered at, given white middle-class women's positioning in imperial relations. Only liminally bourgeois subjects, we work to maximize our claims to full bourgeois (white masculine) subjectivity, a process that cannot succeed if we continually name the operation of gender oppression. Rather, we further our positions by embracing the discourse aimed at true bourgeois subjects. Lorraine's comments are illustrative of this when she talks matter-of-factly about studying journalism and her reaction to news stories of global strife. Her words imply that any *person* with a conscience would respond as she does, by trying to make things better. She does not evince awareness that gender shapes her response, and yet although her conclusion that she must intervene might be the same if she were a man, what impels her is necessarily gendered. The colonial legacy of the good woman is inscribed in her reactions as it is in the altruistic motivations of all the participants.

The importance to many participants of constructing our own subjectivities, our sense of self, is reflected in a number of the reasons participants offer for deciding to do development work. The potential contribution that the development experience affords the process of defining selfhood must be understood in relation not only to our ambiguous and uncertain claims to bourgeois subjectivity, but also to our attempts to refuse certain aspects of this paradigm and its terms for the construction of appropriate femininity.

Consistent with national narratives, Canada appears as a place of order and safety, a good country with (white middle-class) citizens who care about the rest of the (non-white) world. The accepted normalcy of the development worker option and the angst of global guilt that participants acknowledge attest to our need to accept without questioning our role as global do-gooders. A panoptical altruistic gaze incorporates certain blind spots that are crucial to our interpretation of a continuum of need that calls us elsewhere, to zones where relative material deprivation secures our goodness.

CHAPTER 3
DEVELOPMENT IS ... A RELATIONAL EXPERIENCE

This chapter examines participants' stories of relationships with other people in the development context. The centrality of relations with African people in these stories underscores the effects of race in the production of white development worker identities in particular, and bourgeois subjectivity in general, and so makes prominent the significance of racialized constructions of space. There is wide consensus in the whiteness literature that whiteness is a relational identity. Perhaps Dyer sums it up best: "At the level of representation, whites remain, for all their transcending superiority, dependent on non-whites for their sense of self, just as they are materially in so many imperial and post-imperial, physical and domestic labour circumstances."[1] As has been discussed, this dependency was inherent in, and in fact foundational to, the formation of bourgeois identity in the era of empire. In this sense, the relational basis of racism, too, is a colonial continuity. Space is intrinsic to the production of these relational identities.[2] Discursive representations of the "Third World" that impel Northern, bourgeois subjects, especially women, to exercise our sense of entitlement and obligation to intervene globally operate in part through the establishment of spatial difference in the minds of such subjects—equally a colonial continuity. Such constructions of meaning inhabit and give coherence to various conceptualizations of centre and periphery.[3] So established is this spatialized knowledge that it becomes almost impossible to conceive of the "Third World," a "developing country," or, in this case, "Africa," apart from the meanings that have become so firmly attached to these imaginatively fashioned physical spaces. In effect, we inhabit fantasy places that are constituted by relations of comparison in which one geographical area—the West/North—and its people are presented as superior to other places and their peoples.[4] Without these geographic distinctions—which are played out locally in the form of racialized meanings attached to areas designated, for instance, as "Chinatown" or the "hood"—the relational basis of whiteness would falter.

Crucial to bourgeois processes of identify formation, and inherent in the different manifestations of the development binary, are the operation and maintenance of the boundaries that keep spatial differentiation intact. The collapse or threatened breakdown of such boundaries has parlous implications for those whose identities are thereby upheld, and may, therefore, precipitate new dimensions of Othering to sustain "distance."[5] McClintock charts how this operated in terms of class difference when working-class servants entered middle-class homes in imperial England and when the "native" worked to maintain the home of the colonizer.[6] Similar processes of differentiation on the part of those in dominance may occur today when spatial separation is dissolved, so that, in the case of white development workers, it can be theorized that there will be moves to re-establish superiority and recreate spatial meaning when we find ourselves in the spaces of the Other. Stereotyping and even potential violence comprise potential ways of shoring up the boundaries of spatial difference.[7] A commonplace stereotyping move in the development context would be to exoticize the Other by exoticizing their space, and vice versa. Boundary maintenance can also take the form of reasserting images of Africa as the "dark continent." This is a trope that implicitly insinuates a zone of degeneracy in which the purity of whiteness is seen to be imperilled through sexualized debauchery attributed to the Other and fears of contagion that harken back to bourgeois anxieties in the era of empire.[8] As a result, as Mbembe succinctly says, the continent of Africa is "the very figure of 'the strange.'"[9] Like the "Orient" of Orientalist discourses, there is no real place actually corresponding to this imagined geography of "Africa."[10]

As discussed previously, the "Third World" as a whole and Africa in particular are made familiar to Northerners in these terms through discourse arising from the media, especially film, but also travel literature and theme parks. Media present the "Third World" as a spectacle in which the abnormal is routinely showcased.[11] In the geography of modern adventure narratives "elements of normal life are inverted and contradictions are displayed ... [and] the hero encounters a topsy-turvy reflection of home."[12] Theme parks provide direct experiences of a liminal space in which "excitement, danger and the shock of the grotesque merge with dreams and fantasies which threaten to overwhelm and engulf the spectators."[13] However, encountering such imaged spaces can be both liberating and alienating for bourgeois subjects.[14]

This suggests a "carnivalesque" subtext that reinscribes racialized, spatialized difference. The carnival or fair was a feature of medieval times, also a world of "topsy-turvy, of heteroglot exuberance, of ceaseless overrunning and excess where all is mixed, hybrid, ritually degraded and defiled."[15] It was a place where social distinctions were cast aside and participants were liberated from the normal behaviours and forms of interactions, enabling "a special type of communication impossible in everyday life."[16] In the colonial era, carnival gave way to the more sedate fair that recreated many of its original aspects. Displays of exotica from subjugated lands and a temporary reprieve from the usual order available at the fair, however, threatened even while validating middle-class standards and cultural competencies, generating desire, dread, and overall unease with the phenomenon itself.[17] The relationship between the carnival/fair and colonialism is articulated by Stallybrass and White as follows:

> In each case the manners taught [to exotic creatures exhibited there] imitate European forms of culture or politeness and amusingly transgress, as well as reaffirm, the boundaries between high and low, human and animal, domestic and savage, polite and vulgar. We might say that these token transgressions model the double process of colonialism. The Other must be transformed into the Same, the savage must be civilized (like the wild creature who smokes a pipe "as well as any Christian"); but at the same time, the Other's mimicry of the polite is treated as absurd, the cause of derisive laughter, thus consolidating the sense that the civilized is always-already given, the essential and unchanging possession which distinguishes the European citizen from the West Indian and the Zulu as well as from the marmoset and manteger.[18]

Apparent here is the reciprocal connection of strange and exotic beings from fabulous far-off spaces with the identity-constituting effects of colonialism on the bourgeois self. The processes of Othering and interpreting as carnival continue today, for as Stallybrass and White assert, the bourgeoisie goes on ceaselessly rediscovering the carnivalesque "under the sign of the Other," an act that reveals to middle-class subjects our own pleasures and desires, and that is "constitutive of the very formation of middle-class identity."[19] For development workers, the development context, that is, the physical space of the "Third World"—in this case sub-Saharan Africa—unavoidably and undetectably (to us) conjures something of the carnival, due to the normative presentation of the "Third World" as spectacle, as exotic, and as a zone of degeneracy inhabited by Others whose "difference" culturally and spatially makes them distant from "us." Soja notes that in the social production of space, such representations become concretized and consequently seem second nature, so that they are inscribed in our understandings of the place long before we get there.[20] Paradoxically, these images can coexist with those of the Other as familiar. Chambers argues that, in fact, Others are at once exotic and familiar and, therefore, neither wholly one nor the other.[21] This dual movement is part of establishing the "examinable Others" who are necessary to whiteness's invisibility, that is, its ability to *not* mark itself.

Configurations of different or exotic places and peoples are achieved as well, at least in part, in counterpoint to the image of home: home being the nation, or, more specifically, the personal home. The contrast between the two is captured by McNelly:

> [Home is] civilization, but also order, constraint, sterility, pain and *ennui*, while native culture, the far pole of the myth, represents nature, chaos, fecundity, power and joy. The home culture is, moreover, associated always with the ability to understand by seeing, abstractly, while the other culture is associated with black, with the sense of touch, the ability to know by feeling, from within. The far pole of the tropical journey is indeed the *heart* of darkness.[22]

Development workers from Canada and other Northern countries thus carry assumptions of both home and the exotic and carnivalesque with us to the spaces of the Other: signs of "the boundaries in our minds formulated in and by our experiences of Western culture."[23] As we do so, we keep in place the differences on which whiteness relies, but also make central to our experiences our relations with African people, relations that are simultaneously, as Chambers noted, about the exotic and the familiar—about objectifying and humanizing.

This chapter focuses on participants' stories about relationships in the African context. For the most part, the accounts are monologist, to use a term explained by Bakhtin, in that Africans appear as "Others," not "another *I* with equal rights (*thou*)."[24] There are dialogic moments, when the Other/African person figures at least partially as "*thou*," to continue Bakhtin's dichotomy, but even in these moments Othering can be detected. The spaces of Africa are particularly noticeable in participants' accounts, which is to be expected in light of the relational constitution of white identities, which are both reaffirmed and challenged as they enter the terrain of the Other. To start with, the adjustment process is examined, and then participants' relations with African people—the centrepiece of their time in Africa—are presented.

First Encounters

Development workers are usually encouraged by Canadian development NGOs to think about the adjustment process when going to the "Third World" in terms of "culture shock," which purports to describe "the anxiety produced when a person moves to a completely new environment … the physical and emotional discomfort one suffers when coming to live in another country … [where] everything is different."[25] The notion that African people's culture and environment are going to be shocking for white middle-class subjects already implies a carnivalesque world that does not make sense and is not quite real,[26] and calls into play previously known spatial tropes that are productive of Othering. Debbie graphically conveys her initial reaction to Eastern Africa this way:

> I was in a state of shock, you know? It was horrible. And you know, I thought I was quite well travelled, very intrepid, and stuff like that, and you know you feel, you know you feel like a fairly worldly person. And I've been in weird places, I've gone *alone* to weird places, with no money, and having no job. So you think, "Well this is, this is nothing," you know. But—it sounds like nothing you know—but, culture shock I have learned can really hit you at different times of your life and under different circumstances in completely different ways. And *nothing* you can do will prepare you for it—I find.

Most other participants do not utilize the term culture shock, but allude to the extreme strangeness (in our view) of the spaces we have entered. As Vickie says: "But what a world—where you buy a half loaf [of bread] in supermarkets! If you have, if they have coffee you buy it in case there's no coffee in the next week or two." Within this reaction to strangeness, our adjustments are articulated as responses to places and people. This is where the material conditions participants encounter enter our narratives with particular intensity, and African peoples are Othered through undifferentiated foreignness. Our adjustments are really about the recovery of self in the strange new sites of development.

Evidently, encountering the Other in the physical space of the South is initially threatening rather than affirming, especially for white middle-class women, the full extent of white bourgeois positional superiority and the effects of the legacy of white womanhood in the spaces of the "Third World" being new to freshly arrived development workers from the North.

I turn again to Lorraine for her story of what it was like for her when she first came to Eastern Africa:

> Lorraine: Driving from the airport you know, through the, the industrial areas towards the city to the [Canadian NGO's] office downtown, I'm just thinking *"Oh my god! What am I doing here? I am staying here for two years? I had to be insane!* (Both laugh) *What was I thinking?"* But then, you know, I went back for more! … I guess, I mean it was a mistake to uh, to decide to stay in the city. Um, we had the choice of staying in the city or out at the beach to get over the jet lag and so on, and James [her partner] had this idea that, well we should get used to the city right away um, so there we were in the [name of hotel], which I think they closed down the next year. And, you know, sort of cockroaches the size of cats in the bathroom and there's no electricity, you know, and these sort of mouldy, beds. And I'm, you know, waking up at four in the morning bawling my eyes out thinking *"What am I doing here?"* You know, it was terrible, we should have been out at the beach chilling out for a couple of days. But, well, live and learn. (both laugh)
> Interviewer: It's too late now!
> Lorraine: Give me beer so I forget about this!
> Interviewer: How did you deal with the foreignness?
> Lorraine: The foreignness?
> Interviewer: I mean it just, it sounded like there was so much to get used to.
> Lorraine: There was, it was a big shock for a Toronto girl.

Lorraine is straightforward in describing her feelings on arrival. "A Toronto girl," even in the company of her white male partner, reacts strongly and negatively to the "Third World" up close. It appears a zone of degeneracy indeed, with "cockroaches the size of cats," and "mouldy beds," made worse by the lack of electricity. She is unnerved, and wonders what she has done. Several other participants also echo Lorraine's chagrin on arrival. Susan, too, mentions "the *size* of those *cockroaches!*" Tired, alone, and facing the reality of "mud huts" ("I mean I had descriptions of what it was going to be like, but I mean my neighbours were all in mud huts really … at first it's hard to get used to") and a yard full of interested neighbours and school students, Jane says:

> The primary school probably had about 500 students and by the time I got down to my house, they had surrounded my house and they were all in my compound and, it was just like they were all peering in, at me. I was just so tired because I'd been on the night train the night before and I had been travelling all day. I sat down and I started crying and it was like, (laughs) cause you just feel like "Oh what have I done?" You know, "Here I am!" You know when you first get into a house and it's bare and it doesn't really look very nice and, you know you just, well it's like when you go anywhere, and ah, anyway, I, I just shut all my doors and windows and eventually they went away. And ah, then, you know, my neighbour came and introduced himself and things got much better.

Despite Jane's resistance-talk that "it's just like when you go anywhere," this is obviously quite unlike anywhere else she has been, in part no doubt because of the interest her presence stirs in the neighbourhood. African people in large numbers appear overwhelming rather than welcoming for a young white woman. It seems that what inscribes them with Otherness is about more than numbers, however. The fact that these are people "really" living in "mud huts" imbues this account with a sense of *National Geographic*–like exoticness with overtones of savagery. Local living accommodations thus signal a preconceived meaning of the space of Africa.

It is not only the initial, apparently bizarre strangeness of a new place called Africa that generates challenges, but sometimes also the hardships of day-to-day life even for Northern development workers. Vickie's comments touch on one aspect of this: that of commodity shortages. Several other participants remark on the daily difficulties of arranging for food and water. As Erica puts it: "Those were the things that like got me down, more like 'Oh man, I gotta go into town again and like lug, you know, take my knapsack and fill it full of groceries.'"

More disconcerting than the physical challenges, however, were participants' early encounters with the Other, as is evident in Jane's story above. It is noteworthy that with the first move toward individuating (as when a neighbour comes to introduce himself), the undifferentiable crowd becomes less intimidating. The perceived dissimilarities between participants and the people we came to work and live with are couched in terms of cultural differences and yet are evidently racial, as Joanne's account also shows:

I observed a lot. I observed what people were wearing, what they were doing, you know um, how they walked down the street, what they ate, how they ate it um—because they use their fingers, I'm used to eating with a knife and a fork and a spoon um, so how do you eat rice with your fingers? How do you eat this *luku* stuff with your fingers— how do you roll it around in a ball properly and dip it into your sauce? I observed um, and, and used my senses, when I adapted into that culture.

Reifying aspects of African culture leads to presenting African people as Others, and as objects for study: the examinable Others, mentioned earlier.[27] Local food is derogatorily described as "this stuff," a not uncommon response among participants. In a more explicitly racialized revelation, Joanne goes on to admit: "When we first got there, you look at everybody and they all look alike. You know it's hard to distinguish because they all have the dark skin." Here African people are to blame for Joanne's inability to distinguish one individual from another: "*they* all have *the* dark skin" (emphasis mine). Later on in the same story Africans are gradually granted a degree of subjectivity, but initially the term "they" continues to homogenize the people Joanne encounters into what Watson and Smith call "an amorphous, generalized collectivity," from which Joanne is eventually able to discern certain individuals.[28]

For Erica, too, local people are initially indistinguishable, but this time in terms of gender:

It's *hilarious* now to think of it and I was (laughs)—but I, I couldn't tell the difference between boys and girls and, and they weren't all in their uniforms? They were all—and *I could not tell the difference*, I couldn't tell who was a boy and who was a girl. But honestly I couldn't. They all looked so, hilarious you know—their little *things* stuck out of their heads because uh, they don't, most of them don't plait their hair and stuff the way they do in, certainly in East Africa.

Another aspect of relations with Others that initially troubled a number of participants, and that did not always ameliorate, is the feeling of standing out and constantly being noticed, which gender exacerbated. As Carol says: "I didn't like being noticed. I didn't like being looked at, I didn't like feeling different, standing out, for all the reasons that I obviously would." Lorraine, who shares this discomfort, offers the cultural explanation that in the country of her posting, it is not considered rude to stare. This is an experience that figures more often in the stories of the second group of interviewees. Absent from these accounts is an awareness of why participants seemed so interesting and literally noticeable: the inscription of colonial history and the effects of globalization on their bodies. Missing, too, is an acknowledgement that being made to feel conspicuous by virtue of race is a practice reciprocated by white subjects in the North, where positional superiority is not on the side of the person of colour who is so singled out.

Not all the participants disclosed quite this genre of experiences; yet for the great majority of us the adjustment process was clearly disturbing and challenging, even if, as Laura claims, many of us feel that we "enjoyed taking everything in." Time slows down, "the first couple of weeks seeming like months and months 'cause everything's new. Every day was like 48 hours instead of 24 hours" (Linda). Participants coped in different ways, some becoming depressed or withdrawn, some writing home frequently, others turning to baking (that is, making familiar food) or establishing our new homes (which, while not like the ones we left behind, are equally not like those of local peoples in terms of decor and amenities). The issue here is not the specifics of the coping mechanisms but rather what they reveal about what is at stake in the adjustment process: a loss of sense of self. Since home is where bourgeois subjects recreate their identities, home-related activities become important at this point. Similarly, as Kaplan notes, travel, which was especially common during the adjustment phase, is a means of reclaiming the self by reasserting a relationship with the Other in which difference is soothingly re-commodified.[29] What recreating home and travelling have in common is the reproduction of spatial meaning. The familiarity and "Canadianness" of development worker homes offer a reprieve, even refuge, from the foreignness of the new space, and at the same time redraw the boundaries that keep Othering intact. Travel, likewise, revives and reaffirms the spatial representations that development workers have been exposed to before coming to Africa, and thus renders the new context manageable.

In addition to other challenges participants face in adapting to the new situation we have entered, for many of us there are stresses connected to work. Several participants who went overseas as teachers had not taught before or were not confident of teaching "there." For example, Carol says: "I don't think I am that great a teacher." Vickie, who was in a busy medical placement, mentions, "It was hard to work at that pace, since I had been used to going much more slowly." And Laura acknowledges a confidence issue that many of us seem to be implicitly referencing:

There was a lot of things that I was in awe of definitely, and, and particularly what was going on, people's (sighs) … um, just in awe of some of the incredible people that I was working with. And uh, so it, I think it took me quite a while to sort of develop any level of confidence about what I was doing in just in my job there.

The situations participants encounter initially comprise a subterranean threat that at first overwhelms the white, female, bourgeois self. Patti argues that "as long as you have good relationships with people … then all that other stuff doesn't matter." This is precisely the point. At this stage participants do not have relationships with the Other or with sister/fellow expatriates;[30] we are no longer on home ground, nor do we have access to our former homes. The fundamental, identity-succouring place of a "real" home in the bourgeois constructions of self has been lost, and with its loss, as well as the temporary uncertainty of our positional superiority in relations of power, we struggle to varying extents to re-constitute our identities, to recover our selves, in these uncertain spaces where boundary maintenance is failing. Sometimes when we experience what feels like objectification, we engage in Othering more completely, which helps to re-secure the sense of comparative superiority that appears immediately imperilled and in the same moment reproduces the spatial difference we depend on. The extent of threat is implicit in the absence now of any notion of altruism, of our moral imperative to intervene. In the face of African people who for the moment seem more menacing than in need of saving, and spaces that figure more as zones of degeneracy than exotic, the white middle-class development worker's moral self falls silent.

There is, however, another much less common reaction among participants to the newness of the spaces of sub-Saharan Africa: that of consuming the Other. Yvonne says that for her "the adaptation process was very good" because she was "quickly thrown into life," an interesting turn of phrase that implies Yvonne's immediate acceptance in the place where she was posted. In fact, Yvonne went through two periods of adjustment to the same West African country, so her remarks about the first time she arrived there bear looking at. Yvonne describes her earlier encounter with Africa as follows:

But from the moment, almost the moment I landed—and then we, it was almost dark and there were soldiers everywhere with guns. I thought "Ooh!" But uh, the, the culture was so rich in West Africa, I mean the clothing, the food, the noise, the smells, the music. And I'd be just, "Oh wow! This is really Africa!"

Yvonne and Wendy are the only participants to react in quite such unequivocal terms, Wendy also responding this way to her first experience of Africa. In her words:

> When I had gone to [Southern Africa] I was just filled with this incredible sense of *wonderment*, you know, and *excitement* at all the *newness* and everything that was, you know, all the learning, and you're really trying to get to know and understand other people and uh I didn't find that same sense of excitement [arriving in West Africa]. And I don't know if that's because—you know, obviously the cultures are not the same. There are lots of ways in which they are very different, but—maybe it was just ... I don't know. I never really figured that out. Why that wasn't *quite* the same. There were other parts about living there that I really appreciated you know, but the life—maybe it's just that daily life was so much harder that it was, it took so much energy just to get by, you know. Um ... maybe that's why.

Wendy's explanation is framed in terms of the hardships of day-to-day life displacing the wonder of a new experience, and certainly that would seem to be part of what is going on for her, as for quite a number of participants. However, bell hooks's notion of the commodification of Otherness is also important here.[31] For Yvonne, West Africa has lived up to expectations, proving to be, in her words, "really Africa," and thereby reaffirming her white bourgeois identity, since if Africa is really Africa, then white middle-class subjects can remain who we think we are. For Wendy, Southern Africa is likewise a place of wonder, excitement, and learning, where the Other is available to be understood. For both participants the space of Africa is cast in the reassuring guise of desired exoticness. Africans, too, appear as comforting figures, so that gendered threat is diminished, even absent. With bourgeois feminine identity entrenched rather than challenged by the first brush with the exotic and the Other, there is no need to engage in the mechanisms of recovery of self that many other participants employ.

A final remark that must be made in regard to the adjustment process is that, among the first group of interviewees, the participants who have the least to say about the challenges of this period were married, and were overseas with their partners. There is not a clear-cut division, however, between single and married participants, since both Lorraine and Linda are among the latter. The second group of recent interviewees had notably less to say about the adjustment process, presumably because most of them had been overseas before, even if on short-term assignments.

How Do "We" Relate to "Them"?

All participants move sooner or later to the centrepiece of our development stories: engagement in relations with African people. These are
relations in which the movements of recoil from apparently insurmount-
able difference and embrace of romanticized Otherness, the one through
reification of culture and the other through disavowal of disparity, are
played out. Thus, African people are always construed as available to us,
and our assumptions are pervaded by a planetary consciousness such
that, just as we assume the right to be in the Other's space, so are we
(self-) positioned as entitled to intervene in the Other's existence, and
to seek relations with whom we choose. At times these relations also
exhibit a considerable degree of reciprocity, and Otherness is to a large
extent eschewed.

For each participant, daily life in the development context is full of
people: African workmates, domestic workers, friends, neighbours, and
other foreigners. For a minority of participants being a development
worker was nevertheless an apparently lonely time. However, most of
us seem closer to Lorraine's account of a social life that is "*far* more
vibrant when I'm there than it is when I'm in Canada." As Patti says:
"And you know in Africa it's *all* knocking on the door and coming over.
Nobody ever phoned." These comments speak to an extent of engagement with African people that helps to explain the centrality of these relations to our narratives of development work. Involvement with so many
people is in itself a considerable adjustment, since the multiplicity of
relations participants describe is attended by various and interrelated
meanings and effects. With so much interaction afoot, what kinds of
relationships do participants then form, and what do they reveal about
our understandings and negotiations of relations of power?

Our friendships with African people are clearly a mixture of longing
for relationship, that is, for a meeting across difference, and its simultaneous reinscription. We engage in Othering even when we grant subjectivity, although it is important to note that we do both: our resistance
to these terms of the production of our bourgeois identities operates
alongside our perpetuation of them. Whiteness remains for us, however,
a marker of all that is constant, civilized, and home. Our engagement
with sister/fellow white Northerners permits what Grewal calls "the consolidation of the Self enabled by the encounter with the 'Other.'"[32] At the
same time we pursue—and many of the African people in our narratives
reciprocate—human and humane relations of caring and respect with

African people. The cardinal relationship in participants' accounts is friendship with individual African persons. This relationship is, therefore, the primary focus here.

Notwithstanding the significance of friendship, though, there is one additional relationship with local people that is crucial to most participants' adaptation process: our employment of domestic workers. Like bourgeois subjects in the era of empire, Canadian development workers in the sub-Saharan context find ourselves negotiating the presence of the Other within the spaces of our homes. In this case the "Other within" is the domestic worker. Participants remained silent on this relationship until asked about it, and then tended to say little. Most of us expressed discomfort with having chosen or felt it necessary to employ African people to do physical, care-taking labour for us, and strove to find ways to justify or make this situation more equitable. We gave various valid explanations for hiring someone, having to do with the state of the economy, the skills needed for certain types of work, our own busy lives, security, and so on. What domestic workers also so crucially do, however, is to make participants' lives more comfortable. They take the edge off the material conditions that we find frustrating during the adjustment process, they enable us to recreate the space of "home," *and* they configure and assert for us our positional superiority in the privacy of the domicile. The latter effect, turning on a nexus of class and race (domestic workers being invariably from the working or peasant classes), contributes to the recovery of self—an ineffable aspect of achieving comfort in the space of the Other that participants now inhabit, and of reducing the perceived threat of this world.

For these reasons our relationships with domestic employees are important, but since this was not a prominent feature of most participants' stories, I turn now to the relationships that mattered most: the friendships we developed with "them" over "there," which I contrast with our relational experiences with other (white) Northern development workers/expatriates. After this, I discuss participants' efforts to negotiate barriers that we perceive between ourselves and African peoples, and lastly barriers of our own and the Other"s making are considered.

Participants' prevailing perspective is that African people await our overtures of friendship and are willing to reciprocate. This is a view that seems to presume a kind of blank slate, as it were, on the part of local people in respect to interactions with foreigners like ourselves. It is almost as if participants are unable to imagine that where we go, other Northerners are likely to have gone before and almost certainly will come after. This is implicit even when we speak, in terms that respect their subjectivity, of developing relations with African peoples slowly over time. Joanne captures what all participants seem to feel when she says:

> The best about having gone, for me, was the friends I've made and, and the impact that they had on my life and, and how, I became a part of their lives and a part of their culture through them, and I just felt that was so valuable. That everything I, you know, did, you know with groups or anything else, kind of is secondary compared to the friendships I made and the informality of the visits and stuff like that, that was, that was just so nice.

Joanne's comments effectively situate the significance of friendship with the Other to Canadian development workers.[33] There is a tone of reciprocity in Joanne's statement that reflects some of what is best in participants' encounters with African people, signalling as it does a mutual valuing of relations and refusal to objectify.

Relations across Difference

In some instances and to varying degrees participants achieve the longed-for relationships with local people. For example, Joanne describes an incident that occurred well into her contract, where she asks to borrow money from two different West African women neighbours in turn. Her interpretation is that, in responding to her in disparate ways, these individuals did not discriminate on the basis of race, but rather accepted her as an equal. Joanne explains:

> I was going to church, and I forgot—to a ladies meeting and they always had an offering there—and I forgot to take money that day, and I was halfway to church and I thought, "Well, if I go back home I'm gonna be late, and I don't want to really be *late*." So I stopped in at my friend's house who happened to be on the way to church. I said, "Can you loan me some money so I can give an offering?" I said, "And I'll pay you back, when I get back from church, I'll bring it over this afternoon." And she said, "No, I don't have any money." And I, it just, it just hit me as I was talking to her and when she responded to me, I thought, "That is what she would say to one of her friends. She would probably say the same thing," you know? So that I was *white*, she didn't change her response and say, "Yes, here's some money, I know you're gonna pay it back." She would say exactly the same thing to them, "I don't have any money, I can't give you any." And I thought, "Hey, is this a sign that *I* have actually become one

of them, because her response is the same to me as it would be to another one of her friends?" And I thought, "Wow! That's really neat!" And then, I met another lady, as I was walking to church on the road, I met another lady who I kind of vaguely knew and she was going to sell stuff at the market, and I happened to be going the opposite way. I said, "Can you give me a little bit of money, I need, I'm going to church and I forgot to bring something for offering." She goes, "Oh, oh sure, sure, sure," and she gave it to me. And uh, and I said, "Are you going to be at the market all day? I'll bring it to you this afternoon." "Oh sure, yeah, no problem." You know it was like, like you know, like, like anything, you know what I mean, like anybody else, she would have said that to anybody else you know, I mean, if you have it then you give it type of thing, you know. And it's just, it was just amazing. Like, it was such a, like a real *light*, you know, that went off, "Hey, I'm one of these ladies you know. I'm not special to them or anything!" So but, I was actually one of them you know, it was like "Ooohh! They don't see me as—" and when I looked at them, I didn't see them as being a different colour of skin or somebody different, I saw them as people, as my friends.

Here African women grant subjectivity, and by the same token are accorded it from Joanne, who realizes that these are "people," "my friends." A mutually supportive/helping relationship is portrayed between African neighbours and Joanne, who elsewhere in her interview describes ways in which she reciprocates.

Joanne's narrative is more complex than what it might first seem to be, however. Along with an account of mutuality, Joanne demonstrates power-evasive strategies. Frankenberg describes power evasion as "a selective attention to difference, allowing into conscious scrutiny—even conscious embrace—those differences that make the speaker feel good but continuing to evade by means of partial description, euphemism, and self-contradiction those that make the speaker feel bad."[34] Joanne does not notice the racial differentiation that she evinces when she says: "that I was *white*, she didn't change her response and say, "Yes, here's some money, I know *you're* gonna pay it back." She would say exactly the same thing to *them*" (emphasis mine). Joanne also glosses over the fact that she, herself, likely would not have responded with an "if-you-have-it-then-you-give-it" attitude to a similar financial request from one of these women, as she later explains. As Joanne sees beyond the "different colour of skin or somebody *different*," and moves toward a dialogic relationship, Frankenberg's argument regarding "seeing beneath the skin" becomes applicable. Frankenberg points out that the humanist notion of a core self to which other qualities are then added is what warrants the claim that we are all the same underneath, a claim that obscures any suggestion that the white person is an oppressor. The claim to being "actually one of them" can therefore unproblematically proceed.

Farthest along the spectrum of desired intimacy with African people is Carol's relationship with Rebecca, a national of the Southern African country where Carol was posted. Here is some of what Carol says about this special friendship:

> I never felt like I was in a relationship with somebody from a different culture, ever, I never felt that. And um, I, I felt completely at home with her right from the start ... I'm, and I'm sure a lot of that came from the fact that she had had so many friendships, or she had had a couple of very close friendships with foreigners. And I think a *huge* part of it came from the fact that she was albino and never had fit in herself. She was *ostracized* all the way along. She came from a *very* supportive family, *extremely bright* woman, and I, and I think that she was an outsider in a way, as well ... But in a way I think I was a sojourn for Rebecca, I think she liked the fact that I was coming through as a foreigner ... But I thought it was *immediate rapport*. I felt there was *no* issue of race or culture ever, it was just what we, it just never ... between her and I it just seemed *pure* ... So I was a bit taken aback when I, when I thought that what I was to Rebecca maybe was a, was the white friend ... I guess, I guess also that's why I pr—, *prize* my relationship with Rebecca so much, was that it was just *pure*, there were, I didn't feel *that* between her and I. And I thought we were just two people who *talked*, and respected each other, et cetera, et cetera. (emphasis in the original)

This is a dialogic narrative in which the African person is positioned as equal, as *thou* to Carol's *I*, to use Bakhtin's terms.[35] Rebecca appears as having agency, and the relationship itself is "prized" by Carol because of its purity: "*no* issue of race or culture ever," but "just two people who *talked*, respected each other." Mutually granted subjectivity is present in this relationship, and Carol perceives it as clearly beyond the reach of larger relations of power. In her account she and Rebecca realize a kind of oneness.

However, as with all the relations under discussion, there is more than one thing going on. In this case, the idealization of the relationship suggests the "special type of communication impossible in [Carol's] everyday life" that was an earmark of the original medieval carnival noted earlier.[36] As Carol talks about the friendship between them, she demonstrates sensitivity to Rebecca's position: "she was albino and never had fit in herself … I think that she was an outsider in a way, as well." Carol's conception of a pure place of intimacy is founded, it would seem, in part, on a degree of shared subject position as outsiders. At the same time the harmony of Carol's narrative is disturbed by the unsettling suspicion that perhaps Rebecca in some ways objectifies *Carol* as "the white friend," and so does not entirely play her part in validating this "pure" relationship. Carol's willingness to understand Rebecca's negotiation of differences between them reaches its limit at the point where some of the relations of power that inhabit their friendship assert themselves: that is, where it appears that Carol is herself a "sojourn." Carol's refusal to recognize that differences in relations of power are operating in the intimacy she prizes denies Rebecca her personhood, as does Carol's determination to pay only momentary attention to the less comfortable issues that she does acknowledge. In view of Carol's doubts about the ethics of her desire for development work, her insistence on having achieved a relationship that is completely free of inequalities and, therefore, dominance, may be read as a redemption discourse that secures her moral self. Redemption discourses "may present themselves as witness to, or dreams of, racially unequal subjects merging or becoming one, communicating lovingly in spite (or because) of the great chasms of inequality."[37]

There are moments when African people assert the mutual subjectivity that many participants long for, and this occurs in Carol's narrative as well. Thus Carol proudly notes regarding an overnight visit to a rural area: "Rebecca said, "Of *course* she can sleep with everybody else! She's like one of us—right?" And so I was just housed with everybody else." Kris also has an experience where an African friend, Rose, signals a recognition of reciprocal subjectivity:

> Rose said to me when I left, she said "But you're—I *don't* think of you as white. When I'm with you I don't think of you as white. And, you are not a white person like these other white people. You're not like those white Canadians."

Thus it can be seen that some African people appear to desire, as many participants do, relations in which differences of power, race, incomes, conduct, and so on, are diminished to the point of being inconsequential: relationships in which difference is effectively transcended. It seems in such instances that Patti is right when she says:

If you're friends, do you notice that [difference of affluence] even? You know, like are they noticing that you have more or less than they do? I mean they notice it but does that, I mean that doesn't form the basis of the relationship, you know, hopefully anyway.

Barriers We Negotiate

In accounts of sought-after relations with the African people, there is, however, a primary recurrent theme: the concept of "barriers." That participants encounter what we conceive as barriers is perhaps not surprising given the store we set in developing relationships across difference. Barriers that disturbed participants are cultural, including gender relations, and material—the relative and perceived affluence that accompanies the meaning of whiteness in sub-Saharan Africa. Each set of barriers is examined here in turn.

Cultural barriers are mainly framed in terms of differences in which the culture of the Other generates the difficulties, as opposed to relations of power historically produced through, and replicating at the micro level, imperial relations that are reminiscent of colonial precedents. As Norma puts it: "I think there's always kind of um, some sort of barrier, you know in cross-cultural relationships." Debbie explains a little more about such barriers: "I don't think you can get too close to [East Africans]. Even when you're working on the lowest level of the foreigner totem pole, it's very difficult." She goes on to explain that "their knowledge of the outside world is *severely limited*." The hindrance is thus presented as local people's perceived cultural insularity, which evokes a comparison with unmarked Canadian culture that is by implication open, knowledgeable, and willing to engage with the rest of the world—that is, exemplary of planetary consciousness. This kind of discursive move is common in explaining the barriers participants understand as cultural. Not only are Canadian nationalist narratives silently invoked through cultural comparison, but culture becomes, as Said has pointed out, a means of distinguishing "them" from "us."[38] Ultimately, cultural explanations of this kind, rather than locating particular events in time, serve to cast African people as possessing or ruled by what Pratt refers to as "a pre-given custom or trait," thereby making "order [for us] out of apparent chaos."[39] Resolved in the process is the most fundamental of tensions of empire, which endures yet in the development context: the instability of the Otherness of the colonized whose difference must therefore be ceaselessly delineated and asserted,[40] in the process, I would add, affirming white bourgeois identity. However, in the sites of development, this "solution" conflicts with participants' desire for the Other, generating another kind of tension. This tension is evident in Wendy's discussion of her relations with West African people. Wendy utilizes the concept of hitting a "wall" where "we were getting too close to some really critical questions that related to my culture and their culture and how development works ... the values that were gonna be coming into play were gonna be much more deeply-held values." In this narrative, the idea that there is a point beyond which we cannot go in our relations with African people coexists with Wendy's desire for uncompromised intimacy. Several participants echo Wendy's perspective; Patti even uses exactly the same metaphor, explaining that "in one sense we were in a long-term guest status," but adding that with a couple of people she thinks, but is not certain, that "that last *wall*" (emphasis mine) did finally get broken down. Here reified cultural difference intrudes into the assumed availability of African people, inserting a boundary on intimacy and obscuring for white development workers both the historicized effects of racialized relations of power in African spaces and questions we might ask ourselves about the moral legitimacy of our presence there.

One of the most difficult barriers for participants is that of gender relations in the sub-Saharan Africa context. This is not to say that participants were self-identified feminists (very few of us were), or that we arrived with Gender and Development (GAD)[41] theory predisposing us to be critical of the positions of African women (no participants display any predisposition or commitment to GAD or any other development theory). Nevertheless, our Northern, discursively produced presumptions shape a commentary on gender relations that is usually made in strongly critical terms: "how little say women had in this particular development organization" (Patti); "most marriages [are] loveless, women are the slaves to their husbands and they have no say in decisions" (Joanne); "in a culture that is male-dominated, women are invisible" (Margaret); and "so much in that culture is just an absolute disgrace for women" (Erica). There are other remarks as well, too numerous to include here. For most participants there is a tone of anger, and our inability to communicate in local languages—which several of us admit with regret—adds to the distancing effect of these views of gender relations.

However, Patti, Laura, and Kris spoke with some care and restraint, as Patti illustrates:

> I always found treading around women's issues rather tricky because
> I feel that African women have to speak for themselves about what
> are *their* issues and where they need to be quotes "liberated" from,
> you know, the things that are oppressing them or keeping them from
> reaching their potential ... eventually there is questions that come up,
> like the whole multiple marriage thing, depending on which women
> you listen to whether that's a good or bad situation for instance or,
> or child issues, infant and child-, uh family planning and those kinds
> of things. I never had an opportunity to have conversations with
> those women there about that. But I always thought as an outsider,
> yeah, like it looked like, you know, what it looks like to me and what
> it looks like to them—I wanted to be careful. So mostly I felt like I
> tried to watch and listen and learn ...

Here African women, and by extension African men, appear as persons
with agency, who have reasons for their conduct and choices. This stands
in contrast to Patti's previous, more critical comment about women having little say in a particular organization, which demonstrates that even
the non-judgmental position Patti is staking for herself as an outsider is
not one that can be constantly maintained.

As with participants' assertions of other pejorative kinds of cultural
contrasts, our more commonly held negative views of the position of
African women validate our sense of superiority, but this time in gendered
terms, the position of women as a category in Canadian society, as in the
wider expatriate community "there," seeming to us so much preferable
in comparison. As Razack notes: "If African and Asian women are vic-
tims of their cultures, Western women can rush in to save them and, in
doing so, can affirm their own positional superiority."[42] Reinscribing
the homogenized female Other as needing our interventions thereby
affirms the moral obligation we feel to insert our preferable knowledge
and our very presence. Jane furnishes an example of the modelling that
many of us seize upon as a way of intervening without appearing (at
least to ourselves) to impose our values. She recounts often going away
on weekend trips, and says the school girls she knew "followed me and
they were always asking me, "Oh madame, where did you go? Oh that's
so far, madame. You went all by yourself!" So I think they realized that
you could, you could do those things."

However, apart from overlooking the material advantages that made
such choices possible for a Canadian development worker, this perspective also makes it difficult to see the female African as a subject, the gender commonality of our subject positions notwithstanding. Only in Kris's

narrative of a close friendship with an African woman does this dynamic show signs of changing, although this too is not unproblematic. It may be significant that Kris is one of the participants with a longer-than-average stay in the country of her posting. Kris recounts:

> I felt if Rose wants to stay with [her husband], she's my friend, I love her and I'm going to support her. I'm not going to dump on her husband, I'm not you know, I'm not going to keep urging her to leave him. Other [Northern development workers] were urging her to leave him. I felt that it's easy for someone else to urge her, but the, the kids, the fight would follow over the kids, the housing issue, and, and in [Southern African] society too, like it, it's the man who can earn the money that comes, and brings with it the house and the vehicle and all that stuff. It's rarely a woman who can do that. And in coming to terms with supporting *her* decision to stay with him, I moved away from dumping on [Southern African] men, in general, not just one in particular. And seeing, just got out of that expatriate thing that I had also been in for a long time, was like how awful [Southern African] men are.

Although Kris is differentiating herself from such an "expatriate view," this very act secures her moral narrative, thereby undermining the subjectivity she grants her friend. Kris names what many other participants are alluding to: the Northern expatriate community's conviction that African men are "awful"—in Joanne's word, "jerks."[43] The inherent animosity of this attitude colours many participants' notions of cultural barriers and lends an air of abhorrence to the spaces, bodies, and cultural practices of African people. In regard to the latter, Yegenoglu points out that Western subjects take for granted that the Other's culture can be known through the position of its women, a practice that Westerners or Northerners do not hold to operate reciprocally.[44]

The final category of barriers to be discussed here is that of differences in affluence. The historically grounded perception in the sub-Saharan Africa context that whiteness equates with wealth gives rise to a genre of material barriers that require constant negotiation. The affluence of whiteness manifests not only in incomes, but in housing and access to vehicles. Two interrelated mechanisms for addressing the resulting disparity recur in many participants' narratives, each comprising a way of dispelling the wider, power-related implications of affluence, which among other things have the potential to call into question our middle-classness, which is threatened by our relative wealth. One is our assertion that several of us are earning (close to) a local wage; and the second is that we share with African neighbours and friends our higher standards of living. A third approach is to simply accept differences of affluence.

That our salaries and lifestyles more nearly approximate those of African people rather than what many foreigners or "expatriates" have is a distinction that seems of utmost importance to almost all of the participants. An illustration is provided by Wendy, who says: "Even though they [her co-workers] still believed I had more, they knew, they *knew* I wasn't earning more than them. And if I had made an expatriate's salary (sighs) … you know that would have changed things." However, in narratives of this sort African people are diminished as meaningful referents, since the comparison that matters is to other foreigners. A different example is furnished by Jane, who in order to appear "not that much different," decided that "I would never *ever* tell [East African] people that I owned a car, for example, in Canada because I didn't want them to think I was rich." When her parents came to visit and rented a car, Jane explained to workmates and neighbours that it was borrowed, since having the wherewithal to rent a car "was going to ruin my image a bit, you know, or the image that I had been trying to portray." Thereby established is that African people would be mistaken to think we are wealthy, and, to the extent that affluence in this sense conflates with dominance, we are absolved of implication in both.

Housing is almost always superior to that of our co-workers. Kris explains that "it was an, sort of an expatriate house, and there was that sort of split. Like somehow a house got designated as fixed up to expatriate standards." However, this is understood to be a surmountable barrier. Joanne explains, referring to the house she lived in:

> Of course, this was their [African neighbours] impression too—that white people live in you know, cement houses with tin roofs and stuff like that. And it was a nice house and it served our purposes and um, everybody around us had, like straw houses uh, with um, dirt and sticks. But um, but we felt like because we were welcome—we welcomed them, that it wasn't a real barrier too much.

Similarly, Linda says:

> We certainly made people feel very welcome at the home, at our home. And you know, when we were playing cards or, or having dinner together or something it would often be in our home because we had the space and, and it made sense.

She continues:

> I think making our, making um, the dinner table a, a welcome place too was another way [to bridge disparity of affluence]. 'Cause people—if they were up around that time, they'd just stay for dinner. And I think food and conversation always bring people together.

There is a feeling of warmth that is conveyed here in the mutuality of interaction and the welcome extended toward African friends. Although not overly frequent, such recollections are common to most participants' narratives. In a variation on this theme, Kris says, "I didn't want to live in a house that when [Southern Africans] that we worked with, or that I knew as friends, walked in, that they felt that now they were in foreign territory." In this way she attempts to negotiate the standard of living that accrues to her as a Canadian development worker.

In regard to having a personal vehicle, Patti recounts a similar story of sharing:

> We had a car and most of our neighbours didn't. And with our car, we didn't, like if people came and asked us to take them to the hospital or something, we, we would do that. Or if we were travelling [to the city] you know, we would fill up our car with people who wanted to go, and you know, not charge them.

One way of bridging differences with those around us *is* to share what we have in terms of our accommodation, food, vehicles, and things of this sort. The response of sharing our resources can also be interpreted as a kind of resistance move that is connected to seeing African people as people. Such generosity secures for participants a position as good and generous helpers, however, and thus serves to place participants firmly on the moral high ground. At the same time, many of us attest to our being not *really* affluent. Yet differences in housing, furnishings, personal possessions, and the quantity and quality of foodstuffs constitute the development worker home as a foreign space. One effect of this is to continually reinscribe surrounding, exterior space as "Africa" or the "Third World," and thereby reproduce the logic of the development binary and the Otherness of African peoples.

In light of participants' propensity to share the benefits of our relative affluence, it is rather telling that most of us are troubled by the idea of actually sharing money. Patti admits struggling with knowing "when to quote 'help out,' and to, you know—you could always help out, but whether that's the best thing for the relationship of for, for them or for us ... that was hard." Her comments seem to capture a quandary that many participants experienced. Joanne states: "We had a policy that we didn't give out money to people. I mean, otherwise we would have had people at our door all the time." It seems that when it comes to money per se, the differences in affluence can no longer be masked, and this adds urgency to participants' decision to remove this element from the domain of shareable resources. The apparent equivalence between wealth and whiteness, compounded by the harshness of day-to-day life for the great majority of African people, leads some of them to request partic-ipants for money, sometimes after participants have left the country. As Margaret's narrative shows, this after-the-fact assertion of difference causes a painful re-evaluation of the friendships once so gratifyingly achieved:

> You know, the first letters that come you're all excited about. And you're disappointed in some letters because you realize that, you know, that still for people you were a dollar sign. So, you know, "Can you help me, can you do this, can you do that?" We received 22 let-ters, you know, in a period of a couple of weeks, with people saying, "Now that you're home will you help me with my school fees?" "Will you help me with—?" You know, "God has led me to ask you this." And I thought, "Aw, you know, I thought better of these people."

The words "I thought better of these people" suggest a devaluation of Margaret's opinion of African people she formerly considered friends, which is in a sense a move away from granting subjectivity to Other-ing—a reaction to interpreting claims on her relative affluence as betray-ing an underlying objectification toward herself. Margaret goes on to explain that these were not the people with whom she was *really* inti-mate, but not everyone can make this comforting claim. Wendy says:

> I knew from my point of view that they were genuine feeling relation-ships, but from the point of view of those people, how much of that was about *what they thought I could do for them*? Genuinely I feel that they, they care for me. Um, but did they really know me? I mean if I were [West African] and was who I was, would they have chosen to befriend me? With the values that I have, and my personality and all of that, I don't know. And that's kind of sad.

Apart from Wendy's feelings, and the impact on her narratives of self that such uncertainty generates, what is evident here, as in several accounts, is that African people are clear about who is who in material terms in the sub-Saharan development context.

The final mechanism that a number of participants utilize is that of accepting differences in lifestyle as unavoidable. Vickie, for example, says simply, "I lived an artificial life." For Kris, this conclusion is accompanied by an air of resignation:

> Interviewer: Did the contradictions ever get easier to deal with?
> Kris: No, they just became more apparent. I just saw more of them. Some of them I, I just realized that I had worked it out as best I could. That it wasn't—I wasn't going to figure it out any further. No the contradictions never got easier to live with, or to work out.

Resistance to glossing over differences in affluence comes from Debbie, who outrightly says:

> There's some resentment. I mean of course everyone thinks you're rich. And when I first got there I thought, you know, "I'm living like the people. I'm not rich." But *bullshit* (spoken softly but strongly)— you are rich. Compared to them, you're *rich*!! The fact—by the fact that you're actually there, (laughs) you're rich. Even if you didn't pay to get there, you have access to these programs, you're rich!

This is an important discernment of disparities that no other participant quite replicates, yet in a sense Debbie's acknowledgement leads back to the terrain of acceptance. The point is that our responses operate in several ways simultaneously. We see and at the same moment do not want to see how we are positioned, and our negotiations of differences similarly produce multiple and contradictory effects, among which is preservation of moral narratives of self.

Non-Negotiable Barriers: "We" Generate; "They" Impose

Even though we do not name them as such, there are barriers of participants' own making that can be discerned from our narratives, and some that African people impose as well. Among the former are the centrality of relationships with other Northerners, and our understandings and reproduction of racism. Among the latter are African people's views of Northern development workers that appear in our stories.

Regarding friendships with white Northerners in the sub-Saharan context, many participants talk about these relationships as characterized by immediate ease and familiarity. It is evident that cultural dissimilarities that might have loomed large in Canada vanish in the face of the *real* difference, that of the culture of the African Other. Thus,

Wendy becomes comfortably close to a Dutch woman, Kris to a New Zealand woman, Vickie to an American woman, Norma and Carol to American men, and so on, and so on. For married women the partner also plays the role of "significant-other" Northerner. Other (white) Canadians are important to many participants as well. Indeed, this is where our identity as Canadians assumes special importance, since our nationality serves to situate us within the larger expatriate communities where Northern nationalities are to some extent also reified in cultural terms. Despite this, though, Northernness appears productive of, and predicated on, a sense of commonality that can effortlessly surmount gender as well as national differences. At times there are conflicts with other Northerners, as Debbie's, Linda's, Norma's, and Erica's accounts attest. However, as Yvonne, describing her friendships with Australian and Scottish women, puts it: "It was so nice to escape to a place where I didn't have to explain my culture. I could be Canadian, for a little while, and uh, then go back to my [work] world." In other words, these relationships afford a refuge from the carnivalesque—a space of relative normalcy (to us) that replicates the effect of home, where we recompose the selves that are being simultaneously constituted, threatened, and challenged by the Other and the spaces of development. Retreat to such relationships, however, when imbued with the ease described here, must also serve to sharpen the sense of distance from African people.

Most participants avoid specifically mentioning race in our narratives, a remarkable omission in a context where race so effectively demarcates belonging, and developed versus developing. Margaret goes to the extent of saying that, except maybe initially, she did not "think that race really made an issue" in her relationships with Africans. What understanding of racism in the development context do participants then evince? Four participants acknowledged racist thoughts: for example, "I got in touch with some of my own racism" (Bev); but only two participants stated that they had been accused of racism. Kris mentions that during her first months in Southern Africa, her husband's dislike of the country of their assignment led the Canadian NGO's representative to suspect that they "were racist." Laura recounts an incident that occurred in connection with a special event her employing organization was hosting. Two Southern African participants complained to a foreign donor, represented by an African American woman, about Laura's refusal to attend to their request at the time. Laura is asked to meet with the donor:

> I had no idea what the meeting was all about, but then I found out
> it was, it was confronting me about, um ... (sighs) ... about how I, how

I dealt with the situation and how I had tried to maintain too much control and, although it wasn't said, I certainly got the, the feeling it was very much "What are you trying to do—pull, as, as a Northerner, as an expatriate? Why are you trying to keep all the control of this program, and why wouldn't you listen to Joyce when she wanted to do this?"

She responds:

I remember just being *absolutely mortified* by the whole thing, just— first of all feeling very much that they, they totally misunderstood what was happening. And then later on, and then thinking, "Oh my God, you know, maybe I really was very, very um, well, unfair," I'm thinking, "and disrespectful." Uh, so I just I remember leaving, and nothing was really said outright. It was all just sort of complaints without being really very specific about what was, what was happening. Um, I remember leaving and, and being really upset and crying, and not wanting to go home and, tell, talk to anyone about it ...

Looking back, Laura now says:

Although it certainly wasn't said, I, I think probably, you know, they, they were thinking in terms of racism and that kind of thing which, um, which I just was *so astounded* by. But, but now, as I think back on it, I think, "Yeah, okay well that was, but that was a lot of the ways that I did things. I, I always saw that was my, my position, my job to control things."

Kris's and Laura's accounts are interesting, not only because theirs are the only ones where a charge of racism is admitted, but because of their reactions. Kris skirts the issue, framing it in terms of her *husband's* dislike of the country. Laura internalizes the accusation more fully, but goes on to say that, although she sees this as a comment on her way of operating as a whole "there," "it just was *not* a good day, I don't think I could— would have reacted anything differently on that particular day with, with those two people." Thus, she simultaneously extends the critique and asserts a limit to her acceptance of it. Both Kris and Laura thus call into play "containment strategies." As the term is used here, containment strategies are boundaries that participants draw to preserve the story of the moral self. In a sense, this is a concept that takes the idea of Pratt's anti-conquest strategies into the realm of subject formation,[45] since containment strategies work to "contain" awareness of personal participation in, or perpetuation of, domination, an awareness that threatens the moral coherence, and by extension, the unitary cohesiveness, of bourgeois identities.

There are two issues that are also generally pertinent to the discussion of race in participants' relations with Others, however: the ways in which we and other development workers talked about the country of our posting when there were no African people present; and how we responded when we encountered what we interpreted as racism from other expatriates, which turns, of course, on our own conceptions of racism. As Vickie says:

> You probably know that expatriates grumble the entire time. Even though we say, "Oh well, this is Africa," words of resignation ... Where you draw the line between "this is Africa" and being superior and rather unpleasant, is hard to know.

Vickie does not see that saying "this is Africa" has racial connotations, but is concerned about drawing a line between that sort of remark and what she supposes would be "really" racist—in her words "superior and rather unpleasant." Attempting to make this distinction amounts to what McIntyre calls "white talk"; that is, "talk that serves to insulate white people from examining their/our individual and collective role(s) in the perpetuation of racism."[46] However, what is more interesting in Vickie's remarks is her acknowledgement of a parallel conversation taking place among expatriates/development workers regarding the country and its inhabitants (we "grumble the entire time"), to which the African people are not privy. Laura's comments demonstrate this even more explicitly:

> It was, it was awful really, generally. It, there was this, this ... there was such a huge difference having one [Southern African] in a room versus having all white people in the room. And, and the, the inevitable way the conversation of whites would turn to the hardships or the things that they thought were really absurd, happening and yeah, the really, um, really disrespectful comments often, um, to, to absolutely, you know obviously racist comments too at times.

Drawing her own line, Laura reluctantly acknowledges that up to a point she took part in these conversations "around how frustrating life was," but beyond that saw some comments as racist. Similarly, Carol is clear that when she was in conversation with a white American friend about "cultural differences," "just the fact that we would sit around and *talk* about the place we were living, and the people we were living with as almost anthropological *objects* was, in a way, racist," but likewise insists that among development workers like herself "living in huts" the tendency was curtailed. Some participants maintain that "venting" with other development workers just provided a "safe place" where they could "joke about the system or complain about corruption" (Patti), or assert that everyone told and embellished with humour stories about the national airline, or roadblocks, and so on, which were therefore "national stories that were really funny" (Yvonne). While initially stating that such stories have a racist overtone, Yvonne reaches the conclusion that they are in fact simply "national stories" because of an occasion when a group of West Africans and expatriates engaged in this kind of storytelling together. The fact that West Africans joined in seemed to prove to Yvonne that the stories cannot be racist, regardless of who relates them. This is an instance of what Keith and Pile call false equivalence, born of both obscuring relations of power and not comprehending what this storytelling accomplishes for different subjects.[47]

What is also striking in these accounts is how space and African people are configured as carnivalesque: bizarre, comical, and sometimes frightening. Conduct of African people that is perceived as development mimicry[48] emerges as a source of white Northern fun. Here I draw on Bhabha's notion of mimicry. Like the mimicry of colonial relations replicated by carnival in the era of empire, "development mimicry" necessarily presupposes at best an incomplete appropriation and at worst a comical and sometimes disastrous imitation of bourgeois practices and knowledges, both of which are to be expected in the carnivalesque context of the sites of development. This racializing move coexists with the central importance to participants of our relations with African people, and lends deeper meaning to our attachments to other foreigners and to the productive effects of the latter relationships on our identities. No sooner do we invoke a spatial interpretation of our environments and their inhabitants in sub-Saharan Africa than we re-establish our separation from the subjectivity of African peoples, and assert our own comparative superiority.

Noteworthy, too, is that constructs of cultural racism that proliferate in Northern discourses of multiculturalism quietly infiltrate the discursive repertoires of Northern development workers. Kris demonstrates this when she says: "I realized that I had, that there were racist explanations that came to mind, to me, without me thinking—like they were *there*, they were automatically *there*." A kind of double move can then occur without troubling our view of our selves as moral. That is, we at once participate in the expatriate discourse of Othering and continue to develop with African people relationships that manifest some degree of reciprocal subjectivity: the friendships that we value enormously. It could be said, in fact, that at times the latter enhances our ability to do the former.

To hold these contradictory positions while enabling our selves to remain whole requires that we draw the line to which Vickie refers, between permissible Othering and what we cannot avoid understanding as racism. Participants do this either by denying that what we say when alone with other white Northerners is *"really* racist"—there are a number of mechanisms we employ to effect this containment strategy, including white talk—and/or by distancing ourselves from *those other* expatriates who make what we see as racist comments. The latter containment strategy is one that McIntyre found operative in her study of white student teachers: "When being a member of the white race requires that the participants reflect on the history of white racism and the consequences of racism for people of color and for their own individual and collective white psyche, they separate themselves from 'those whites' and stress their individuality."[49]

Lorraine illustrates:

> The way people would *talk* sometimes to [East Africans] I found embarrassing, you know, I just hated to be—you'd be out with people that you thought were a certain way, that they didn't you know, that were just humans and, and thought of—and didn't think anything less of an [East African] than they would of anyone else and, you'd uh, just you know, it would come out in the way they addressed someone, you know. It was just, I don't know, barking at people basically or calling them "boy" or whatever, you know. We'd just sort of make a mental note not to bother with these people anymore 'cause it was embarrassing to be associated with this sort of behaviour, you know.

These encounters with *real* racism secure oneself as not racist, and therefore moral. As Lorraine explains, "I certainly heard a lot of racist talk which used to just shock the hell out of me. You know, 'cause I don't—I guess you assume that people are there in some ways with the same mentality as you, you know?" With a moral self-conception safeguarded through comparison to other whites, one's perpetration of racism becomes less detectable, and as Razack points out, there is then no need to take responsibility for it.[50] An acceptable (according to our standards) degree of Othering can now take place without requiring our notice, reassuring us of our comparative superiority as white bourgeois subjects.

Even those few participants who recognize our participation in racism seem able to incorporate this acknowledgement into a narrative of a virtuous self, or to keep the awareness of our "own racism," as Bev puts it, from becoming overly disturbing. Our venturing to the space of the Other (at least in part) to act out our moral imperatives as bourgeois feminine subjects *and* in fulfillment of the Canadian national narrative that we are the "good guys" of the world places our moral narratives of self squarely on the line. The fact that racial difference obviously matters a great deal in the sites of development threatens to implicate us in racism—a prospect not to be easily countenanced in narratives of the moral bourgeois self. We need to avoid confronting too substantially issues around race that might rupture our basis for being "there" and, by extension—what is really at stake—our image of self. The affirmation of our presence in moral terms is also important as an antidote to this unwanted possibility, and contributes to our inability to act on African people's rejection of our presence, when this occurs.

Local people who interact with Canadian and other Northern development workers must contend with the consequent inequities, both material and otherwise, that are played out in day-to-day experiences in the workplace and at home. There is not only a multiplicity of relational layers being negotiated at any one time, but a range of relations, and degrees of mutual proximity. It must be assumed that African peoples negotiate our presence unceasingly, in ways that are either not perceptible to participants or not mentioned in our narratives. As is evident in Carol's story of intimate friendship above, however much an African person desires close relations with us, she (or he) can rarely afford to entirely let go of an awareness of what we represent: our comparative wealth, our foreignness, our whiteness, our relative position of dominance, and our temporariness. At times this truth will out. This is an awareness that seems to have escalated over time for both African peoples and Canadian development workers; indeed, the more recent stories of the second group of interviewees particularly emphasize the effects of differential affluence.

Since participants assume that African people are available for us to know, it does not and cannot occur to us that what we experience as a wall may be produced by their need to assert some boundaries in response to our insistence on relations. As Vickie recounts:

> One of the nurses said to me, "You don't think we're unkind, do you, but we don't really make friends with expats because we know they'll

go away in two years and what's the use of getting close to someone who's going to leave?"

To her credit, Vickie accepts this perspective. However, unless an African person or persons explains to us in so many words that the desire for relations is not necessarily reciprocated, participants tend to draw on the racialized cultural interpretations that inform our white middle-class and Northern discursive repertoires to explain the distances we cannot overcome. This is so even when we recognize, as a number of participants do, that initially African people watch us carefully to determine, as Linda says, "what kind of volunteer you're going to be."

In a few cases, within the work environment, individual Africans react more strongly. Debbie's story goes like this:

> Debbie: But I mean, I, I could have told you it was an *invalid* placement from square one anyway. We were told that *we weren't wanted or needed* from the very beginning.
> Interviewer: By whom?
> Debbie: One of the—the Dean of Academic Affairs. They were quite bitter you see, they've had a lot of whities come and go and tell them what to do, and rewrite the curriculum, and they're quite bitter towards foreigners.

Vickie, too, is similarly informed by a hospital administrator: "Everyone [national of the country] who's trained in [Southern Africa] eventually goes across the border into South Africa." When she asks if that is why all the medical staff are expatriates, he says: "Yes, of course. If you weren't such fools to work for this money, then the government would have to pay [us] better." Erica also struggles with co-workers who at first do not distinguish between herself and another Canadian woman whom they dislike, and having won that point finds herself immersed in a situation of racial tension, which:

> centred on the fact that we [white foreigners] shouldn't be there. For about five or six months there were terrible divisions ... there was *real animosity* ... [An African colleague] built this little barrier in the staff room and the whites were supposed to sit on one side and the Blacks on the other—like this little mini-apartheid thing going on. Oh, it was just unbelievable!

Participants' responses to these and other incidents when they occur manifest containment strategies. Our determination to continue as development workers in the face of such direct confrontations bespeaks an enactment of domination that we disguise from ourselves in various ways. Debbie stays on until eventually there is simply no work for her to do; she then leaves before the expiration of her contract, having finally internalized a feeling of not being wanted, which has a painful impact on her self-image. Vickie agrees with the administrator but pursues her own goals in her work, departing only when she has achieved them and when the administrative burden of her job shows no sign of improving; and Erica questions whether she should stay but settles the matter when she decides she is "doing a way better job than most people." She subsequently engages Southern African colleagues in debates about the issues under contention, gaining her co-workers' confidence, which enables her to conclude that she felt "trusted."

What is remarkable here, as well as rather dismaying, is that some blatant critiques about participants' presence are being made to our faces in these and a few other incidents, but to no avail. African people reject us, but still we stay, and our ability to disregard or reinterpret what is being said unavoidably diminishes the subjectivity of those who dare to speak out. These comments do have an impact on us, but conceivably not the one that the African persons making the comments might have expected. Based on our reactions to these confrontations, it must be surmised that African people do not easily share with us their more critical views of our presence.

Even where no such criticisms are voiced, doubts arise, and in response there are lines participants contrive to avoid crossing in our stories about being "there" that maintain our claims to goodness. Carol's words are indicative of this:

> Interviewer: Did you ever think that maybe you shouldn't be there?
> Carol: I think I got to the point where I realized that I was just justifying things. I don't know if I'd stayed longer, um, if I would have just started to feel completely immoral for me to be here, I've got to leave. I don't know if I ever would have come to that point or if I just convinced my—the one half of my brain so thoroughly that it was okay to be there, to stay.

Carol literally sees herself persuading "one half of my brain," that is, drawing a limit to the disruption she will permit in her dialogue with herself about the ethics of participating in the development context.

In the foregoing accounts of African rejection of our presence, and our own doubts, the disregard we show for such frankness and/or our capacity to simply incorporate this as evidence of the genuineness of

our relations with African people—and, paradoxically, of our innocence—demonstrates an enactment of domination that relies on the
positional superiority of whiteness. Taken in combination with much of
what is said about "their culture" (versus "ours") and some of the discussion about friendship across differences, the operation of racism as an
organizing theme in the understandings of white Canadian development workers begins to be inescapable, and yet its significance as a barrier to relations with African people remains imperceptible to
participants.

Concluding Remarks

At its core, the theoretical framework of this book concerns processes of
identity formation of white middle-class (Northern) women. Referencing this conceptual base while examining the accounts of Canadian
women who are former development workers in sub-Saharan Africa
amounts to reading our stories of being "there" in terms of narratives
of self. Not only am I tracing the continuities I have identified as seminal to bourgeois constructions of subjectivity from the era of empire, but
by so doing I am pursuing our understandings and negotiations of our
positions in relations of power in the development context. This leads
me to scrutinize our accounts with a view to what participants attempt
to secure. Put simply, on the whole, the decision to go overseas as a
development worker actualizes the colonial continuities of entitlement
and obligation to intervene globally. In this respect, what is especially
noteworthy is the apparent disappearance of altruism from the stories
participants disclose once overseas. In its place is the centrality of relations with local people. Beyond the commonality that both narratives of
altruism and relations with African people are means of making white
bourgeois selves, how are these connected?

Already prefigured in Northern discourse by a tone of spatially sanctioned surreality, the situation we had envisaged as needing our interventions and the African people we have come to save/learn from/
experience take on a more distinctly carnivalesque cast when encountered
directly in the Southern development context. Often initially more menacing than desirable, the strangeness of the space of the Other, and of
the bodies that occupy the space, precipitates a necessity to recover the
white bourgeois self, which seems initially to be unravelling and overwhelmed. Reinscription of preconceived spatial meaning and development of relations with the Other are crucial to the resurrection of this

"underground self with the upper hand."[51] However, there is a constant tension for us in these connections born of our need for African people to be "different" and our simultaneous desire for the kind of pure meeting across and beyond difference that Wendy, Carol, Joanne, and other participants describe. Our evolving relations with African people are earmarked by our ongoing identification of cultural differences in which comparative racialized superiority is implied. As Stephens notes, "Once the language of "more than," "less than," "better than," "worse than" comes into play, the relationship between knowledge and power becomes more explicit. This can and has been interpreted as yet another form of racism."[52] It is the refusal or affirmation of the superiority inhabiting our articulations of difference that is respectively necessary to granting equality and to Othering. Seeing African people as fully equal, that is, "just like us," however, is risky because it erodes the ethical basis for our presence "there": if too many of "them" are "just like us," "they" are not in need of "development" by "us," so why are "we" "there"? It is evident from participants' narratives that the carnivalesque meanings ascribed to the spaces of Africa keep intact the Otherness of African peoples; both space and race hold the development binary in place and, with it, our moral grounds for being "there."

The importance of relations with African peoples in participants' narratives notwithstanding, it is hardly surprising that participants are sparing in our acceptance of the Other into more fully reciprocal relationships. Conversely, too much difference, as for instance when the Other appears threatening, overwhelming, or outright rejecting, also undermines our certainty that what "they" need is "us" (our knowledge, our solidarity, and so on), and challenges our assumptions that African people are available for us to experience. Hence bell hooks argues that "the acknowledged Other must assume [reassuringly] recognizable forms."[53] This comforting (for us) way of Othering, then, not only colludes with and is produced by discursive processes of white bourgeois subject formation, but can be seen as keeping inviolate the justification for our presence in the lives of African peoples and their organizations. Securing the moral imperative for our interventions by means of containment strategies in turn safeguards our narratives of self, which are bound up in the ethics of the decision we make to do development work. This complex process is most apparent, although not exclusively so, in participants' relations with African women, where our views of gender subordination are inscribed with explanations of cultural inferiority that seem to necessitate showing a "better way" to our African "sisters," who are the very people with whom we most often seek deep friendships. The morally questionable (because inherently racial) dichotomized view we have of "us" and "them" is further revealed in the readiness with which participants enter into easy friendships with white Northerners from different countries, and in our anecdotes of encounters with racism where homogenized "we's" and "they's" act on each other. The tales we tell, however, are of our earnestness and innocence: our struggles for true relations across difference and the ultimate purity of our participation in these relationships.

CHAPTER 4
NEGOTIATING SUBJECT POSITIONS, CONSTITUTING SELVES

Two intertwined themes that have already been discussed bear further elaboration as an introduction to this chapter, which focuses on shifting subject positions and new narratives of self: the ambivalent positioning of white middle-class women as bourgeois subjects, and that which underlies this positioning, the active legacy of colonialism. The process of bourgeois identity formation in the era of empire was, as Stoler and McClintock have shown, bound up in race and gender.[1] To be really *middle-class* was to be white and male, and to demonstrate approved cultural competencies, including appropriate moral behaviour. Similarly, to be truly *white* was more than a question of skin colour; it meant being male and bourgeois, able to display correct class standards in the performance of identity. Conversely, possessing all of these qualifications save maleness relegated white middle-class *women* to an ambiguous position in relation to claims to full bourgeois status and, by extension, to genuine subjectivity: the gender equivalent of "white, but not quite," rendering white women at once and always bourgeois insiders/outsiders. This is one of the enduring legacies of the incomplete process of bourgeois identity formation from the nineteenth century, a legacy still enacted within and by means of ongoing imperial relations.

The notion of a palimpsest expresses the idea that what has been formerly inscribed remains partially visible through that which is newly written over it. This, I suggest, effectively encapsulates the colonial continuities of gender, which produce for white middle-class women an ongoing, sometimes unacknowledged liminality of positioning in the project of bourgeois identity formation. During the era of empire, "to be a middle-class man was to be a *somebody*,"[2] an appropriation of public space that signified the private, domestic sphere as the proper place for the making of white bourgeois femininity. Although the decisiveness of this split has been blurred over time, particularly due to feminist contestations, to fully be "somebody," in all the ways that count, still remains the domain of white middle-class men, and the public realm. Thus, Dyer concurs that white women do not attain to the heights of whiteness.[3] Neither, it could be argued, do white middle-class men, since notions of bourgeois identity that circulate today reference a mythological fantasy, which is at once a norm and an ideal, and which shapes social constructions of white masculinity in heroic terms. Bourgeois constructions of femininity, on the other hand, focus on "goodness" in the perpetuation of class standards and appropriate behaviour.

What was inscribed in colonial times on the uncompleted slate of gendered white heteronormative middle-class identity still shows through, competing with and subverting newer writings that make contrary claims. By this I mean the work of discourse in professing that *nowadays* women are equal to men, even as processes of gender subordination proceed apace and preserve for white men the dimensions of true bourgeois subjectivity. Always simultaneously insiders and outsiders, white middle-class women are discursively produced to aspire to the mythological bourgeois ideal/norm even as we are fitted to accept and perform a subordinate, feminized variation thereof. As in colonial times, our best chance of more fully accessing bourgeois subjectivity lies in our proximity to the centre by means of relations with white middle-class men, attained through proper performance of femininity and feminine (hetero)sexuality.[4]

The liminality of white bourgeois women's claims to subjectivity structures the making of female selves. Subjects but not-subjects, white bourgeois women strive in the face of this subordination to prove their/our adeptness at bourgeois cultural competencies even as they/we struggle to refuse some of these very terms for accomplishing subjectivity. That white women do indeed internalize dominant middle-class notions of planetary consciousness, and a concomitant sense of entitlement and obligation to intervene on a worldwide scale, is evident in the participants' narratives drawn on here. Tracings of the goodness of colonial bourgeois womanhood configure our efforts to claim a moral self. Apparent, too, in our accounts of development work in sub-Saharan Africa, as discussed in the last chapter, is the operation of (favourable to us) racialized comparison in the form of our continual assertions of difference in relations with Others, another inheritance of empire that is productive of white bourgeois identities, including those of middle-class women.

In respect to the latter legacy, Sharpe contends that the middle-class Englishwoman in the colonial context oscillated between "a dominant position of race and a subordinate one of gender."[5] Inferred here is an instability that is reflected in the conflicting subject positions occupied by white women in the sites of development today. As Sharpe notes, this was—and is—an amplification of the dynamics of ambivalence bourgeois women experience(d) in the metropole. On the whole, however, the unquestionable positional superiority of middle-class white women to colonized men meant that the colonies provided a kind of proving grounds for Englishwomen to attempt equality with Englishmen.[6] The result was that British women in West Africa during the era of empire were granted the status of "honorary men."[7] Furthermore, as Grewal asserts, the lived experience of being part of empire enabled white women to feel a sense of worth and equality with men.

These histories and continuities remain prominent in the palimpsest contours of white women's identities, and collaborate with micro-level enactments of imperial relations of power to shape our narratives of self in the overseas context. I propose that the racially inscribed development arena, discursively construed as only problematically suitable as a locus for the enactment of bourgeois feminine goodness, in actuality affords white middle-class women a field for forging images of self not available to us in the same terms in Canada. For participation in the development enterprise comprises simultaneously an act of gender transgression and fulfillment, and the spaces of development grant a kind of "temporary liberation from the prevailing truth and from the established order," as previously noted in respect to the experience of carnival.[8] Indeed, a feeling of carnivalesque release, born of racial and Northern-development-worker status, pervades our accounts of being white women in sub-Saharan Africa.

As was discussed previously, narratives comprise a mode for the construction of self, and through remembering events subjects are able to give meaningful and organized interpretation to their lives.[9] Ochberg usefully sums up:

> One does not make something of oneself once and for all … Instead individuals continually rediscover themselves in new situations in which they might be unmade: revealed as flawed. The work they do, via narratively structured and publicly performed action, rescues their self-ideal from the risk of its negation.[10]

Building on the discussion of our relations with Others overseas, this chapter explores the making of white feminine selves in relations of power in the sub-Saharan development context. Following Ochberg, key subject positions that participants occupy in this situation are analyzed: whiteness, its subsidiary—(Northern) development worker—and woman. As well, the ambivalences we express about occupying these positions, the work we do to keep in place coherent narratives of self in the face of multiple and contradictory positionings, and the self-images we convey in relation to our development experiences are articulated. In keeping with the chronology of participants' accounts, discussion of the subject positions identified above serves to fill out the description of development worker experiences begun in the previous chapter. Here attention shifts away from relationships with African peoples to our negotiation of positionings in relations of power, and then to overall, summative comments about this episode in participants' lives (including our return to Canada), in which can be read new narratives of self, and from which our desire for development can be understood.

Considering Whiteness

What is immediately noteworthy in respect to participants' experiences of being women "there" is that it was almost impossible for us to extricate gender from whiteness within the development work context, and that even when we did make this distinction, it is apparent that our stories about being women in sub-Saharan Africa are really about being *white* women. The significance of whiteness in shaping our experiences in the sub-Saharan African development context cannot be adequately conveyed unless explored primarily from that subject position, which is the focus here. Such an examination makes more clear the depth of participant involvement in relations of power and domination. There is a carnival tone of marvellousness that permeates virtually all participants' accounts of experiences in the sites of development, and that essentially accrues to us because of the privileges and status of whiteness. Although bound up in part in perceptions of white people as wealthy—which our trappings of abundance seem to affirm—this is more than the effects of relative affluence, which have already been addressed. In the words of Memmi: "Daily one experiences [her] power and importance."[11] Participants realize this, however uneasily and incompletely. As Susan sums up: "This is maybe where the white person comes in because you're a *big person*, you're a *big fish in a pond* there, you're flying in these airplanes, and visiting people and talking to church—like the *presidents* of churches and stuff." In Joanne's words: "I mean when you're white of course you're influential and I mean, you know all these—I mean I never associate with mayors or anything here, but boy in [Central Africa] we associated with all the, the wing—the wingdings." Erica puts it this way: "I think that people do give you this sort of distance and uh, you know, respect that you don't necessarily deserve, just because you're white ... the old sort of 'Sahib' kind of complex or something—I don't know."

Even those of us who do not state things in quite such unequivocal terms nevertheless acknowledge receiving preferential treatment in small and big ways because of being white. Particularly, we often mention being thrust to the head of the line in banks, at bus stations, and so on. Many participants describe getting to do things, such as swimming at the pools in the most expensive hotels in town, or excursions to tourist spots and neighbouring countries, that we take for granted that African people cannot do. Erica furnishes a prime example of the latter:

> I wouldn't say it was jealousy [about her frequent out-of-country travelling] because a lot of times you know, like people [her Southern African co-workers] were curious about it but, these are people that are *never* gonna leave [Southern Africa] except for maybe to go to [name of capital city] ... I always felt that they're in such a *fabulous* continent and they'll never see it, even though they're Africans.

Participants also acknowledge having access to and acceptance in the wider expatriate community and all that it offers: invitations to social events, house-sitting opportunities in luxurious houses, and networks of friends and acquaintances that extend in many cases to bilateral and diplomatic circles. In respect to the latter, Vickie tells the story of "SLUGS":

> The secretary to the ambassador, who was a very outgoing social sort of woman, made a little club which had the wonderful name of "SLUGS"—"Sun Up in L— [name of place] Unique Group of Singles." And we met at seven o'clock each Thursday morning in one of the hotels downtown for breakfast. So that once a week, you met anyone else who was a single woman. And this was just wonderful. A lot of the members were people working in embassies or USAID, or anything like that, and you could bring guests.

It is noteworthy that "anyone else" is a racialized term in this account, although not recognized as such. Not all participants would join such a group, or think it "wonderful," but many of us talk of moving in and out of these realms at will.

The implications of being thus positioned as powerful are troubling for participants, however, since whiteness clearly betokens dominance in relations of power. Patti says of the resulting dilemma: "The biggest struggle for me was to feel that different from them." Her words echo a profound impasse that is shared by virtually all participants. Here the impetus to bridge difference emerges as a negotiation of power relations rather than a culture gap, the latter comprising the usual avowed disparity through which we frame our travails in developing relationships with African people. Carol is the most candid about this when she says in regard to her position in sub-Saharan Africa:

> I guess I, um, I guess it's a general—generally true that I don't know how to deal with having power by virtue of my race. Um, I think it's harder for me to handle that than having no power by virtue of my gender. Um, just because it comes to me for no reason other, for no reason that I've earned.

This quote is important because it encompasses themes in participants' struggles with power relations. Aside from the view that power is something that one either has or not,[12] there is the supposition that we "have no power" because we are women, the discomfort of recognizing that we are, to some extent, in a position of dominance in sub-Saharan Africa, and that race is implicated in this conferred status. However, also at stake is the preservation of participants' claims to goodness and, with these claims, our hold on morality. The "good woman" described by Britzman—"self-sacrificing, kind, overworked, underpaid, and holding an unlimited reservoir of patience"—would cease to be good in these *feminine* terms if she were positioned as powerful.[13] Because it is implicated in domination, power is placed in opposition to goodness in the schema of white bourgeois morality as a whole, but particularly so for women, as Patti's and Carol's uneasiness demonstrates. As unitary subjects, our accounts of ourselves cannot readily or safely admit such contradictions. Hence, the struggle to curtail an acknowledgement of dominance that is evident in Patti's and Carol's remarks pervades participants' accounts of being white women development workers overseas. This is not to imply that many participants articulate a concern about power and its accompanying privileges in as specific and candid a way as Patti and Carol do. Yet, regardless of how subterranean our admissions of power differentials may be, participants are plainly, although by no means uniformly, ill at ease with having comparatively more importance and more opportunities, including many that would not be available to at home.

The crude meanings of these dimensions of white privilege, if unmasked and/or not negotiated, threaten to situate us as oppressors. The resulting imperative to find ways of coming to terms with this configures countless stories that participants tell of being white in sub-Saharan Africa. There are two main responses that participants employ. First, several accounts contain individual variations on the theme of proving that in contrast to the wider expatriate/white community, we are "good whites." Second, some of us deny the meaning of whiteness altogether.

"Good white" is Kris's term: "I really wanted people to *not* think I was one of those white people [referring to white settlers]. I wanted to be a *good white* person." Similarly, Yvonne, as coordinator of a Canadian development program, was at pains to be fair with an employee suspected of stealing, in part because:

> *Those* expatriates would have sacked the first month, and would have
> shouted and screamed and uh, taken them [African employees] to the
> police, or whatever. And um, yes, because I believed that they should
> understand the kind of organization they were working for. Didn't
> they know, that this is how [name of Canadian NGO] operates?

The identity of a "good white" then becomes a way of negotiating the effects of the subject position of whiteness in relations of power in the overseas development context. To this end some of us deliberately eschew the expatriate community. Wendy, for example, says that she had "seen so many expatriates in [Southern Africa] who sort of spent their lives drinking beer and complaining about life in the country where they were, you know, and I didn't want to do that." I suggest that, in fact, the procedures mobilized by participants against the charge of affluence discussed in the last chapter are similarly intended to secure, in our own minds and in the perception of African people, the idea that we *are* "good whites" (because we are not *really* wealthy, we share our resources, and so on). The implications and connotations of whiteness are, thus, contained (however imperfectly) in our narratives.

The other strategy for denying the power implications of whiteness is prompted by African people's recognition/assertion of our place in imperial relations. Where this occurs, participants' response is to view this as a misinterpretation on the part of African people who are wrongly adhering to a colonial past. This denial is given urgency by the threat such perspectives pose to participants' stories of difference from other expatriates: the reference point that truly matters. Diane's account is illustrative:

I think for me the most frustrating thing is that many people that I've—many Africans that I've worked with in Africa, in the six countries that I've been in, tend to assume um, I don't know how you can say it—assume a sort of colonial relationship, a colonial style relationship, where they would view *you* as the colonizer and they are the one being *colonized*. And so they tend to be quite um, ingratiating and subservient initially. I mean it's a real mindset and worldview that people have. And it's just that people can't overcome that sort of, you know, difficulty immediately. So in that sense the colour was really um, frustrating for me because it sets me up as a colonizer when in fact that wasn't my purpose for being there. And it's not my motive for being involved in this kind of work.

Here African people situate Diane as *just like* other white people, both presently and historically, and in doing so aver the continuing operation of imperial relations. This upsets her narrative of difference by virtue of motivation, that is, her claim to goodness and a moral self. Diane defends herself, re-establishing the rightness of her motives, but in the process relegating Africans to an ignorance that they seem helpless to overcome—in itself a "colonial" repetition.

Margaret is more impatient:

To talk about colonialism, or being white or being Black or being Chinese, or whatever, is, that's just one of the, the givens of life. My history is given, world history is given, my race is given, my gender is given, so how do I *understand* that and then use it to move *forward*?

Margaret's denial of the ongoing significance of whiteness in the postcolonial context comprises a containment strategy that forecloses reflection on her positioning in relations of power.

It should be noted that, for a few participants, being white meant being seen as a target for theft, a reality that especially impacts the accounts of the more recent development workers. Whiteness also means standing out, an uncomfortable experience that is also noted with greater frequency by more recent development workers, as previously mentioned. Yet, clearly coexisting with such hazards of specialness are a dazzling array of advantages, as has been discussed. While it must be emphasized that not all overseas narratives are framed in fabulousness, nor are the effects of whiteness felt to the same degree by all participants, it is evident that talking about being white "there" reveals aspects of carnival-like pleasure and opportunity. The subject position of whiteness generally conveys a sense of ongoing adventure and excitement in which participants appear as important figures, and Africa is cast in the same exhilarating light as colonial woman traveller Mary Kingsley described it: "a rousing jolly good time"[14]—rather than a space where we respectfully act out our altruism and express a commitment to social justice.

Exploring the Positioning of Northern Development Workers

In this context, the term development worker functions as virtually a subsidiary of whiteness since "Northern" (which is conflated with whiteness) is assumed in the very concept of "development worker." However, the significance of each of these subject positions gives added potency to the others: "white," "Northern," and "development worker" being mutually constitutive subjectivities inscribed with a discursive and material global effect derived from and expressive of colonial genealogies. This is not to deny that people of colour from countries such as Canada may also become development workers, and share in some of the positional superiority that Northern white development workers experience, but rather to identify the prevalent assumptions and meanings that inhere in these terms. How participants talk about being Northern development workers, and our participation in the development enterprise, itself an instrument of imperial relations, is examined here.

The subject position of development worker does not seem to generate as much recognition of specialness on our part as does that of whiteness. Patti demonstrates an unusual cognizance of the power relations in which development work is situated when she says that "just by being white and by being educated and having economic resources behind us, even if we are volunteers, that is, represents a lot of power in, in one person in a situation." Although direct remarks of this kind are not often present in participants' narratives, it seems that many of us have some similar consciousness about our positions as development workers, if only because we are at pains to blend in, and to not appear (at least to ourselves) as inordinately influential.

The scope of action available to participants in our roles as development workers exposes further dimensions of our elevated positionings in relations of power in sub-Saharan Africa. The four participants who were program coordinators for Canadian NGOs describe a scope of responsibility that far exceeds what they do, and have done before, in Canada. For some other participants the terms of the job itself are grand in range, as was the case for Debbie, who worked with other expatriates to "design the whole curriculum and materials to go with them, tapes, the whole thing" for the national public school system in the country of her assignment. The majority of participants worked in more ordinary situations, as teachers or community workers of various kinds. What is notable even in these settings is the range of responsibilities and the influence each woman wields. In contrast, though, participants generally portray our employment as development workers as if we were describing jobs we do here in Canada, in that we seem to take for granted the scale of action and responsibility that is ours. Paradoxically, often our achievements in our postings are in fact contingent on our special status as development workers, in terms of the kinds of things we get to do, or initiate, and the people we know. Linda, for example, describes an innovation she helped her partner introduce in a school situation. To give the students practical experience with running a small business "we brought back [Canadian used] clothes, and they ran this business where they sold used clothes. And we were able to get a bunch extra, so that was there. And again it was one of those highs." Laura also talks of the fundraising she was able to do at receptions and other social affairs in the bilateral aid and diplomatic communities. However, in retrospect she problematizes her conduct:

> Reflecting on it now I think, "Well, okay, I mean I was able to do those things because of who I was, but how sustainable really was that for the [name of Southern African NGO]?" Like there's not too many of the rest of the staff who could do that same kind of thing. So, should I have tried to do, tried strategies that only I had access to?

The self-critique that sometimes occurs when participants are looking back on our development experiences from the perspective of our lives in Canada is taken up in the next chapter. Here the point is not Laura's questioning of her behaviour later on, but what seemed appropriate to her to do at the time. This was, it turned out, largely not "sustainable" by her employing organization since fundraising of this kind was, as Laura suspects, essentially contingent on who she was "there": a white Canadian woman development worker.

Kris and Yvonne are the exceptions to the normalizing moves in participants' narratives. Kris compares her position as a white Northern woman coordinator for a Canadian development program to being a chief executive officer of a middle-sized company in Canada. Yvonne, also formerly a coordinator for a Canadian development NGO, talks about her work in terms of "finally having real power." The awareness exhibited in these comments is perhaps a reflection on the positions these participants held. It seems that power relations could not entirely escape their attention under the circumstances, and in response, they embrace the influence they were able to wield rather than attempting to deny it.

However, even where some of us at times recognize the scope of our work, as Kris and Yvonne do above, we do not link what we get to do as development workers with historicized and ongoing global relations of domination. We show little consciousness of our non-accountability as development workers. It is as if we largely take for granted that we are specially positioned in the hierarchies of our employing organizations, and are unaware that our African supervisors, when we have them (and most participants do), are hard put to rein us in when we overstep the bounds that apply to our co-workers. Rarely, therefore, do we seem to understand that there is an important connection to be made here regarding some of the barriers we acknowledge in our relations with local people. Laura describes a situation like this, the effects of which she came to comprehend as a result of a post hoc dialogue with a close African colleague:

> Some of the other staff were, were really frustrated by the access that I and Lisa [another Canadian development worker] both had to the Executive Director. Our, our style of working was such that you just, you know if you had a question, you just sort of walked in and if she wasn't busy you just, you just asked her and felt quite free to sit down and chat and laugh and um, deal with whatever issues you needed, you wanted her input on. Um, and I think we also kind of thought that by us going in and, and operating that way, that, that would be like a role model for other people to feel that they, they should also not be so inhibited. But in fact it had the opposite—a very different effect.

Overlooked in this narrative are the special privileges that accrue to Laura and her Canadian co-worker as foreigners, that is, as Northern development workers in a country with a colonial history that is still a part of people's lived experiences, and the impact of the presence of two such development workers on a middle-sized African NGO. Instead, Laura imagines that she is modelling a better way, which African colleagues should learn to adopt, so that they can become less "inhibited" in their work relations. Laura, however, accepts the critique of her

behaviour offered by her former African co-worker. That this feedback
comes belatedly attests to the risk African people incur by making such
comments to a Northern development worker, as does the fact that it does
not come from Laura's former supervisor.

In narratives not very different from Laura's, the stories of most of
the participants who were volunteers show us exercising a unique status
within relatively ordinary kinds of employment. Even as schoolteachers,
participants assume exceptional prerogatives, as Erica illustrates:

> I was handing them out [condoms to students] and the headmaster
> just *screamed* me out once—basically that I was, you know, promoting
> promiscuity. Well, "Come on, it's happening, let's put a condom on
> and admit that," you know. So, again like that was another thing I
> remem—I, I was faced with disciplinary action. And actually it was
> reported to the [Canadian NGO's] office in the country that I was,
> was doing inappropriate ah, activities or whatever, and I just thought,
> "Oh screw it. Someone's gotta do it."

Here Erica positions herself as not having to abide by the rules that
apply to teachers from the country where she is posted. When challenged, her attitude becomes defiant. The "know-better" development
worker stance, with its civilizing mission overtone, is very much in evidence. Attempts by the school to discipline or otherwise curtail her
behaviour are unsuccessful, and she is able to continue teaching—an
unlikely outcome for a Southern African in similar circumstances.

Laura's and Erica's accounts characterize the relationship many participants portray with the African organizations that employed us. Despite
our claims to being on equal footing with African co-workers, despite our
efforts to bridge "difference" in cultural and power relations terms, when
it comes to our personal expectations and standards—the white bourgeois cultural competencies that are most important to us—it seems
many of us become uncompromising. Then we may choose to make use
of our special status, while our assertions of moral justification enable
us to misinterpret or disregard these micro-level enactments of domination. Nor do we perceive that these actions are at all connected to racialized relations of power.

This is not to suggest that participants are without some awareness
of how we are positioned as "special" employees in the organizations
where we work. In fact, a counter-theme of attempting to refuse to exercise privilege is present in many participants' narratives. Jane, a teacher,
relates an incident where her African colleagues turn to her and say, in

reference to a problem facing all of them: "What are *you* going to do?" Jane's response is, "I mean, you don't want to tell people how to run their country." Finally a meeting is held, and she and the other teachers write a collective letter to the authorities concerning the issue at hand. In a parallel manner, Carol also attempts not to impose herself: "I kept quiet for the first year I was there. I really didn't say anything [in staff meetings]." These accounts indicate a degree of discomfort on the part of Jane and Carol, as well as thoughtfulness about how to perform themselves. Such moves, of course, can and do coexist along with the more prevalent normalizing narratives that obscure how we are positioned in dominance by virtue of being Northern development workers.

There is, however, a yet more cogent story that most participants tell ourselves about the innocence of our subject positions as development workers. As a result of our overseas experiences, virtually all participants espouse critiques of the development enterprise as a whole. We speak of wasted money, of ineffective projects that are imposed on local people, and of a proliferation of highly paid Northern professionals who have no real commitment to development. Interestingly though, regardless of how unexceptional our postings might be, most of us see our work as representing in at least some respects an *alternative* to what is going on around us. I term this the "myth of alternative development." Participants who were teachers, for instance, believe ourselves to be particularly conscientious (Jane) or hard-working (Erica), or we think our work is more meaningful in some vital ways than what other expatriates appear to be doing. With these perceptions we distance ourselves from the development enterprise as a whole, so that our critiques of it have the effect of enshrining us in virtue. Margaret, for instance, insists that what she was engaged in doing was oppositional, which in some ways it seems it was, since among other things she was teaching people "the rules" for accessing Northern project grants. However, Margaret goes on to say: "I'm glad that the organizations are there, I'm glad that development is going on, I just don't want, I don't see myself as being identified with it." It is as if taking an oppositional stance in certain regards is sufficient to place us outside of, or to safeguard us from being implicated in, the impact of the development enterprise, which we recognize as questionable and sometimes harmful. Lorraine sums up this exonerative move when she says, "Because I believed in the work that we were doing, I guess the microcosm justified the macro for me, for that time."

Only two accounts of a more rebellious reaction to our critiques of the development enterprise are offered by participants. One concerns

Erica's decision to challenge the justification for having development workers at the annual meeting of the Canadian NGO under whose auspices she was in Southern Africa. Erica's confrontational contesting of the status quo is unsuccessful and unwelcome. Carol recounts a similar, but unrelated, incident. In this case she is the supporter of another person's questioning of development, which occurs again in the context of a country meeting of volunteers from a particular Canadian NGO. These are important moments of serious interrogation, which require some courage on the part of both Erica and Carol. They are taking unpopular and unsanctioned stands, and are censored accordingly. At the same time, though, much as these narratives near a point of recognizing personal complicity in what is being challenged, that crucial boundary is not crossed. In fact, mounting or supporting such fundamental questioning may have the effect of securing the limits that the implications reach. Erica and Carol have their very serious doubts, but they do not push the limits further, either in the context of the meetings they describe, or in relation to themselves. In Erica's case, this is despite her African colleagues' telling her to leave, as mentioned previously. The logical conclusion of Erica's and Carol's questions would lead to a rupture that would require the ultimate action: a refusal to continue to participate as development workers. Both Erica and Carol remain in their postings, but their uncertainties continue to trouble them.

That participants constitute less of an alternative to mainstream development than we imagine, even when we ask fundamental questions, is evident in the previous discussion of our enactments of domination, as well as in our persistent realization of bourgeois notions of planetary consciousness, morality, racialized relations of comparison with African peoples, and internalized acceptance of white privilege in the development context. Our avowals of alternative practice resonate with Said's charge of the "horrifyingly predictable disclaimer that 'we' are exceptional, not imperial,"[15] and betoken another containment strategy.

Gender Complexities

Compared to the dominance-conferring effects of whiteness and Northern development worker status, participants' views of themselves as women are even more complex. Initially, it seems that Sharpe's point about the variable positioning of British women in the colonies in relation to gender and race is operating with force as assertions of experiences of gender subordination are presented alongside narratives of

whiteness and development worker privileges.[16] Participants feel themselves being ranked as less important than expatriate men, and sometimes African men too, and discriminated against in the same ways as
African women. However, there are also stories of gender transgression
in which participants stake a heroic attitude or slip the bonds of the
social constraints of femininity. These will be discussed below. First,
though, participants' accounts of subordination through gender are
addressed.

The most frequently recurring theme in participants' stories of being
women in sub-Saharan Africa is an assertion of a hierarchy of status in
which we, *as women*, are located on the second or sometimes third tier.
Within that hierarchy, white women clearly rank below white men, as
Lorraine explains:

> I hated that, I always felt like James's [her partner] wristwatch, in
> any setting whether it was professional or social and um, where we
> were going to an [East African] thing. People from [African] NGOs
> would come in to find out what we were all about, or whatever and
> they'd immediately look to James. There'd be four of us in there,
> two [East Africans], one male, one female, and James and I. And
> they'd look to James and ask—right he's the, the white guy, he must
> be in charge. And it, he, James would sort of introduce us all and
> they'd sort of look at me and say, "And what do you do?"

This ranking is directly or indirectly referred to by most participants,
although there is some disagreement about whether white women are
placed below or above African men. In Lorraine's account, we are second to white men, but this seems to be an unstable location that is highly
dependent on specific circumstances.[17] In Carol's view, as in several
other participants' accounts, "the white men and African men were pretty
much in the top rungs in the echelon." Participants' identification of
such a ranking system is significant for what it can reveal and conceal concerning our positionality as white women in the development context.
Here is, on the one hand, an acknowledgement of special status and, on
the other hand, an irrefutable means of diminishing this status and
denying its importance in power relations.

A common manifestation of the theme of hierarchy is heard in the
refrain that "men are taken more seriously." Although, as mentioned
above, the category "men" is at times extended to Africans as well as
Northerners, the usual implied point of comparison is to white male
development workers. This is not only a more frequent correlation but

an especially galling one, as is apparent in Lorraine's remark above, that she felt like her partner's "wristwatch." Denoted here is the exceedingly elevated position that many participants perceive white male development workers occupying in the overseas context.

From participants' critiques of gender relations in their countries of posting, it is foreseeable that African women would be perceived to be placed at the bottom of such hierarchies. Participants' indignation at this injustice toward African women, *as we understand it*, exacerbates our reactions in instances when we feel we are being treated by African men as less than competent because we are women. So strong are some participants' responses to gender subordination in Africa, especially as it affects us, that Margaret, speaking from this standpoint, is able to infer that as a woman she was invisible: "In a culture that is male-dominated, women are invisible ... there's no advantage to ah, to being white and female. As I said the advantage was in becoming invisible." This is an unusually extreme conclusion, but not different in what it accomplishes than, for instance, Joanne's more typically tentative comment that "I was seen with a little bit more respect than what um, women in their society [were]." Both perspectives serve to gloss over the potential for participants to recognize how we are also positioned as dominant. For whether African *and* expatriate men, or *only* expatriate men, are thought to be held in higher regard than white women in the development context, the point is that a male someone or someones are positioned as more powerful in connection to us, thereby eclipsing our view of our own privileged locations in relations of power.

The conviction expressed by many participants that "there," in the sites of development, we are circumscribed as women is strengthened by the particular kinds of subordination participants experience. These episodes seem to us flagrant in comparison to what we encounter (and are educated not to perceive) at home. It is noteworthy, however, that there are almost no accounts of sexual harassment. Debbie mentions one incident at work, and Norma describes a problem one time on a bus, but other than these remarks the issue does not arise. To some extent, the gender subordination that participants find so objectionable appears to be a function of the new (to us) ways in which it is manifested, since often the incidents described are petty and the participants who are affected are able to overcome the initial inconvenience caused. What seems particularly irksome is that local mechanisms of gender regulation are extended to us *despite* our whiteness so that temporarily, at least, race takes a back seat to gender. For example, opening bank accounts was cited by at least two participants as a situation where being white had no effect on exclusionary and paternalistic rules for women.

Many participants mention feeling constrained to dress modestly, for instance, to wear a skirt, because of being female, and some note that special occasions such as traditional ceremonies could also lead to gender determining what, and with whom, participants would eat. However, these occurrences are also interpreted as matters of personal choice, or as valued cultural opportunities. A fine line is drawn between what limits in terms of gender and what is accepted on cultural grounds, the latter contributing to a tacit narrative of being good/not enacting dominance, as in choosing to wear skirts to show respect. It is interesting to note that operating here is another explanatory function of "culture," a term variously employed to different ends by participants. As in previous instances, when it comes to gender subordination, home or Canada is construed as a space of comparative enlightenment. This is evident in Diane's words: "In a very practical sense ah, people in Canada are more aware of the issues surrounding gender. Not that we're dealing with it too much better, but at least people are aware of it." Diane goes on to say that "essentially I don't think it's, it's not a whole lot different" in Canada, and yet there is an initial spontaneous reaction that in Canada we are more "aware," intimating more civilized or advanced, in respect to "the issues surrounding gender." Erica simply says that we "know better."

As noted earlier, most participants recognize that gender is usually inextricable from whiteness. This is the case for the more recent group of interviewees as well. Thus, there are also narratives revealing the obverse of experiences of gender subordination, that is, gender transgression. In these accounts, the development context can be seen to more closely approximate for participants the colonial notion of a proving grounds where white women can attempt to achieve equality with their male counterparts. There are two particular narratives of gender transgression that recur in participants' accounts. One is what might be called "heroic," the other that of being "liberated from gender."

In striking contrast to the position of African women in our narratives, virtually all participants tell stories of our overseas experiences that inevitably, and to some extent inadvertently, have the effect of casting ourselves as heroic figures. References to place, as savage, exotic, and wild—the topsy-turvy of carnival—and stories of survival in these spaces are frequent. Visiting family members and Canadian friends appear in a number of accounts and are presented as overwhelmed by how participants are living. Laura's parents prove to be the sole exceptions once they are in Southern Africa; prior to that they, too, see their daughter as residing in a frightening place. Norma tells the story of her parents' visit while she was in Southern Africa. Before leaving to return home, they confided in expatriate friends of hers:

> They cried every night (laughing) before they went to sleep because of my living conditions. (still laughing) I didn't know that! They wouldn't tell me, they wouldn't—they never said a word, never said a word when they were there (laughs and laughs).

Of course, in addition to a non-technological lifestyle, there are physical conditions that are genuinely difficult to cope with, such as shortages of foodstuffs and water, bad roads, and theft. However, unless a participant is very careful in both the content and manner of speaking, to mention contending with these challenges is to automatically reference African tropes that circulate in Northern discourse. It is as much *how* participants talk about these things that seem to convey the latter, as *what* is actually said. There is a tone in use at times when many of us speak and a way of describing situations and events as immutable backdrops that render participants' experiences as travails and cast us as larger-than-life heroines of the stories we tell. This is apparent in Norma's recounting above, particularly in her laughter at her parents' concern, which implies that, unlike them, she is tough enough to handle the circumstances in which she is required to live as a development worker. Absent from her narrative are the facts that her living conditions are by her own admission superior to those of African co-workers and neighbours, that unlike them she felt she always had more than enough money, and that she frequently leaves for the relative affluence of South Africa. Nor does she acknowledge that the conditions creating temporary hardships for a Canadian woman development worker touch her less than they do African peoples. To speak of these matters would alter the heroic light in which this story places her.

Participants also talk about some of their experiences in terms that suggest a temporary liberation from the usual constraining constructions of gender to which they are accustomed at home, a carnivalesque effect in which race is unevenly recognized as instrumental. Thus, comments range from being pleasantly surprised at feeling valued in the work situation, as Joanne does, to, in Debbie's evocative phrase, being "the goddess of the town." (Debbie says this in reference to another woman development worker who is going to a rural area where there are no other foreigners.) As Jane avers, referring to being a *white* woman: "I think I could have done anything [I wanted to]," and Erica concurs that she was allowed "certain eccentricities" because she was white. Norma adds: "Being a white woman—people, I don't think people really knew what to expect so I remember thinking that I had uh, in a lot of ways, you had a lot of freedom." Yvonne's comment is that "I think in some ways being a woman opened more doors than for the male [development workers]." Patti too says: "I wasn't always aware of the constraints [of gender], you know, because I was a foreigner and I could get away with seeing and doing and being in different places that maybe normally women would never have been able to be."

There are several more comments of this kind. In addition, quite a number of participants speak about feeling safe doing things in sub-Saharan Africa that they would not do in Canada, such as hitching rides. This is not to say that there are no counter-discourses of fear, but the conviction that many of us express that we were protected by both African and expatriate men is noteworthy for its resonance with the lingering trope of white womanhood in the spaces of former colonies. Africa is still discursively and historically construed as a questionable place for a white woman, but once participants are stationed there colonial legacies produce not so much peril as safeguarding. Altogether this evokes a sense of feminine empowerment[18] by virtue of whiteness. Yet often our narratives work to straightaway undermine this recognition.

Joanne gives an apt illustration of how freedom from normative Northern gender constraints together with heroic self-posturings inscribe participants' actions in the carnival spaces of development. Joanne's account is a little long, although slightly abridged here:

> One time I went to the market to buy some stuff one morning, and there were these guys taking food from all the villagers who had come into the city to sell their stuff. And that really, that *really bothered* me that *these men* would be taking their food—these villager's food that *they had walked how many miles* to come and sell, so that they could get some money so that they could buy soap or like they could buy medication for their child who was sick or something. That really irritated me. So I went up to these guys and I said, "Why are you taking their food?" They said, "Because they have their prices too high, and we're price-fixing." And I said, "*I beg your pardon*, you're price fixing these villagers, but you *aren't* price-fixing all the merchants who are selling pens, and paper and cloth and, and shampoo and stuff. You're not price-fixing them. You're price-fixing

the villagers who supply us with food." ... I said, "Who told you to do this?" "Oh, the mayor." "Oh, the mayor did—okay, um, um," I said, "Well, you know, I don't think you should be doing this. You should probably give the food back." ... So they were putting the food over on a pile over there and so I went over to this pile and I said, (shouting) "Whose food is this? Come and get it!" And they said, "We're not giving it back now. We're gonna give it back later." I said, *"You're giving it back right now in front of my eyes!"* (aside) That's how they said it, "in front of my eyes"—you know "in front of my eyes you do this." I said, "In front of my eyes you are giving this food back—not later, but *right now in front of my eyes!*" I said, "Whose food is this? Come and get it! *Would you come and get your food!*" (almost shrieking). So they finally came and got their food.

Joanne's behaviour in this situation shows, among other things, the exercising of a status that is not bound by gender. Without hesitation she challenges a group of local men carrying out what she considers a reprehensible deed. Even though she learns that they are under instructions from the mayor, she orders the men to return the produce, and when they refuse she intercedes to ensure that the owners retrieve it. Later on she tells the mayor about this incident, and commands him: "You better tell them *not* to do that again because that's just not right." To which the mayor apparently responds, "Oh yes, I will tell them *never to do that again!*" Interestingly, Joanne asserts that she would do the same thing in Canada if a similar situation were to arise. She seems unaware of, or unwilling to confront, her positioning in relations of power in the African context that she called on in acting as she did.

Joanne's story is cast in especially strong terms, but it demonstrates, if in a somewhat exaggerated way, the kind of freedom many participants seem to feel entitled to actualize in the liberating (for white subjects) spaces of development. Although this incident does not occur in connection with Joanne's job responsibilities, her position as a development worker in the relations of power is obviously implicated in her actions. Similarly this is an account about being a white Northerner, who considers her own sense of justice sovereign and to whom local hierarchies do not powerfully apply. It is also a story of a saviour, whose heroism is cast in terms unimaginable for Joanne in Canada, and as such it is a narrative of gender transgression. Although not necessarily as grand in scale, such implicitly self-augmenting stories are recurrently told by all participants.

Considered in their totality, the unstable positions within relations of power experienced by white women development workers in the sites of development appear from the foregoing to be more complex than moving between the subordination of gender and the domination of race. For the one inheres in the other, so that what we experience is more than push and pull. Rather, it can be argued that what is operating is a simultaneity of effects rendered more complicated by the domination nexus of whiteness, Northernness, and development work intersecting with, and affecting, gender. As Haraway notes, individuals cannot be viewed as occupying at any given moment all or merely one of the subject positions produced through gender, race, nation, and class.[19] This is apparent in participants' narratives, so that what is traced here is in a sense an artificial separation of what our accounts inevitably conflate. However, examining each of the key subject positions at play in the concept of "white woman development worker" is useful for what is revealed. For in our narratives regarding each of these positionalities the same pattern is present: an undermining of resistance moves, which would otherwise acknowledge a degree of dominance, the result being the achievement of containment, even forgetfulness, regarding our positions in relations of power, through narratives where we are "good whites" (unlike other "expatriates"), where what we did was "alternative" to mainstream development, and where men are taken more seriously than we are. These explanations reposition participants as innocent, and secure the fundamental story at risk here of being unmade: the narrative of self as moral subject. We act as Ochberg suggests, to rescue our self-images in this case, from the risk of negation posed by too much recognition of our part in the oppressive operation of imperial relations in the development context.[20]

Yet, the interplay of domination, subordination, and negotiation is not the whole story of the construction of feminine selves in the carnivalesque spaces of development. The palimpsest tracings from the era of empire that inscribe as liminal the bourgeois subjectivity to which white women can presently attempt to lay claim are apparent in a transfigured form in the subject positions discussed above. Processes of gender subordination remain detectable, but appear less potent than the nexus of whiteness, Northernness, and development worker status in shaping the intricacies of participants' positionings in the relations of power obtaining in sub-Saharan Africa. Despite inherent instability, the accumulation of the consequences of being so positioned in dominance operates in pervasive and productive ways. The overall outcome is a realization of gender transgression even as the "good woman" aspect of bourgeois femininity is being actualized. To be sure, as mentioned earlier, there is a sense that participants transgress gender boundaries when we decide to become development workers in the first place, that is, to go to live in the proscribed (in gender terms) spaces of the South, and to participate in the masculinist project of development. While it is clear that our engagement in development work does not disturb Northern gender hierarchies, our stories nevertheless show release from the strictures of normative constructions of white femininity, an extent of emancipation that seems to be tolerated by our white male counterparts, perhaps in part because of their own corresponding realization of some of the epic aspects of mythical bourgeois masculinity. Faced with the numerically overwhelming physical presence of the Other in foreign/exotic spaces where conduct, particularly in terms of gender relations, is not "up to" bourgeois standards, the *laager*[21] response of whiteness seems to entail extending a degree of insider status and an elevated positioning in power relations to white women development workers, albeit in gender-specific ways.

Claiming Subjectivity

As a result of these multiple processes several participants reach the conclusion that we were, in fact, "*honorary men,*" a term that suggests a way of encompassing our cumulative positionings as white women development workers. This uncanny choice of words, which exactly reiterates McEwan's statement noted earlier in respect to British women in colonial West Africa, is made independently by at least five participants.[22] Thus, Jane's comment is: "You're different. You're not a woman, you're not a man, you're like an honorary man if you're a white woman." Where participants do not use this precise designation, it is nevertheless evident from our stories that this is how we see ourselves. What is being referenced in these comments is participants' narratives of self, *and* the identities we were able to thereby construct, and that were constructed for us, in the sites of development. This is a new narrative of self approaching true (white male) bourgeois subjectivity, which, in Davidoff's words comprises the "identity and destiny" that "real" (white bourgeois) women can "only approximate and never fulfil."[23] That participants see ourselves as more fully subjects is evident in our summative comments about the impact that doing development work had on our self-images. Yvonne says: "The whole experience really raised my self-esteem, and my sense of my self-worth and capability." Other participants voice similar convictions. These are points at which the undercurrent of empowerment that runs through many parts of our narratives breaks surface. There are feelings of increased confidence (Joanne, Lorraine, Linda, and Diane), of personal strength (Erica), of being valued (Joanne and Bev), affirmed (Margaret), useful (Vickie), respected (Jane and Kris), unique (Yvonne), appreciated (Margaret, Laura, and Norma), known (Patti, Vickie, and Kris), important (Bev), and of simply feeling good about oneself (Jane and Joanne). The names of participants are noted in conjunction with a number of the terms each specifically uses, but since one effect infers others, several of these adjectives would be applicable to many of us.

Some verbatim quotes are presented below because a list of adjectives does not adequately convey what so many participants aver:

Jane: There I was somebody. I was really, I was well-respected.

Bev: I was feeling like actually what *I* was doing was important.

Patti: You're *known* anywhere, whereas here you just sort of blend in. So that you know, you're a big fish in a little pond ...

Joanne: For my sense of self-worth, it definitely makes me feel good about myself.

Margaret: What I felt affirmed in was that, whatever I was, was appreciated.

Erica: Certainly it made clear to me how *strong* I am.

Diane: Before I went I did have, you know, questions about "Am I the right person for this?" and "Can I really cope or have what it takes?" and so on. I don't think I'll ever ask myself those questions again.

Lorraine: People were so welcoming. They always made you feel welcome and wanted.

Laura: I know my confidence level increased an awful lot. I probably was a lot more self-confident about myself and my work in a lot of ways than I am here.

Kris: I could be whatever I wanted to be. I had all this responsibility and I was an important person.

It is important to clarify, too, that while many participants evinced a strong self-image prior to going overseas, there is a considerable difference between that self-concept and the development worker one. As Joanne says:

It [being a development worker] made me much more self-confident and, and—not that I was ever *not* self-confident before, but I think it's just made me more aware of that—of my skill and what I'm able to give back to society and to the—my friends and the people I work with.

For just one participant was the development experience described negatively in terms of impact on self. Having been told from the outset that she, as a foreigner, was not wanted, Debbie's job came to a premature end through no fault of her own, and she returned early to Canada. Importantly, Debbie had internalized some of the rejection she encountered through the lengthy denouement of her posting. Here she describes the effect of these experiences on her sense of self-worth:

Well, it's taken a while to recover. In fact, that's what it came down to, to be honest, at the end of the day it came down to self-esteem. That's why I quit. Because if I felt that if I stayed any longer, I really couldn't respect myself. It wasn't working.

For Debbie what is so painful is the erosion of what most other participants gained: her self-esteem or image of self, and with that her greater claim to subjectivity—instead, in its place, is a diminishment of sense of self. Susan and Wendy also found the overseas experience difficult personally, although in quite different ways. They are the only other participants who speak in a less-than-glowing manner about the impact of doing development work on their images of self.

Yvonne, on the other hand, whose self-esteem grew through her development worker experiences, concludes: "There was *nothing* that I felt I couldn't do if I had to do it. I wasn't always successful in every negotiation or anything, but I *knew* that there was *nothing that I couldn't do*." What is remarkable is that a number of participants agree, saying almost exactly the same thing. Described here is the feeling of being "someone": a personage of dimensions and importance approximating those of the middle-class male "*somebody*" in the era of empire, as per Hall's reference at the beginning of this chapter.[24] My contention is that this is more than gender transgression or novel experiences of affluence that exceed middle-class normality in Canada. Because of the multiple and repetitive ways in which the experience of really being "someone" occurs, it infuses participants' narratives and shapes our images of self. I propose that these effects are deeply transformative because our incessant relations-of-power experiences as white Northern development workers operate *in mutually strengthening* ways to provide profound affirmations of self. These accrue to us through our recurrent assertions of difference in relations with African people and through continual validation (and protection of) our stories as moral subjects.

Memmi contends that such experiences in the colonial context produced a superhuman concept of self.[25] While this may be so for white male development workers, I am arguing for an understanding of who we, as white middle-class *women*, get to be where such conditions yet obtain: in the overseas development context. And that, I propose, amounts to a realization of our always-immanent "true" bourgeois selves. The self that is thereby produced is cast in terms that not only exceed the reach of proper bourgeois feminine constructs, but that also signify our claims to a fullness of subjectivity, which, I would argue, we ordinarily cannot achieve on home ground. Tellingly, Wendy in fact refers to a separation between what she calls "two worlds" and "two selves." In the African world, Wendy was "more able to be who I am," an assertion echoed by Yvonne, who says she was "my most authentic, genuine, happy person," and by Kris, who describes having "become myself." Here the expressions of identity suggest a correspondence with Seshadri-Crooks's argument about whiteness: that it "promises wholeness"—in a sense, a self-perception of wholeness does seem to be attained at this point.[26]

It is not surprising, therefore, that participants' reflections on the development worker experience as a whole bespeak happiness. As Jane says: "I was really happy to be there. It was great!" For Joanne it was "a highpoint in my life"; for Vickie "a very rewarding personal experience"; for Debbie it was "very rich, very intense"; for Norma "a big adventure"; for Diane "the most challenging and rewarding thing I've ever done"; for Kris a time of "being very happy"; and for Erica "a defining moment in my life." There are other comments along this line, but the point is that this seems to be a period in participants' lives that we recall with joy and excitement. No doubt, the distancing effect of time glosses over memories of the wear and tear of daily life in sub-Saharan Africa. Yet participants speak in these euphoric terms toward the end of a lengthy interview process in which we have discussed in considerable depth various and sometimes difficult aspects of our development experiences. Consequently, it seems that these summative remarks are not so much the result of nostalgia or the idealization of hindsight as they are indicative of how we view the persons we were as development workers.

If, as is argued here, the carnivalesque spaces of the Southern development context afford white women development workers a libratory claim to "true" bourgeois subjectivity, what happens to this sense of self where the conditions of its constitution no longer obtain to the same extent or in precisely the same ways? Here I look at our images of self when we return to Canada, where our liminality as bourgeois subjects is daily reinscribed, our membership in the middle class offers considerably more limited material benefits, and our dominance in relations of power is less dramatically drawn. In keeping with the storyline of our development experiences, it is fitting to end this discussion of the constitution of self with participants' homecomings.

Yvonne is particularly articulate about the way returning to Canada affected her self-image. She says that "the time I spent in [West Africa] really, really did a lot for my self-confidence. The question now is how to recapture that. And I don't have an answer ..." Later in her interview Yvonne expands on this predicament:

> I think the length of time to get, to get—to, to re-adapt, I think the length of time is so hard. Uh, the absolute feeling of *being alone*, as if nobody values the work I've done. I, uh, I can't still yet present myself in a very confident manner. I always think that everybody here knows so much more, has experienced so much more, everybody seems so slick, and so well groomed in their suits and uh, uh (sighs). And yet, I *know* that the skills I have could so easily be adapted to the work I could be doing here. And uh, but I, I'm still feeling insecure, as if there are *so many* qualified people out there and why would anybody acknowledge what I can do?

In Yvonne's account, that "authentic, genuine, happy person," who was capable of facing any challenge in the development context, has all but vanished. Yvonne is looking for work, and this of course has a diminishing impact on self-image. Yet unemployment, even of a prolonged nature, seems inadequate to explain what has changed for Yvonne. Rather, this points to a loss of identity, or as Kris more moderately sums up: "I was *someone*. Now I'm not no one, but I'm just ordinary." Lorraine and Joanne, on the other hand, evince continued confidence in themselves. How are these divergent constructions of self to be understood in light of the arguments being made here regarding the constitution of white women's identities in the sites of development? A number of commonalities in participants' readjustment processes bear mentioning in this regard. The two most recurrent themes are that of being silenced upon the return to Canada, in the sense of not feeling able to refer to or talk about what we did "there," and that of rejecting Canadian affluence and some bourgeois values. Although the latter is actually more frequently mentioned than the former, I start with the issue of silence because it is fundamental to understanding our rejection moves.

The feeling of being silenced is acutely felt by many participants. As Carol summarizes:

> I find it extremely difficult to articulate the things I have spoken with you about ... Often people ask me what were the most valuable lessons I learned from my years in Africa, but I can rarely, if ever speak the truth on these matters. What I do say turns out to be trivial, silly and laughably naive.

Debbie puts it this way: "I don't even bother to usually explain the whole story to people." These comments reflect not only isolation due to the inability to share our experiences meaningfully, but also with this closure comes a shutting out of the persons we now take ourselves to be, the identities we now claim. We cannot express these identities if we are repositioned by everyone around us as our "old selves," or as no one out of the ordinary.

It is not surprising, then, that Kris says "there's no space here except when I'm with a couple of friends who were also in Southern Africa, for me to acknowledge having been there. I can't reference it in my conversation." Joanne's coming-home experience is one of returning with a number of other development workers who were in Central Africa at the same time, and staying connected to and working with this community of people. This makes a crucial difference to maintaining some aspects of the "new" identity she staked for herself there, and elucidates the significance to participants of holding on to friendships from "there."

What also prevents participants from referencing the experiences we have had is, I suggest, that the selves we describe in these accounts are transformed in ways that are disruptive to the national narrative operating in collusion with social constructions of femininity. As has been discussed, development work is crucial to Canada's story of global benevolence. However, the tales we tell as white *women* development workers only partially conform to what is discursively sanctioned, since interwoven in our accounts of appropriately feminine "helping" and "goodness" in carnivalesque spaces are gender-transgressive depictions of us in heroic modes. This disturbs the contribution we make to the discursive perpetuation of the fantasy of development. Our stories, and our performance of self, cannot be unproblematically welcome since they implicitly trouble the Canadian development narrative, just as our claims to a fuller subjectivity move us disconcertingly toward white bourgeois insider status and so unsettle gender relations at home.

Unable to assert what we feel we have achieved as development workers, many of us carry on an internal dialogue about the materialism and relative ignorance of the people we meet and know back home in Canada. Several of us speak of bringing values we have acquired in sub-Saharan Africa into our lives here. Lorraine, for instance, tells of sometimes feeling compelled at work to explain to colleagues who come straight to the point upon seeing her that "they'd be very rude if they were in [East Africa] and they didn't greet me and ask about my family and home and children." Almost all participants talk about ongoing dismay at the amount of choice available in supermarkets, and the "trivial" (a frequently used word) concerns Canadians have. An example that particularly upset Joanne was a debate friends were having about choice of wallpaper. Laura typifies participants' reactions when she says, "You walk into a supermarket and just see so much stuff [and are] so appalled at the materialism and wastefulness of Canadian lifestyle." With an enlarged frame of reference about the realities of life for some people in other parts of the world, which sometimes leads us to recognize such hardships at home too, participants thus position ourselves as not just moral subjects, but "more moral" than other white middle-class people we know.

It can be theorized that this becomes a way of holding on to some parts of our new identities, and retaining *at least in our own minds* a claim to genuine bourgeois subjectivity, of which morality is a crucial constituting element. At the same time, the perception that Canada is a country where people, including women, *have* everything—where no *serious* inequities exist—collaborates with our experiences of the "inferiority" of gender relations in sub-Saharan Africa, which affirmed for participants that Canadian womanhood is "advanced" and "liberated." What results for many of us is a (further) eclipse of awareness that gender subordination is operative here, and indeed instrumental to the shape of our own lives. This, too, has the effect of focusing our attention on claiming bourgeois subjectivity, while paradoxically foiling our efforts to perform ourselves as more fully bourgeois subjects.

Two other factors that emerge as important in the readjustment process, and that affect our hold on being "someone," are employment and motherhood. While prolonged unemployment is not a sufficient explanation for Yvonne's loss of self-image, it is nevertheless an important factor. For participants who come back to jobs, the transition is easier. If the able-to-do-anything development worker self is compelled to recede, a new job-related identity is there to take its place. And where the work context allows at least some use and recognition of skills and knowledge honed overseas, the result is a degree of affirmation that also enables some retention of a sense of greater bourgeois subjectivity. As Joanne says:

> I'm still developing a lot of my skills in that area of leadership. But some of them were *really* starting to come out when I was in [Central Africa], and I found that as, as I looked back on it I thought, "Wow! I don't know if I'd be doing some of these things now if it had *not* been for my experiences in [Central Africa]." So um, for my self-worth, it definitely makes me feel good about myself …

For three participants, returning to Canada was followed by the birth of a first child. This is a transformative experience, not only in terms of lifestyle, responsibility, family commitment, and so on, but in comprising a unique fulfillment of the terms of bourgeois femininity. Done "properly," that is, in the context of a sanctioned relationship (heterosexual marriage), motherhood is met with approbation and accrues esteem. As such, it affords another way for white middle-class women to fulfill a key construct of proper femininity, which brings us closer to the centre of approved feminine bourgeois subjectivity. Lorraine's comments illustrate this:

> Oh, I can do anything now. Although I think that also has to do with having a baby but um, when I came back it was just yeah, I just, yeah, I can talk to anyone—you just, I just [have] a different kind of confidence. Things don't faze me.

Lorraine is clearly holding on to much of the identity that was produced through her development worker experience. This does not seem to have been the case for Erica, the third participant to have a first experience of motherhood after returning to Canada. This has to do, I suggest, with the difficult emotional and financial circumstances in which this occurred, Erica having been a single mother.

For most participants, as Bev puts it, "in development work the difficult thing is coming back." It is evident that a fundamental, underlying distress that many participants encounter on returning home is an underground struggle not to lose our new-found sense of self. For as Yvonne's desire to "recapture" the person she was in sub-Saharan Africa implies, and participants' frustration at being silenced and our continued embrace of an actualized planetary consciousness affirm, this expanded identity seems like an expression of who we truly ought to be able to be. And so I would suggest it is, for this self represents an unprecedented facsimile of the masculine bourgeois subjectivity to which white middle-class women are produced to aspire to but can never fully attain. There are other spaces where white middle-class women make our selves in terms closer to this mythical identity. It is not always necessary to journey to and live in the carnivalesque spaces of the Other for this to happen, and conversely, being in these spaces does not automatically or uniformly produce this effect, but the sub-Saharan sites of development are evidently particularly conducive to the making of white women's bourgeois selves.

Concluding Remarks

At the outset of this chapter it was suggested that the notion of a palimpsest can be aptly applied to describe the positioning of white middle-class women as bourgeois subjects. Essentially, here I have been examining what happens to our bourgeois liminality in the Southern development arena, and how our positionings in relations of power shape our constructions of self. I have tried to capture the almost-euphoric sense of transformation that infuses many aspects of participants' reflections and stories. I argue that this response is directly linked to white women's ongoing exclusion from/proximity to bourgeois subjectivity, which although still eluding our reach, is more fully realizable "there." Since my attention has been thus primarily focused, it may seem that such pervasive change is being proposed as an inevitable product of prolonged exposure to positions of increased dominance. There does seem to be a relationship in this respect between such confident transformations and duration of time overseas. It is noteworthy that participants who stayed overseas for four years or more tend to speak more strongly of their new-found sense of self, although some participants with shorter periods of development worker experience also describe themselves in this way.

However, of greater importance than the fact that some participants reveal more dramatically transformed narratives of self than others is that the extent of internalization of these narratives exceeds what temporary experiences of "empowerment" might be expected to produce. As has been shown, we embrace our new identities as our "*true*" selves. Previously self-conceived in positive terms such as "strong" and "confident," these words now seem to convey fresh and fuller meanings as we demonstrate an able-to-do-anything attitude. In other words, we bespeak ourselves as more complete bourgeois subjects. I have proposed that this internalization of changed self-images is produced through the operation of white women development workers' positionings in relations of power and attendant material benefits in the sites of development, *together with* affirmations of the self as superior—through racialized comparison with the Other—and as moral. I would like to expand on this here.

More complex than the oscillation between the pulls of gender subordination and racial domination, participants' shifting nexus of subject positions of dominance—white, Northern, and development worker—interplays with and produces frequent absolution from less powerfully inscribed (for us) hierarchies of gender. The resulting sense of gender transgression resonates with the notion of carnival as a space of liberation from established hierarchies. In this space of development white women enjoy, as Memmi says of the colonialist, "the preference and respect of the colonized themselves, and [are] part of the group of colonizers whose values are sovereign."[27] I invoke Memmi not only because his words immediately connect the content of this discussion to colonial antecedents, but because he raises both relations of comparison with the Other and the sovereignty of the values of the colonizers. Participants were previously shown to be engaged in ongoing processes of Othering and desire in relations with African peoples. Each process is productive of affirmative self-images: the former offers reassurances of white superiority, while the latter secures innocence and the story of the moral subject. These very processes operate through the multiple positionings in relations of power discussed in this chapter. Participants' assumption of the status, relative affluence, and influence of the fluctuating whiteness/Northern/woman/development worker nexus, produced through imperial relations manifesting at the micro level, relies on an already-existing, deeply internalized, and often unrecognized (by development workers) acceptance of white superiority. Equally crucial, though, are moves by which our stories of ourselves as moral subjects are preserved, often through the use of containment strategies, as we actualize a sense of obligation and entitlement to intervene so as to "help" in the world—a scope of action sanctioned by the planetary consciousness of bourgeois subjectivity. The interplay of these continuities of bourgeois subject formation from the era of empire pervades our narratives and, I would argue, is fundamental to comprehending our abiding attachment to our new images of self derived from the development context.

By the same token, as Ochberg notes, the selves we make are susceptible to being unmade.[28] My argument is that it is this risk that cuts short and otherwise subverts our resistance moves time and again. In the next chapter, I will examine resistance more closely. In closing, though, let me add that if, as mentioned at the outset, the lived experience of empire gave white women a sense of self-worth and equality with men, it seems that the same could be said of white women's experiences in the sites of development. This is something that development work does for us as white women, which we are not well equipped to understand. Consequently, our abilities to negotiate our positions in relations of power, and to resist the ways in which we are implicated in dominance, are compromised. In the development context, we are treated as important personages by African peoples, and granted special status within white communities in *laager*-mode: we become "honorary [bourgeois] men." But it is the enactment of colonial continuities central to the formation of bourgeois selves in the spaces of development, where power-over relations are amplified for white middle-class women development workers, that produces our new identities as "true" subjects in our own eyes and, in conjunction with subsequent experiences of the erosion of this claim to subjectivity on returning to Canada, creates much of the regenerative capacity of our desire for development.

CHAPTER 5
PARTICIPANTS' RETROSPECTIVES: COMPLICATING DESIRE

This book articulates the contention that development experience is constitutive of new dimensions of identity formation for Canadian women development workers and that this is key to our desire for development. It is clear that for the participants, doing long-term development work can often have a transformative effect on images of self. In this transformation I have been tracing the operation of gendered colonial continuities that locate bourgeois women as permanent insiders/outsiders in respect to achieving "true" bourgeois or white/middle-class subjectivity. This is not to imply that the participants in this study either undergo a homogeneous, always-predictable kind of change, or that we now claim this elusive subjectivity as completely our own; we nevertheless show evidence of having attained a close (or closer) proximity to it—a heady experience that, for at least some of us, seems to blur the lines between nearer approximation and full attainment. This newfound self is what we try to hold on to through the reassertions of the normative liminal positionality of femininity on our return to Canada.

While this is only one aspect, albeit a central one, of what the research has uncovered, it is emphasized here because it connects to an element of participants' narratives yet to be read: a kind of chronological postscript necessary not only to achieving closure in terms of the development worker story, but more importantly to further exploring resistance and elucidating what is at stake in participants' understandings of our positionings in relations of power. Therefore, this chapter examines how the development worker experience sits with participants after some time has passed. Although it may seem that participants look back on having been development workers as an unqualified "good thing," in fact half the participants retrospectively problematize the *moral* propriety of having been involved in the development enterprise overseas. For most who raise after-the-fact concerns, this kind of critique appears as a contradiction that does not substantially reconfigure other stories we tell of how we value the development worker episode in our lives. However, there are two participants for whom this is not the case, and their stories are discussed at the end because of they proffer important insights into whiteness.

The Moral Basis of Bourgeois Subjectivity

A moral theme runs through the colonial continuities that have been traced in participants' stories, as it does through the historical origins of bourgeois subjectivity from the era of empire. Historically, whiteness has incorporated a moral lineage that intensifed from the time of the late medieval period.[1] The centrality of the moral was made exigent by capitalism in white conceptions of selfhood but has a discursive basis in philosophy and draws on Judeo-Christian religious underpinnings.[2] Rabinow has shown that the advent of capitalism required various kinds of disciplinary technologies,[3] among which was "the self-regulating individual."[4] Being accountable to oneself is seminal to capitalism's self-regulating subject, but the one inheres in the other. The self-regulating subject was made possible, as Foucault contends, through the very notion of a *rapport à soi*: "the kind of relationship you *ought* to have with yourself,"[5] which turned on a post-Enlightenment view of the individual and his (self-evidently gendered) identity. In this view, the self was a divided entity: "it was an object: "me, myself," something of which "I" could become (self-) conscious and subject to (self-) restraint or indulgence."[6] In the process of self-awareness, individuals relied on adherence to internalized moral standards and the operation of reason in the objective application of these standards. The valorization of the notion of the *rational*, self-commanding unitary person that was advanced in the philosophy of Kant and Rousseau is central to modernity's project.[7] Kant posited that "the rational being utters the commands of morality to himself. He obeys no one but himself."[8] Rousseau profoundly influenced the concept of the sovereign individual, arguing for a moral law that man is able to apprehend through reason. However, the practice of self-accountability originated with Christianity, and was normalized through the confessional from medieval times,[9] and later on in Victorian England through the sweeping impact of the Evangelical movement, which required self-examination and accounting to God.[10] In metropole and colony alike, the infusion of Christianity into nineteenth-century bourgeois moral values exerted a powerful influence that was crucial to processes of middle-class self-definition.[11] This, I suggest, combined with the by then commonplace acceptance of the sovereignty of the liberal subject, who practiced a *rapport à soi* to produce the bourgeois individual that capitalism needed: a self-regulating, *moral* subject, accountable to him- or herself in ethical terms. As Goldberg states, "Social relations are constitutive of personal and social identity, and a central part of the order of such relations is the perceived need, the requirement for subjects to give an account of their actions."[12] This is a foundational aspect of white middle-class subjectivity that is still very much in play. Moreover, the bourgeois subject was, and needed to be, a moral subject, not only in his or her own eyes, but also *in the view of others*. This also remains the case today.[13] This is not to infer that a moral foundation to social life is the exclusive purview of bourgeois subjects, but rather that the moral basis of this subjectivity is inflected with specific meanings that articulate with the material privileges of class and Northernness, allowing for the actualization of moral choices and living out of personal goals in terms not available to the majority of peoples in the world.

Thus, the imperative of moral "goodness" suffuses white middle-class identity. The particularly gendered nature of bourgeois subjectivity's relationship to the moral realm has been previously discussed, the niceties of ethical choices and behaviour being the special purview of women. However, the line of argument presented here suggests a convergence of forces from colonial times that generate a deeply felt imperative to "get it right" on the part of "true" bourgeois subjects (white men) and their liminally positioned female counterparts. I propose that the concept of self as a moral subject or a "good person" is in actuality what containment strategies and other moves to innocence both protect and secure. Furthermore—and this is what is really at stake—because subjectivity is conceived in unitary terms, there can be no subject apart from the moral self. The two are conflated, so that if morality is lost, the sense of self or personal identity is ruptured. Although it can be reconstituted, it will be in different terms, and the process cannot but be arduous. In this schema, internalizing and perpetuating morally reprehensible attitudes and practices, if recognized as such, is personally as well as socially construed as a person's "singular badness/shame."[14] This precipitates a crisis of not being (seen as) good, and produces an urgent need for what Flax refers to as "innocent knowledge":

> By innocent knowledge I mean the discovery of some sort of truth
> that can tell us how to act in the world in ways that benefit or are for
> the (at least ultimate) good of all. Those whose actions are grounded
> in or informed by such truth will have *their* innocence guaranteed.
> They can only do good, not harm, to others. They act as the servant
> of something higher and outside (or more than) themselves, their
> own desires, and the effects of their particular histories or social
> locations.[15]

The necessity for this kind of knowledge is no doubt felt with particular intensity by middle-class white women, since on home ground our tenuous claim to bourgeois subjectivity rests on demonstrating our superior
moral sensibilities. There are many such knowledges available to bourgeois subjects. I suggest, though, that development work constitutes a
particularly compelling expression of innocent knowledge because it
addresses the issue of how to act in the *world*, as well as how to fulfill the
imperative to "help" or "improve"; in other words, participating in some
aspect of the development enterprise seems to guarantee a place on the
moral high ground of white middle-class subjectivity, and speaks particularly to feminine constructions of that subjectivity. At the same time,
bourgeois subjects are assured that when we intervene it is an innocent
undertaking, that is, our actions bear no connection to the perpetration of domination or other immoral processes or relations. Quite the
contrary, "helping" in this context is a manifestation of the moral fabric of bourgeois subjectivity, as colonialism's civilizing mission was in its
day. Planetary consciousness and the related sense of entitlement and
obligation to intervene elsewhere appear to be unproblematically "good."

Yet the operation of these colonial continuities sets up a paradox
that today's moral subjects cannot easily perceive or acknowledge: namely,
the prevailing form of planetary consciousness, which comprises a comparatively derived view of self as superior to Others, and the resulting
moral imperative and entitlement to intervene in/"improve" the lives
of those very Others, rests on assumptions organized by racial difference. This is actually a disjuncture in terms of colonial antecedents
because, whereas in the era of empire racial difference was understood
as accepted—*and* acceptable—knowledge among bourgeois subjects, in
contrast today the recognition of race is disavowed in white-dominated
multicultural nations.[16] In the late twentieth century and early twenty-
first century those holding and/or acting on identifiably racist beliefs
have faced social condemnation, a response which arises from the consensus that racism has been discredited by science and that it leads to

morally despicable behaviour.[17] Beyond this there is an additional threat to the moral self posed by recognizing the violence of racism, which Bannerji identifies.[18] The impact on white subjects is described by Jensen as a kind of fear: fear that bourgeois subjects' underlying, lingering racism will be found out by non-white people.[19] While the need remains for bourgeois subjects to feel that our actualizations of the helping imperative are innocent, the work required to keep this story intact while "doing good" elsewhere is complicated by the fundamentally racialized underpinnings of the development binary, which Goudge's analysis reveals: "The more I have reflected on my experiences, the more I have realised the crucial role of notions of white superiority in maintaining the whole structure of global inequality. The aid industry is deeply implicated in these structures."[20] The racial dilemma thus posed has important implications for some participants' post hoc thoughts on the rightness of our development worker odysseys.

What Do We Think of It Now?

How do participants feel in hindsight about our time as development workers? Although three participants had been back in Canada for only a matter of months at the time their interviews took place, the rest had returned at least one year earlier (of these, three had been home for more than five years). Over half have stayed involved in development: one participant was on the verge of leaving for another assignment in Africa when she was interviewed, and three were employed in Canadian development NGOs where overseas travel went with the job; the other "involved" participants were doing workshops and/or volunteer work with Canadian development NGOs, and one person was on her way to Southern Africa on a study tour when I met her. This would seem to reaffirm the strength of the regenerative capacity of our desire for development. However, despite many things—our ongoing development connections, our accounts of euphoria and empowerment, our emphatic assertions that we would do it over again, and our moves to conceptualize our role in the development enterprise as alternative or even oppositional—despite all this, half the participants, the majority of whom have stayed connected to development work, express ambivalence now about having gone overseas as development workers in the first place. In so doing, we pick up threads of uncertainty that are woven into our stories of being "there." It may be relevant to note, however, that none of the most recently returned participants are among those to express these doubts, an omission that can be understood as resulting from the struggles to hold on to self through the readjustment process. Perhaps, too, the passing of time lessens the intensity of our attachments to having been "there," allowing for more probing interrogation. It is also apparent in some accounts that it is university studies that occasion, and afford the space for, deeper reflection. I mention this with caution, however, since as Roman asserts, access to some kinds of knowledge can have the effect of producing knowing (white) subjects, rather than unsettling domination.[21]

No Misgivings

Participants' uncertainty has its degrees, so that an apt analogy might be the layers of an onion. On the outside, the biggest layer, making up about half the onion, are participants like Linda who do not espouse any misgivings, and for whom the development experience appears to remain unproblematically a special time. As she says: "When anybody asks me about my time in Africa or something, you know, you just sort of *come to life*. There's a lot of pride in all the new things that you did. It was just such a *wonderful* time!" Linda would like to go again, some day, but not to the same place. Lorraine is more representative of some other participants who would be included here too, although perhaps on the inside of this layer. Reflecting back in a more balanced manner, and mixing enthusiasm with reservations borne of her development critiques, Lorraine shows no noticeable apprehension about "what she has done" by becoming a development worker. Lorraine's assertion of alternative practice holds firm, even after the fact. For about half the participants then, the development worker experience continues, even as it recedes in time, to be seen as a treasured moment in the making of self: a view not undermined by any lingering criticisms of the development enterprise or our part of it.

At the next layer, the critiques of development that arise when participants are overseas and that are pushed aside at the time by claims to exceptionality—the myth of alternative development—appear to infiltrate our memories of having been there, and begin to dilute our certainty about our own participation, but only up to a point. By curtailing the extent of critical scrutiny, these participants manage to evade, if only barely, direct encounters with the question of whether we *should* have been development workers. For example, Bev says: "I didn't really know, but that will continue to bother me like it has you ... what really can my role be?" It is telling, I think, that Bev was about to leave for another overseas posting when I interviewed her. Susan too exhibits this kind of doubt:

> (Sighs) Hmmm ... It [having been a development worker] um, stated again, the questions: What, what *are* we really doing here? What *can* we contribute? Do we really have something to contribute?

Yvonne's comments take this to a larger perspective:

> I think that really all the work that [name of Canadian NGO] and the—we [development] types, what we were doing, *really* is not getting us anywhere. The problem is just too big.

Vickie adds a related, self-deprecating note:

> Perhaps I had had a rather inflated idea of the virtues and importance of Western medicine and my moral obligation to bring what I could to the Third World.

And lastly, Wendy raises an issue linked to Vickie's remark: "I think the problem is to think that you're going there for them. Because you're really going for yourself." She goes on to say: "I mean we don't need to send teachers any more, that's pretty clear—not to teach. Because they have teachers a lot, in lots of those countries." However, Wendy's subsequent declaration that her current work is a continuation of her social justice commitments previously expressed through development work attests that for her the (Northern) development worker model remains consistent with social justice. She goes on to conclude: "You had to be careful about what you send people to do," a statement in which the practice of "sending" people remains uninterrogated. Here lies the boundary of this line of questioning.

Wendy's delimitation strategy can be read in what Bev, Susan, Yvonne, and Vickie have said, for the seemingly heavy uncertainties expressed at this point in the interviews are belied by insistence elsewhere that something of value was achieved; *and is achievable* by going "there." Vickie, for example, goes on to say: "In the big picture, I was part of the problem. In day-to-day affairs I was useful in a limited way." Similarly, Susan was sustained by the work she saw the other Canadians from the same Canadian NGO doing, and Yvonne thinks that every Canadian volunteer had something to contribute. Thus, the implications that seem to inhere in the questions raised are prevented from reaching their full potential: that is, from unsettling narratives of alternative practice, and by extension raising the issue of whether we should have gone "there" at all.

Doubt Deepens

There are two more layers to this "onion" though, and these are where doubt deepens. What is particularly important in these accounts, apart from growing expressions of uncertainty that take up more air time in the completion of participants' stories, is the multidirectional relationships, already beginning to be detectable, in respect to the moral foundations of our misgivings, the subjectivity of the Other, the boundedness of the questions we raise, and our images of self. Patti's comments are illustrative. Noted previously for her recognition of what she calls "a global connection" in which the wealth of the North is procured "at the expense of people who don't have that," Patti asks where she should physically locate herself in this unjust world:

> We [Patti and her partner] do struggle with that. Is the, is the place of integrity in the world right now, is it to go out there? Cause most countries in Africa have people there who can do whatever job we would do, you know, as far as the work we would do or the contribution we would bring. I mean, highly trained people who probably can make better applications of things in their own context than we can. Although sometimes an outside perspective does—a person on the outside can see things or make connections for people that, when you're caught up in your local mode of thinking you can't, or you don't have the freedom to look in that direction, or whatever. But therefore we need to have people from Africa coming here ... I feel I want to be part more of an exchange that's going on. And I enjoy living there. I really appreciate the community social values that are there, that I feel lacking in North America. So, there's sort of a selfish motive involved too. And I like, I like wearing wrappers,[22] you know? Some of it's not terribly glorious, you know it's not very ideal—or I don't know, altruistic. And, and even on my own, from my own faith perspective, I wonder whether it is of value that you know I, here at work I try to do the education part of it rather than going there with *questionable* results of most of these typical development approaches, you know. Again sort of the imposition of my own world view on people there, as opposed to "Can we be a catalyst for them to figure out something about their own situation?" Or together figure out something about their situation and also our situation at the same time? Maybe that's it.

In this *rapport à soi* can be seen both reflecting on the past and decision-making about the future, since Patti and her partner were at that time considering the offer of another posting in Africa. The back-and-forth discussion Patti is having with herself, where she repeatedly raises a cri-tique and answers it, indicates considerable qualms competing with a desire to resolve her moral uncertainties at least to the extent that par-ticipation in overseas development seems permissible once more. In effect, Patti's answers to her own questions keep the debates in check by curtailing further scrutiny of, for instance, the feasibility of any real exchange of the kind she wants to imagine as possible. Thus, through the evasion of key issues, her position and her narratives of self remain morally intact, although Patti's uncertainties persist, fuelled by her moments of recognition of the African people as fully human.

Laura, who presently works with a Canadian development NGO and travels overseas for her job, also articulates considerable misgivings about having been a development worker:

> (sighs) Well, uh … for, for a long time I guess I've, I've certainly been wrestling with the, the whole experience of, of being in [Southern Africa] and, and what that meant and if, I should have been there and what was the impact on me, what was the impact on other people I worked with. Um, and, and having difficulty with, with things par-ticularly I guess around the privileges, that, that I had as, as some-one from the North … [Referring to critiques encountered in graduate studies] I became more skeptical of, of any kind of aid doing—development doing—any good at all. But I, I never could quite sort of come to terms with "It would be better if all aid money was simply—people, the whole industry—was just withdrawn." I can, can never quite think that that is going to (sighs) um … not be absolutely frightening. So I guess a part of me has to actually resolve—I couldn't keep looking at myself right now. But, but there are some things that are done that are useful.

Laura goes on to say:

> Development is a such a contested kind of, of field and, and (sighs) by participating in any way, you're still participating in that whole proj-ect of, of development. And, the amount of time and energy and angst you spend on trying to figure out how you could be there but, but not be as bad as the whole picture, uh, is stressful.

Laura's tone is concerned. Her *rapport à soi* is quite seriously disturbed by the incongruity she acknowledges now between what she initially saw as an altruistic contribution ("I certainly did have some feelings of altru-ism around it all, when I first went") and what appears now as a "con-tested field" where her impact on African people is questionable. She asks herself if "I should have been there." It is notable, too, that Laura's growing discomfort with what she has done appears to have been consolidated by her university studies. Laura keeps trying to negotiate a moral space for herself as she continues to look for what is useful or beneficial in the development enterprise; thus, she speaks against simply withdrawing the "whole industry," making an argument that recognizes the potentially violent effects on Southern peoples of such a draconian solution.

Laura does not seek easy answers for herself, as is demonstrated in her story of refusing to accept an African development critique she discovers in her studies:

> I, remember just wanting, wanting to latch on to one [African development critique] that was ah, this Zimbabwean guy that talked about how, all, all the problematics around coming across these development workers. That recently he'd seen this new breed of development workers which were women who, had Birkenstocks and you know, white Canadian, or white Northern women who had spent a lot more time listening to people and finding out what people wanted to do and not being so pushy and blah blah blah blah kind of stuff. And saying that, that he, he quite liked this new breed of development worker. And, and "woman" was definitely the biggest part of that picture. So I, like I kind of wanted to be able to latch on to that but I knew that I really couldn't totally either.

This careful self-scrutiny is consistent with Laura's willingness to critically reflect on her development worker narratives at various moments during her interview. However, Laura's other response to her moral quandary is to state that if she could make the choice again, knowing what she knows now, she would not become a development worker. Read against the tenuously reconciled contradictions of her present concerns and her current employment, Laura's declaration that she would not "do it over again" appears as a strategy to wipe the slate clean and redeem a purer narrative of moral subjectivity. Unable to turn back time, Laura perseveres in the field of development, still questioning but securing for herself what seems to her a less contested (because based in Canada) position than that of an overseas development worker. Through all these moves Laura is able to hold at bay the deeper implications for herself of the fundamental question she has begun to name: whether she "should have been there." Laura acknowledges that "a part of me has to actually resolve" this, and it would seem at least a part of her has done so, however uneasily.

The last participant whose comments are included here, before examining the final layer of the "onion," is Erica. Now in an executive position in a Canadian development NGO, Erica talks about the doubts that haunt her from having taught social studies to high school students in Southern Africa:

> And there I am, teaching all the—these kids their local traditions, you know … But it was always filtered through *my*, my judgments of their culture. And uh, and uh, I *tried* not to for a while, and then thought I was just being very ineffective in hiding any biases so, I just like brought them out into the open and so we would talk about things like violence, and sex, and attitudes toward women and girls. And uh, and I made it pretty clear, like I just, I disapproved of a *whole lot of stuff*. And uh, *really*, was that appropriate for me to be doing that? I don't know, I still don't know … So, I, I really, I, I struggled with that more than anything else for the—for the two years … But it's clearly not what I was brought there to do … I was *desperately* aware of it *all the time*, thinking "This is *inappropriate!*" I just kept thinking like "That is *just wrong!*" and uh, that, that I was there teaching *that* in particular. So, so you know clearly I, I was invasive in, in that way and I, well I just, I've, I've never *really* totally come to terms with it. I don't, I mean I feel very comfortable with what I did but, I just, but I also realize that, that was not my role … to me those *are* the issues, like really, and it's hard—you have to *question really, how useful you are*. You're—it's like—it—it's not a pleasant process to go through, I don't think.

Erica goes on to say, though, that this was "really a *defining moment* in my life." She later explains:

> It was the beginnings of something that is enabling me—I, I really believe in this organization where I'm at now—and that experience has enabled me to be a better development worker. I've learned from it. I think if you learn from it, it's not wasted.

It is noteworthy that Erica's concern about the impact of her development work dilemmas on African people gives way to a narrative that re-centres the importance of her own learning. The erasure of any harm she may have caused in the process evokes Keating's eclipse of the African domestic worker in the vignette described in the introductory chapter.

It is not possible to draw precise comparisons regarding the intensity of participants' evident retrospective anguish about our involvement in the development enterprise. Erica does not exhibit the nuanced self-critiques or global concerns that Patti and Laura do. Yet Erica sounds impassioned in her conviction that some of what she was doing as a development worker was morally questionable ("I just kept thinking like 'That is *just wrong!*'"), an inference in which the subjectivity of her students plays an important part. I include her comments here because this assessment on her part disturbs even now her story of development work as a "defining moment" in her life, and because of the moves Erica makes to recuperate the morality of her narrative so as to avoid asking the "should-I-have-been-a-development-worker" question.

I have been contending that what is at stake in our justifications of our participation in development work is the construction of our selves as moral subjects. The extreme pressure being brought to bear on the coherence of that image of self is revealed in Erica's story; in fact, with each layer peeled away in the accounts under examination here the tension mounts. Where Patti and Laura are able to achieve a faltering and imperfect appeasement of the uncertainties that persistently unsettle peace of mind about the rightness of having been development workers, Erica contrives to close more firmly the door of doubt regarding what she has done. She restates her comfort with the choices she has made, and stakes a redemption claim to the effect that the work she is doing now has been made possible by that earlier, if somewhat dubious, period as development worker: the ends justifying the means. This seems a necessary interpretation on her part, for Erica is deeply invested in actualizing her strong and otherwise identity-affirming commitment to development work, which she later emotionally describes in these words: "It's *my love!*" It is the passionate assurance in Erica's tone that also distinguishes her redemption move from Laura's, while at the same time betokening a morality tale more in need of justification, and so perhaps nearer to dissolution.

The Centre Cannot Hold

The "centre cannot hold" is a phrase from a well-known poem by William Butler Yeats; appropriately, another phrase from the poem serves as the title of a well-known novel about Africa by Chinua Achebe.[23] The rest of the stanza reads:

> Things fall apart; the centre cannot hold;
> Mere anarchy is loosed upon the world,
> The blood-dimmed tide is loosed, and everywhere
> The ceremony of innocence is drowned;

> The best lack all conviction, while the worst
> Are full of passionate intensity.

In all the narratives considered thus far, participants have succeeded in holding together a story of personal integrity, to borrow Patti's concept. What happens when the moral self can no longer be rescued? The accounts of two participants take the uncertainties arising from having been development workers beyond the point where the coherence of this narrative can be maintained. Among participants' accounts, this questioning comprises the core or bottom-most layer of the "onion" under consideration here, and pushes critiques of the development enterprise closest to their logical conclusion; that is, to seeing ourselves as implicated in, rather than an alternative to, our own criticisms. In the accounts of Carol and Kris the effects on unitary subjectivities of more unrelenting moral self-interrogation can be traced, and when this happens, "the centre cannot hold."

A graduate student with no active links to development at the time of her interview, Carol has been referenced several times because her accounts often reveal careful self-scrutiny. Carol recognizes that becoming a development worker is about being "somebody who, because of whatever circumstances of privilege, has the privilege of going over and having themselves dismantled, so they can *reconstruct themselves as best as possible*" (emphasis mine), a perspective that goes some way toward the argument being advanced here regarding development and the making of white feminine selves. Carol says of herself now:

> Maybe I still don't know how to live a life that, that is as harmless as possible. Um, and I don't know that it's—I don't kn—I don't even know how to find out what that life would be sometimes. So ... (sighs).

Having realized after returning to Canada that "despite it all, I was still on the one side of the line [of world wealth and privilege] and not the other, and that I just always would be," Carol adds:

> The easier thing would be to not think too much about it and sometimes I don't. And I have the privilege to do that. So I guess coming to terms with it is a slower thing. You can only, I can only let myself know as much as I'm able to know at a time. I mean I know it's—I knew many, many things, many things that I didn't articulate until later. I *know* I knew them somehow, I know they were there. But not able, not letting myself articulate it is I guess part of being able to live with myself.

Although Carol admits that sometimes she doesn't "think too much about it," it is clear that she does struggle with acknowledging her position in global dominance, which she admits she "knew" was operative when she was in Southern Africa. Her statement about only letting herself know so much at a time reflects an awareness of what is detectable so frequently in participants' accounts: strategies of containment that are imperative to living with or protecting our (moral) selves in the context of, or in relation to, development work. These comments from Carol serve as a precursor to a letter she sent after a post-interview check-in phone call.[24] Much of that letter is presented below because it articulates an unresolved moral struggle to come to terms with having been, *and* having relished being, a development worker:

> The thing that I want to write about in follow-up to our interview is the question of honesty. I think the main gist of what I will write came out in our interview, but perhaps this note will sharpen the point. You said that I was very honest in my opinions of the development process and my role in it ... In one sense, I think you are right about my honesty, but in another sense I think I am very dishonest about what I claim to know. While it is true that I have thought a lot about the whole foundations of the development process, the power imbalance and racism involved in it, and while I have recognized, to whatever degree I have, my role in that powerful and racist process, the fact that I can recognize it only by removing my *self* from it is profoundly dishonest. The fact that I do remove my self from my understanding of what it meant for me to be in Africa is the reason why I spoke to you so bluntly and objectively about my beliefs. I think that we have many ways of knowing things. I further believe that some ways of knowing are more effective than others. I may "know" with my reason the things I related to you, but I don't always hold that knowledge in my heart—I do not always feel it passionately. I think if I had, it would have made it intolerable for me to stay in Africa, and I think it would make it much more painful than it is for me to think about it now. If I really knew, in my heart, what my mind seems to understand, I could certainly never say that, given the chance, I would go again to Africa and that I would not give up my years there for anything. I think it is only once we hold our knowledge in our hearts that we can *really* claim knowledge. Without that, I'm not convinced we always act appropriately and for the right reasons.
>
> I think we are not *urged* to behave according to the principles laid out by our understanding unless we also *feel* the rightness of those principles. This is the sense in which I think I have largely removed

my self from my understanding of the things I related to you. I can admit them only by not allowing myself to feel them too deeply, and in doing that, I have removed the better part of my self, the part that I think makes us most human, from the process of understanding. In this case I think I am very dishonest, and this is my current struggle.

Here is a race critique of development in stronger terms than that which was expressed during Carol's interview. Naming the racism leaves no way out for Carol as a unitary subject; having been a development worker, she now sees herself as clearly implicated in racialized domination, and suggests some awareness of the violence of what this entails as she refers to "the development enterprise" as "that powerful and racist process." This sets in motion an irreconcilable moral crisis. Carol realizes that "given the chance, I would go again to Africa and that I would not give up my years there for anything": her desire for development is undiminished by her first-hand knowledge of the development enterprise and its effects. The usual recourse to containment strategies is stymied by Carol's unrelenting self-examination, which also works against narratives of a moral self, causing Carol to conclude that she is "very dishonest." She is able to admit this "dishonesty" only by not feeling too deeply (that is, "removing" herself from) the contradictions between what she "knows" to be right (knowledge held in her heart, that would lead her to "act appropriately and for the right reasons") and what she profoundly desires (the years in Africa that she would not give up "for anything"). The contradictions of her positioning become unbearable, and with the rupture of her claim to an integrated moral narrative of self, Carol sees herself losing her humanity: "I have removed the better part of my self, the part that I think makes us most human, from the process of understanding." The confident, more fully bourgeois subjectivity that was constructed through the development experience has been lost. This longed-for sense of self deeply informs Carol's unyielding attachment to her African experiences. As well though, it must be acknowledged that some of Carol's investment in her time in Africa can be read as desire for connection with African people as subjects, as *thou*: a desire arising from her close friendship with an African woman, Rebecca, noted earlier. Such a devastating outcome—the removal of what makes her most human—leaves Carol in a place of struggle, with no end in sight. This stands in contrast to Erica's successful containment of critiques that threaten this kind of rupture. When the moral centre of unitary subjects is compromised, "things fall apart."

This is evident, too, in Kris's narrative. Kris has had a longer commitment to development work than most other participants, and is still involved in preparing people to go overseas. As she says: "It's not just the years I was there. But going there was what organized who I was and what I did for years before that." Kris was critical of the development enterprise while she was overseas ("I used to think that a lot of it was really bad ... but that some of it was good"). Now though, due in part to graduate studies, Kris's critique, like Carol's, has reached new levels, and with a similar recognition of race and violence:

> It's bad enough as it is, imposing our agendas and all that, but it just feels to me like there's this onslaught of white people from the North ... and it's, it's in, it's racialized, it's epistemological, it's, it—it's overwhelming. And, and at the same time people's economies are so much worse, and they have so much more to contend with, to have any hope of getting their kids through school, and in the midst of all this they have to deal with all of us finding ever more ways and reasons to come and be in their faces, and in their organizations, and in their lives. So ... I ... don't think we should ... any more.

However, like Carol, Kris cannot bring herself to say that she would not do it all over again if she had the chance:

> I don't know. (sighs) It's hard for me to say that I wouldn't, because it would mean—I think of all the people I wouldn't know.[25] And it's like saying I wouldn't be who I am now ... So I don't know that I wouldn't.

Such irresolution comprises an untenable enough position for Kris to sustain; however, the moral certainty expressed above that she should *not* have been a development worker is what more deeply torments Kris's view of self. This stems from her incapacity at this point to contain her critiques of the development enterprise and so save herself/her *self* from being implicated in it. In fact, Kris recognizes that her development experience is productive of her identity ("it's like saying I wouldn't be who I am now"). Kris further explains:

> I thought that what we were doing was different. I thought that there was the space to do something different ... And now I don't know how different it was. (sighs) And I don't know even if it was different, if that was enough reason to do it.

For Kris the myth of alternative development no longer comprises an effective containment strategy. As a consequence, Kris faces a paralysis in her *rapport à soi*:

> It—it's hard. (sighs) So, I don't know. I remain like not knowing what
> I think of anything to do with it. I've been thinking of it in so many
> different ways that in the end I don't have a conclusion. I don't know.
> I don't know.

This soon gives way in her narrative to a view of self as immoral:

> I went through from the time when I became disillusioned, like when
> I began to think that being a woman working with other women
> didn't actually solve everything—didn't, didn't uh, overcome other
> differences—I've gone through about three years, almost three years
> of feeling increasingly that I really made a mess of my life—I really
> made a huge mistake with it. I *shouldn't have* gone there. I *shouldn't
> have* done that. I *shouldn't have* been ... and, I can't bring back those
> years. And it's not just the years I was there.

Kris repeats three times that she "shouldn't have" been a development
worker, and regrets the time that cannot be retrieved. Three years is a
long period to sustain such a severe self-critique and yet be unable to say
that she would not do it over again if she had the chance. The conclusion Kris draws is that she has "really made a mess of my life—I really
made a huge mistake with it." So crippling is this narrative, particularly
in combination with her "I don't know" refrain, that the loss of image
of self here echoes Carol's forfeiture of her "humanity," and illustrates
the dire consequences for bourgeois women not only of failing to make
the "right" moral choices, but of recognizing the harm of the choices that
were made.

   In Carol's and Kris's stories, such unrelenting questioning, that is,
deeper resistance to having been drawn into the (overseas) development enterprise—which they both now comprehend as racist and violent in its effects—unravels the narratives of the moral subject, producing
a fragmentation, even a dissolution, of self-image or identity that almost
exactly replicates Frye's description of her own response to realizing
that she was implicated in racism:

> I had come to realize that not only my acts but my capacities for self-
> criticism and correction were contaminated by racism, and that there-
> fore there seemed to be no way to fix what was wrong with me. I
> wrote:
>
> > It all combined to precipitate me into profound and unnerving dis-
> > trust of myself. All of my ways of knowing seemed to have failed
> > me—my perception, my common sense, my good will, my anger,
> > honor and affection, my intelligence and insight. Just as walking

requires something fairly sturdy and firm underfoot, so being an actor in the world requires a foundation of ordinary moral and intellectual confidence. Without that we don't know how to be or to act; we become strangely stupid ... If you want to be good, and you don't know good from bad, you can't move.[26]

In a different interpretation from Frye's, however, I posit that these accounts reveal how the basis of claims to a coherent narrative of identity in bourgeois terms, and to appropriate white femininity, is forfeited because the core of unitary subjectivity, the moral construction of self, has been discredited. This seems a high price to pay for failing to contain critiques, a failure ironically brought on by the effort to pursue an even purer moral path in these participants' *rapport à soi*. These accounts of persistent self-scrutiny and ensuing moral anguish reflect the bourgeois need for a moral narrative of self—a need that is heightened by the relationship between proper white middle-class femininity and goodness, to which Canadian narratives about development seem to give expression.

However, where Carol appears to be stranded in her struggle with the effects of her moral dilemmas on her image of self, toward the end of her narrative Kris shows some signs of moving forward:

So I finally have reached the point of accepting that that's who I am and that's what I've done, and I did it as best I could. And maybe the ways in which [name of Canadian NGO] was an alternative had more to do with things that I didn't even understand, with being the same person who was there all the time, and being a person who really did care about ... what [Southern Africans] thought about what we did.

Kris speaks in a subdued voice. She has reached a new view of self: not the "empowered," able-to-do-anything subject seen earlier in her interview when she appeared as a newly made "someone" whose self-image approached fuller dimensions of "true" bourgeois subjectivity, but a more tentative and accountable self. Given the moral chastisement present in the preceding quote, Kris's acceptance of what she has "done with her life" implies having come to terms with not "getting it right." Indeed, Kris is able to acknowledge now that she does not know whether she was part of a development alternative, and importantly, she reframes the meaning of such an alternative in terms of her impact on African peoples. The significance of the subjectivity of the Other is also noticeable in Kris's inability to claim she would not change her decision to take the development path because of her relations with some African people ("It's hard for me to say that I wouldn't, because it would mean, I think of all the people I wouldn't know.").[27] Here the Other appears as *thou*, a subject whose importance to Kris forestalls any straightforward way out, despite her moral distress at having been a development worker.

In these aspects of Kris's story, in Carol's meticulous struggle for honesty, as well as in the harsher racist critiques of the development enterprise that precipitate both individuals' ethical dilemmas about having been development workers, can be read a resistance that is distinct from what has been identified up to now in participants' accounts. For Carol's and Kris's acknowledgements of being implicated in what they name as a hegemonic project are tantamount to equating having been development workers with having participated in a process of domination contingent on racial difference. Implicit here is a degree of recognition of the violence that inheres in racism's impact.[28] I suggest that it this recognition that precipitates the dissolution of their moral narratives of self. However, in this painful process, Carol and Kris are in fact refusing, at least partially, continued accession to a subjectivity whose terms rely on a morally sanctioned, normative acceptance of the development enterprise. Furthermore, through their loss of certainty, Carol and Kris demonstrate a performance of self in which the effortlessly marginalizing confidence of white middle-class subjects is diminished. I use the word diminished because also apparent in both accounts is self-absorption—itself a mark of privilege—with the choices that an individual bourgeois subject makes: an evocation of that larger-than-life self that first sought to intervene elsewhere in a beneficial way.

Although Carol's and Kris's focus is on the rightness of their actions in relation to their current understanding of the development enterprise, inherent in this concern is a shift toward granting subjectivity to/recognizing the humanity of African people whose lives are so directly affected by Northern development work. Carol and Kris may now be susceptible, if only in their *rapport à soi*, to being called to account for specific ways in which they enacted domination at the micro level in the overseas context. They may already be contending with such implications, as in fact a few other participants do, and did even when overseas. Laura, for example, demonstrates willingness to accept the critical feedback she receives after-the-fact from an African co-worker, mentioned previously. The particularity of such incidents seems to render them more vulnerable to containment strategies, however, so that isolated negative comments or self-critical insights, while sometimes giving serious pause, need not trigger the kind of moral crisis with which Carol and Kris are grappling. This is illustrated in Laura's conclusion to the feedback she receives:

> There's a few of those kinds of things that you know, hit me—it's not just a flashing kind of insight but they hit, you know, like a hammer on the head sometimes and you go, "Oh my God! How could I have?" But I did.

In view of the isolated "hammer-on-the-head" impact produced by the internalization of particular insights, it cannot be assumed that confronting broader complicity as global subjects in macro-level processes of racialized domination unleashes a stream of specific self-critiques. As Carol puts it, not letting ourselves articulate more than is bearable appears fundamental to being able to live with ourselves/our selves.[29] Carol and Kris have already pushed the limits in this direction, to their cost. That they simultaneously rely on containment strategies is evident in their failure to connect their positions globally to, for example, their positioning in dominance in Canada, or to articulating more fully the violent effects of at least some of their participation in the development enterprise.

In and of themselves, the narratives of only two participants would perhaps not warrant the attention given to Carol's and Kris's dilemmas here. However, as I have tried to show, these participants seem to take further what troubles several others in the aftermath of the development worker experience.[30] Where in other accounts it is only possible to infer that containment strategies are implicitly protecting moral narratives necessary to constructions of self, Carol's and Kris's stories enable such readings to be made directly. Thus, the foundational effects of being able to claim to be moral are affirmed here, particularly for feminine bourgeois subjectivities. Conversely, what can be seen as well is that the consequences of relinquishing such a claim are not to be faced lightly, for thereby threatened are our very narratives of self. This is a conclusion that elucidates the imperative white women feel to make the right moral choices. There is a considerable cost in recognizing and holding oneself accountable for "getting it wrong," especially to the extent of confronting unintended participation in inherently racialized domination, not to speak of an implicit awareness of its violent effects. This has troubling implications for the chances that bourgeois subjects will attempt to understand and refuse the ways in which we are complicit in enacting domination—and for dismantling whiteness. Speaking from a white feminine subject position, Frankenberg concurs: "But my awakening is never complete. Although the initial transformation was one of earthquake proportions, there is always room for another aftershock, always need for further awakening. White antiracism is, perhaps, a stance requiring lifelong vigilance."[31]

How Can We Resist?

In this book the term resistance has been used to describe: (1) opposing global injustice, which participants try to resist initially through doing development work, and then by critiquing the development enterprise and staking a claim to alternative development; (2) refusing the gendered terms of our own production as white middle-class women, some of which participants attempt to reject by going overseas in the first place, and by gender transgressive actions when we are "there"; (3) resisting our dominant positioning as white Northern women development workers in the overseas context, which we negotiate by sharing affluence, refusing privilege, and so on; and (4) countering the common-sense view of development-work-as-benevolent that is fundamental to the Canadian national narrative, which some participants resist when we begin to reconsider the moral implications of our own work in development. The fifth and most crucial meaning of the term "resistance" is, however, the one discussed in reviewing Carol's and Kris's moral struggles: resisting the racialized terms of our own constitution as bourgeois subjects—in other words, refusing whiteness. While implying and incorporating aspects of the other resistance endeavours, the latter relies on relinquishing claims to innocence, and so entails compromising moral narratives of self.

Using resistance to describe the latter seems in some respects a misnomer. I continue to call our efforts resistance for want of another, more apt term. My trouble with resistance is that, despite attempts here to imbue the concept with a nuanced meaning, it nevertheless seems to retain an all-or-nothing connotation. This derives in part from its more common political usage where that which is to be resisted appears in similarly clear-cut or monolithic terms. However, as is evident from the various ways in which we enact resistance in this study, as the term is used here resistance never comprises a total response. On the other hand, neither is it absent from our actions, even when we are at our most compliant. I use "resistance," then, to reference certain kinds of awareness and resulting choices made by participants.

Of these, refusing the terms of our constitution through whiteness and its colonial continuities is of a different order from the rest, for it reconfigures narratives of self, and changes performances of subjectivity. It seems to me that, of the resistance moves made by participants in the study, this poses the most significant challenge to micro processes of domination, for this is where refusal to see our complicity starts to give way to accountability for our actions. Refusing whiteness in this way exceeds other resistance moves precisely because it does not become subverted when our moral narratives begin to be encroached upon.

Writing about a "politics of accountability," Razack says:

> We need to ask: Where am I in this picture? Am I positioning myself as the saviour of less fortunate peoples? as the progressive one? as more subordinated? as innocent? These are moves of superiority and we need to move beyond them ... Accountability begins with tracing relations of privilege and penalty. It cannot proceed unless we examine our complicity. Only then can we ask questions about how we are understanding differences and for what purpose.[32]

This explanation of a politics of accountability echoes the deeper resistance struggles of Carol and Kris, and, to some extent, those of participants like Laura and Patti, who continue to ask questions about the ways in which they may be complicit in enacting domination inscribed with race. What this study contributes to Razack's conceptualization of a politics of accountability is an articulation of a process toward responsible bourgeois subjectivity, and an indication of what is at stake—and what must therefore be challenged in such subjects—if a genuine "tracing of relations of privilege and penalty" and examination of complicity are to be attained. Furthermore, what is clear is that a politics of accountability is not achieved through a once-and-for-all epiphany: just as white bourgeois identities are continually in process, drawing on discursively circulated and normalized comparisons with Others, a planetary consciousness, and sense of entitlement and obligation to intervene that secures moral narratives, and being shaped by constructions of gender, so, too, the interruption of the effects of these colonial continuities must persistently be reiterated in site-specific ways. It is apparent that the necessity to maintain a moral narrative of self works against an ongoing excavation of micro-level perpetuations of dominance. Yet it would seem that this very need for a moral view of self is, ultimately, what can be called on in challenging the invested innocence of white bourgeois subjects. It appears, too, that the particular moral urgency white women are produced to assume may render us especially determined to refuse to acknowledge our complicity in, *and* to track our perpetuation of, domination. Herein lies both impediment to, and potential for, change.

CHAPTER 6
SUMMING UP, DRAWING CONCLUSIONS

Through the 1980s and 1990s, and into the present day, Africa, along with other parts of the South, has been increasingly discovered anew as a terrain of Canadian engagement and training for, among others, women's studies programs, social work students, professional internship programs, and high school learning tours, as well as programs of development studies and burgeoning university-to-university linkages. Canadian development workers—and it can be assumed, other students, trainees, and so on—find ourselves positioned in relations of power in the South in ways that often challenge and contradict our reasons for going overseas in the first place. Underlying our negotiations of these positions are our investments in both what we see of the issues that trouble us and how we understand, or make sense of to ourselves, the dilemmas that result; these meanings shape our efforts to resist perpetuating and acting from dominance. Underlying all of this is what directs our gaze "Southward" and frames our comprehensions.

For these reasons I have attempted a theorization of how it is that white middle-class subjectivities are produced through the historical antecedents of the larger relations of power in which we are located, and how these colonial continuities are productive of the subject position of development worker. It is from this perspective that I have traced the ways in which white middle-class Canadian women negotiate and (often inadvertently) constitute these same relations in our day-to-day lives in the development context, and the possibilities for us to resist complicity in these processes. In light of the disproportionate participation of women in development NGOs in Canada, the growing numbers of female "volunteers" in the South—most of whom

are white and virtually all of whom are middle-class—and my own subject position, I have been especially concerned with how constructions
of white bourgeois femininity are imbricated in our commitments to,
and ways of living out, the development worker experience.

The stories I have drawn on come from middle-class white women
like myself who have served on long-term contracts in sub-Saharan Africa
primarily in the 1980s through the first half of the 1990s, although I have
added affirmations and complexity here and there by referencing the
accounts of a more recent group of interviewees. It is noteworthy that so
little changes in these narratives over time. Indeed, a recent analysis by
Cook of expatriate women in a city in northern Pakistan reveals a "profile" that is interchangeable with the kind of composite picture that
emerges from my interviewees:

> A subject "profile" of a Western woman in Gilgit ... takes shape as I
> assemble the pieces of this theoretical puzzle. She is discursively con-
> stituted; multiple discourses of power are manifested in, constituted
> through, and articulated by her practised, heterogeneous, and
> ambivalent subjectivity ... Finally, she is relationally and ambivalently
> constituted as she lives in the contact zone through material realities
> and discursive complexes that operate cross-culturally. Her subjec-
> tivity is also conflicted in this space due to the ambivalence of dis-
> courses of authority, her contradictory constructions of the Other,
> and her conflictual participation in discourses of power. She repro-
> duces, resists, and modifies oppressive discourses simultaneously.
> When she is on a civilising mission, she tends to consolidate herself
> against negated Other women and men so she can actualise a liber-
> ated and liberating Self. But as a marginal gendered subject, she suf-
> fers from a lack of "authority" similar to that experienced back
> "home."[1]

Cook goes on to say:

> Western women frequently violate boundaries between "public" and
> "private" space, even if it provokes danger. As their colonial counter-
> parts did, they travel and work as "honorary men," and enter places,
> such as men's dining, work, and recreational areas, from which many
> indigenous women are normally excluded.[2]

And, a final quote from Cook:

> By choosing to leave home, Western women in Gilgit disrupt dis-
> courses of femininity, and thereby enhance their self-definition as
> independent individuals. Their individualistic strategies of escape

through travel both enact a discourse of the bourgeois self and initiate a form of gender power for women: entering a global world
enables them to transgress gender norms at home; to shape a self-
confident, somewhat elitist female identity; and to gain some sense
of control over their lives. The feelings of independence and confidence Western women achieve from travelling helps them to realise
other, "freer" selves.[3]

Cook demonstrates here striking similarities in what two disconnected
researchers uncover in respect to Northern women development workers in very different parts of the globe. The profile Cook articulates
regarding expatriate development workers in Pakistan could well
describe the women I interviewed and development workers in other
studies mentioned in the opening chapter of this book. The themes of
"honorary men" and self-realization are key to my participants as well
as to the women whom Cook studied. There are many other points of
convergence in the narratives of the respective development workers,
but the ones presented here adequately make the argument. In these
overlaps lies an affirmation of what Cook and I each explore. The works
of Baaz and Goudge also contain striking similarities to my study, in
terms of both their conclusions and the quotes they present from interviewees.[4] Taken together, I would suggest that these convergences
demonstrate that Ridley's comment on the colonial era still resonates
today: "The essentials of the colonial encounter are pre-formed within
the European psyche, pre-recorded in the deep waters of European life
and merely waiting for actual faces and landscapes to take up pre-
ordained roles."[5]

The differences in the various development worker studies now circulating consist in the theories that inform our readings, and, of course—
and by no means insignificantly—the limitations of our own seeing. In
light of the reading I have brought to bear on understanding white bourgeois feminine subjectivity and the desire for development, what can be
understood now that was not (as) apparent before my research was undertaken?

First, the importance of post-colonial studies in theorizing whiteness is patent. The presence and effects of key colonial continuities in
the operation of Northern discourse, mediating between subjects and
the social, are constitutive of the narratives of always-unfinished, white
bourgeois subjectivities. Participants' accounts of our development
worker experiences attest to these discursive colonial legacies through
their effects, which shape our understandings, more than through direct

references made in so many words. It is apparent that we take up our subject positions in terms of some of these very continuities.

When Northern involvement in other people's development is considered in these ways, the persistent gap between, on one hand, Northern theoretical concerns about getting development approaches right and doing "real development," noted by critics such as J. Ferguson, and on the other hand, African insistence on the imperative to define and control development processes, becomes more comprehensible.[6] The development enterprise, seen in this light, appears to be of constitutive importance for white Northern subjects, securing for us key aspects of what colonial relations accomplished for our predecessors; thus, the development enterprise is not only produced through imperial relations, but is necessary to their operation. Uncovered here is a macro-level dimension of Northern desire for development, which is also operative in the experiences of individual development workers.

Where colonial discourse could in good conscience enlist racialized perspectives in support of the need for a "civilizing mission," indeed for the colonial project itself, today Northern involvement in the development enterprise is supposedly free of such thinking—as presumably are white bourgeois subjects, especially those who engage in development work. Yet, racialized assumptions continue to underwrite the discursive constructions of the space of the "Third World," notions of the North as more advanced, and so on, and as such inhabit the very concept of development as seen from the North. Although the participants in this study showed virtually no knowledge of development theory as such, we demonstrated the effects of racialized Northern discourse in our silent weaving of these same racialized suppositions into our altruistic motivations for becoming development workers and into our efforts to establish relations with Others. We also exhibited a repugnance toward racism that reveals the risks of acknowledging our own complicity beyond certain points, the latter being the boundaries secured by our "containment strategies."

One consequence is what I would call the "paradox of the Other": that is, our ongoing justifications to ourselves for our presence "there" are contingent on repeated assertions of racialized difference or Othering that cannot be acknowledged as such in our *rapport à soi* because we are not supposed to engage in the process of Othering. We want some African people to be subjects with whom we can form equal relations, and yet simultaneously we require Africans to take the position of Other. This Other can be then construed, often through putative "cultural" limitations, as needing our presence in order to "improve" in some way, affirming directly what racialized discourse in the North persistently infers: the superiority of the white bourgeois subject who bears the knowledge that counts.

These subterranean effects befuddle participants' intentions to grant subjectivity and, ultimately, to effectively refuse our own dominant positionality in relations of power. At the same time, the necessity to think of ourselves as moral prohibits substantial reflection regarding how we are implicated in these issues, that is, by participating in enactments of domination to which race is central. We are crucially invested in *not* seeing ourselves in these terms because of our need to remain innocent in order to protect our own moral selves, and in order to continue to *make our selves*.

The possibilities of genuine resistance, by which I mean generating an alternative practice of development that would be viewed as such by *African peoples*, and more consistently and effectively refusing to enact domination in our interactions in the spaces of the Other—in short, rendering the development enterprise less of a white space—are constrained not only by what we understand as domination and racism, but also by the powerful production of our investments in what we do and do not want to see. The likelihood of our engagement in a politics of accountability is accordingly diminished. For as Narayan says, "good will is not enough."[7] Nor, I would add, are critiques framed within the discourse of doing good or "helping" likely to be very penetrating. In order to actualize and support an alternative development practice and to more usefully negotiate the shifting nexus of power relations inhering in our subject positions as white women development workers, we need the conceptual means to more clearly situate ourselves as global subjects, that is, as subjects in positions of dominance not only worldwide, but within Canada as well. Entailed here is an understanding of the development enterprise in relation to the historical and ongoing operation of imperial relations, but also—and of equal importance—a comprehension of how our desire for development is produced through continuing processes of white bourgeois Canadian identity formation, in which the work of discourse plays a key educative role. Although contributing to an understanding of Northern/Canadian macro-level investments in development, it is the relationship between identity and desire for development that this book more clearly elucidates.

What Does All This Imply?

What is illuminated here is not confined to our interactions in the spaces of the Other; for in Canada, too, bourgeois subjects are located in corresponding, although perhaps less clearly pronounced, positions in relations of power vis-à-vis non-white and First Nations peoples. This positionality, which is in constant flux and in which the ongoing effects of gender subordination strike a discordant note for white middle-class women (who aspire to a fuller bourgeois subjectivity), also has a global dimension, so that when we travel elsewhere, we continue to be privileged. The analysis offered here illuminates the need for white bourgeois subjects, especially women, to consider our investments in innocence in relation to the making of our selves, or, put more bluntly, in not seeing our participation in domination. This particularly pertains to our decisions to go overseas as development workers, but equally encompasses our positions here in Canada and in relation to the rest of the world. This study also, importantly, attests to the possibility of moving toward a politics of accountability.

It may seem surprising, in light of the foregoing, and particularly in view of the synthesis of African development critiques briefly presented here, that I do not propose that we should *all* stay home and desist from international links. I make this statement with reluctance, because I do accept the concerns of African development writers, as I understand them. At the same time, however, I am well aware that the Northern-regulated development machine, with its subtly constitutive effects for bourgeois subjectivity, grinds on whether or not we participate in it. Accepting the presence of Northern volunteers, interns, and experts is almost *de rigueur* for African NGOs, whose personnel are, it seems to me, well aware of the positive funding implications of such "co-operation" and adept at negotiating our presence in their organizations. It must be acknowledged, too, that some—perhaps many—Northern development workers do make constructive contributions. Moreover, our remaining aloof within Canada does not safeguard us from responsibility for who we are in global relations of power and in the history of our own country, or change the nature of the development enterprise. Indeed, I would contend that the development worker is, in many ways, a metaphor for the positionality of white bourgeois subjects worldwide.

I am *not* suggesting, though, that Northern bourgeois women (and men) should embrace development work and other initiatives in the spaces of the South as we have been doing up to now. At the very least, the extent of our physical presence overseas bears substantial reduction, and, as the study shows, much personal work is needed in order for us to develop a politics of accountability prior to any such engagement. Key aspects of what such work might entail can be identified from this book: a historical awareness of the origins of current global and national (that is, within Canada) relations of power; an understanding of African and other Southern critiques of development/Northern interventions; a comprehension of the structuring of subject positions, such as Canadian, white, woman, and development worker, through the discursive and material operation of interlocking systems of oppression; and, most importantly, recognition of our own complicity and investments in perpetuating processes of domination. This is in one sense a broad approach to an anti-racist or anti-oppression pedagogy.

As has been demonstrated, race is crucially implied in Northern notions of development itself, in the dominance of white bourgeois subjects globally, in the production and behaviour of Northern, and particularly Canadian, development workers, and in how we understand and negotiate our positions in relations of power in "developing countries." Yet racism itself cannot be either easily acknowledged or identified by white women/bourgeois subjects, not only because of our need to appear innocent, but because race operates in collusion with other systems of oppression, is normalized in Northern discourse, and thus silently informs our discursive repertoires. Consequently, addressing "racism in development work" in a head-on fashion may become the pursuit of both the violent and the elusive: violent, because of the brutality displayed in examples that are glaring enough to *not* be denied as racist by the dominant group; and elusive, because of the ephemeral discernibility—to the dominant group—of the operation of racism in ways "routinely created and reinforced through everyday practice."[8] Because race inevitably infiltrates the heart of the making, and potential unmaking, of moral bourgeois subjects, and by extension our participation in the development enterprise and our desire for development, the acknowledgement of racism in development work is a contentious matter for practitioners. As such, racism is an issue that has challenged personnel in a number of Canadian development NGOs who have been striving to come to grips with it as something that can be addressed through policy and awareness training. This book has much to offer such anti-racism initiatives.

The research makes clear the fundamental investment of white bourgeois subjects in maintaining our stories of innocence, or of not seeing our participation in domination: namely, the need to prevent the potential shattering of moral narratives of self. This seems to have particular ramifications for white women, due to our internalized onus to be "good" as a way of performing appropriate bourgeois femininity. Therefore, educators and others undertaking anti-racism/anti-oppression work with students, interns, and so on, or individuals acting out of their own personal commitment, can anticipate encounters with self-saving containment and anti-conquest strategies on the part of white female subjects in response to exposure to the learning areas outlined above. Being able to theorize in advance the reasons for such opposition moves, though, should serve to strengthen anti-racist pedagogical approaches. The analysis of the research reveals that substantial breaching of these moves can produce moments of rupture in which white women begin to experience a dissolution of unifying narratives of a moral self. This is what anti-racist educators actually need to work toward, and recognizing such moments for what they are, allow them to happen, rather than attempt to "manage" the discomfort of bourgeois subjects, or otherwise rescue them. This point is of utmost importance to anti-racism pedagogy, for in such moments a profound and perturbing new awareness is being internalized regarding complicity in perpetuating and personally perpetrating racialized dominance. To short-circuit this process is to interrupt the possibility of comprehending the violence of the dominance whiteness enables. To foreclose this is, in turn, to undermine the prospects of bourgeois subjects' refusing whiteness, and attaining greater accountability for our positions in power relations. Just as importantly, this book cautions educators not to expect once-and-for-all transformations of white subjects into accountable allies, and makes clear the long-term and never-complete nature of anti-oppression work. It is likely, for example, that short workshops can at best only open up a degree of uncertainty in the minds of some participants.

For white women seeking to refuse our participation in domination, this research also gives invaluable indicators. Our self-confidence is a sign that we are positioning ourselves as dominant; whereas when we feel fragmented in anti-oppression learning about relations across differences, this is as it should be. It seems we cannot attain a place of increased accountability without such self-disintegrating reworkings of our moral narratives. Another cue that we are retreating to dominance is a feeling of innocence, or of not being implicated in the operation of systems of oppression apart from gender subordination. Similarly, the heroic response is one that we should consider suspect. When we feel compelled to "help" by rushing to the rescue of a situation or persons, espe-cially—but not only—Others elsewhere, we need to ask ourselves to what extent colonial legacies of racialized relations of comparison, planetary consciousness, obligation, and entitlement are at play, compounded by our internalized socialization as good women. Forgetting our history as white subjects is key to absolving ourselves of responsibility for who we are in the world, since accountability for the ways in which we are impli-cated in perpetuating relations of power cannot be attained in an ahis-toric fashion. Lastly, it is apparent from the narratives of the participants that, to state what may appear to be the obvious, an accountable bour-geois subject *can* be called to account, which means she (or he) seriously, if painfully, engages with critiques offered by the Other. In these and other respects the research offers a kind of gendered road map to decon-structing whiteness and moving toward a *more moral* position of account-ability. I use the term "more moral" in view of the fraught meanings and effects of claims to morality that are revealed in this study. Never-theless, continually working toward a position of accountability is, ulti-mately, the way in which bourgeois women like myself can aspire to morality.

The research here demonstrates that white bourgeois feminine sub-jects need to both pursue the quest for a moral narrative of self and limit the extent to which this narrative can be unsettled in a given moment. Serious challenges to our deeply held innocence can there-fore be expected to be met with initial hostility. The longer-term effects of such challenges may nevertheless be profound, as witnessed by some participants' enduring struggles, sometimes years later, with uncertain-ties that first surfaced in the development context. In such struggles I see cautious hope for change: in ourselves as white bourgeois subjects, our ways of engaging in international links and relating to Others, and our willingness and ability to be held accountable for who we are within our nation and the world.

I began this work by identifying that Canadian women development workers like myself are invested in not seeing our participation in dom-ination. I hoped that moving away from a preconceived conclusion, and asking how we negotiate and understand our positions in relations of power in "developing countries," would enable me to think more posi-tively about our investments. I also wanted to explore how we resist being implicated in enacting dominance. As I look back over the years it has taken to conceive, carry out, and write this book, it seems to me that my conceptualization has indeed changed, although not quite in ways I would have anticipated. Although it is valid to say that white Canadian women development workers are invested in not seeing our participation in domination, now it seems to me more useful to consider our investments in innocence in relation to the making of our selves. Inferred here is the need to safeguard moral narratives of the self, which are so crucial to our endeavours to resist acting from dominance. Therefore, with a more measured perspective I conclude that, for white middle-class Canadian women who undertake development work, the crux of our power relations dilemmas is as follows:

Whatever else it may mean, development work is also, deeply, about the making of white bourgeois subjectivities at home and abroad. For women like myself, the development context can be a space where we actualize a fullness of subjectivity that we take to be who we truly are, for this is the self we are produced to want to be. Herein lies a deeper meaning of what Keating and her film refer to as a "life-changing" experience, an experience that eclipses its effects on the very Other whose "need" we long to assuage and whose friendship we seek. Consequently, in the end, our desire for development, while a manifestation of the helping imperative, can be more accurately understood as a profound desire for self. And it is this, as much as the ways in which we are discursively produced as white middle-class women to understand the sites of development, that shapes our seeing, our negotiations, and our resistance to our positions in relations of power once we are "there." We need to understand this if we want to become more accountable, and, thus, find for ourselves a "place of integrity" in this world.

NOTES

Chapter 1

1 Lulu Keating, *The Midday Sun*, Don Haig, producer (Canada: Missing Piece Productions, 1989), Women's Television Network, Toronto, 30 September 1995 [film]. The term "development worker" is used here to reference Canadians and other Northerners who, under the auspices of Canadian non-governmental organizations, do development work on long-term (that is, two years or more) contracts overseas in "developing countries," regardless of what titles, such as "volunteer" or "cooperant," are attached to this work.

2 Goudge, in her critique of international development work as played out in Nicaragua over a period of ten years, refers to this Northern-centric emphasis as "narcissism," which she notes as a potent force in North–South relations. Currently, for example, the Canadian government's Youth Employment Strategy's international placements, including ones in "developing countries," are justified as providing skills and work experiences for *Canadians*. Thus, this perspective may take on slightly different variations, but the essential point remains the same. Paulette Goudge, *The Whiteness of Power: Racism in Third World Development and Aid* (London: Lawrence and Wishart, 2003), 138.

3 "Developing countries" is employed throughout this book to encompass the countries of Africa, Latin America, the Caribbean, and Asia, in short, the former colonies. These countries are also collectively referred to as the "Third World" or the South, as opposed to the "First World"/North/West, which includes Europe, North America, Australia, and New Zealand. Although my interchangeable use of these several terms obliterates the very real distinctions between them, I do so on account of their apparent equivalency in Northern discourse. Usually, however, I refer to North and South, recognizing that these binarily related terms have a regrettable homogenizing, even essentializing, effect. Nevertheless, despite these pitfalls, North and South signal discursive as well as material relations of power that are important to acknowledge.

4 Jan Nederveen Pieterse, *White on Black: Images of Africa and Blacks in Western Popular Culture* (New Haven: Yale University Press, 1992), 235.

5 Hannah Longreen, "The Development Gaze: Visual Representation of Development in Information Material from Danida," in *Encounter Images in the Meetings between Africa and Europe*, ed. Mai Palmberg, 221–32 (Uppsala: The Nordic Africa Institute, 2001).

6 Through such discursive processes difference is repeatedly asserted, and boundaries between the unmarked norm and that which is different or Other are actively maintained. Lawrence Cahoone, "Introduction," in *From Modernism to Postmodernism: An Anthology*, ed. Lawrence Cahoone, 1–23 (Oxford: Blackwell, 1996).

7 Ibid.

8 Edward Said, *Orientalism* (New York: Pantheon, 1978).

9 Mary Louise Pratt, *Imperial Eyes: Travel Writing and Transculturation* (London: Routledge, 1992); David Theo Goldberg, *Racist Culture: Philosophy and the Politics of Meaning* (Oxford: Blackwell, 1993).

10 Casey Blanton, *Travel Writing: The Self and the World* (New York: Simon and Shuster Macmillan, 1997).

11 Caren Kaplan, *Questions of Travel: Postmodern Discourses of Displacement* (Durham and London: Duke University Press, 1996).

12 Inderpal Grewal, *Home and Harem: Nation, Gender, Empire and the Cultures of Travel* (Durham: Duke University Press, 1996), 1.

13 Said, *Orientalism*.

14 Ibid., 26. It should be noted that this discursive framing of the "Orient" is gendered. Yegenoglu makes the point that the veil is also a fundamental feature of Orientalist discourse, symbolizing the "veiled, disguised and deceptive" nature of the "Orient." Meyda Yegenoglu, *Colonial Fantasies: Towards a Feminist Reading of Orientalism* (Cambridge, MA: Cambridge University Press, 1998), 48.

15 Pieterse, *White on Black*.

16 Marxist theorist Antonio Gramsci also discusses this concept in terms of "alternative" and "oppositional" cultures in his discussion of the subaltern, which Gayatri Spivak draws on in her landmark 1988 essay "Can the Subaltern Speak?" in which she largely initiates post-colonial theory's use of "subaltern." Homi Bhabha derives his working definition of subaltern groups from Gramsci as well: "oppressed, minority groups whose presence was crucial to the self-definition of the majority group." Homi Bhabha, "Unpacking My Library ... Again," in *The Post-Colonial Question: Common Skies, Divided Horizons* (London: Routledge, 1996), 210.

17 Ghassan Hage, *White Nation: Fantasies of White Supremacy in a Multicultural Society* (Annandale, NSW, Australia: Pluto Press, 1998), 17.

18 Teun van Dijk, *Elite Discourse and Racism* (Newbury Park, CA: Sage, 1993).

19 Sherene H. Razack, *Dark Threats and White Knights: The Somalia Affair, Peacekeeping, and the New Imperialism* (Toronto: University of Toronto Press, 2004), 9.

20 Stephen Lewis, "New Hope for Africa," *Globe and Mail*, May 25, 2000, A15 (emphasis mine).

21 Hard data on the demographics of just who goes overseas are scarce, being kept on an organization-by-organization basis and rarely attending to race. However, the accounts of seventeen former development workers whom I interviewed for a recent study, and who had been overseas under the auspices of six different NGOs, affirmed this gender/race pattern. I make these assertions, moreover, both from my overseas experience and from my more recent years of facilitating pre-departure preparation workshops for development work candidates with

one of Canada's premier volunteer-sending organizations, which does keep records specifying gender. This agency's statistics show that through the 1990s, approximately 60 per cent of its overseas volunteers were women (J. David, personal communication). Lewis's account likewise confirms a predominance of women among Northern "volunteers." From my own experience, this was not always the case. On the contrary, single women in particular rarely used to go overseas to do development work prior to the 1990s. On the home front, Bourke's 1993 study for the Ontario Council for International Cooperation (OCIC) attests to a clear racial composition. *Hold the Ridim,' Ride the Ridim'* showed an overwhelming white majority among the staff and boards of OCIC's then seventy development NGO member organizations. De Wolfe's earlier research on the gender demographics of such Canadian organizations revealed that in Canada the majority of staff in development NGOs are female, although when it comes to management males predominate. Eloise Bourke, *Hold the Ridim,' Ride the Ridim'* (Toronto: Ontario Council for International Cooperation, 1993); Alice de Wolfe, "Private Funding Programs: The Gendered Division of Labour in Charitable Development Assistance" (master's thesis, Department of Education, University of Toronto, 1988).

22 Pratt, *Imperial Eyes.*

23 Kalpana Seshadri-Crooks, *Desiring Whiteness: A Lacanian Analysis of Race* (London: Routledge, 2000); Robert J.C. Young, *Colonial Desire: Hybridity in Theory, Culture and Race* (New York: Routledge, 1995).

24 Foucault, quoted in Ranjana Khanna, *Dark Continents: Psychoanalysis and Colonialism* (Durham and London: Duke University Press, 2003), 33.

25 Bronwyn Davies, "The Concept of Agency: A Feminist Poststructuralist Analysis," *Journal of Social Analysis* 30 (1991): 42–53.

26 Barbara Heron, "Desire for Development: The Education of White Women as Development Workers" (PhD diss., Toronto: University of Toronto, 1999); Derek Gregory, *The Colonial Present: Afghanistan–Palestine–Iraq* (Oxford: Blackwell, 2004).

27 Bill Ashcroft, Gareth Griffiths, and Helen Tiffin, "Preface," in *The Post-Colonial Studies Reader*, ed. Bill Ashcroft, Gareth Griffiths, and Helen Tiffin (New York: Routledge, 1995), xv.

28 Said, *Orientalism.*

29 Alfred J. Lopez, "Introduction: Whiteness after Empire," in *Postcolonial Whiteness: A Critical Reader on Race and Empire*, ed. Alfred J. Lopez, 1–30 (Albany: State University of New York Press, 2005).

30 Goudge, *The Whiteness of Power.*

31 Ann Laura Stoler, *Race and the Education of Desire: Foucault's History of Sexuality and the Colonial Order of Things* (Durham and London: Duke University Press, 1995); Anne McClintock, *Imperial Leather: Race, Gender and Sexuality in the Colonial Contest* (New York: Routledge, 1995).

32 Lopez, "Introduction," 3.

33 Ibid., 5.

34 Alison Bailey and Jacquelyn Zita, "The Reproduction of Whiteness: Race and the Regulation of the Gendered Body," *Hypatia* 22, no. 2 (2007): 7–16.

35 Vron Ware and Les Back, *Out of Whiteness: Color, Politics, and Culture* (Chicago: University of Chicago Press, 2001); Vron Ware, *Beyond the Pale: White Women, Racism and History* (London: Verso, 1992); K.E. Supriya, "White Difference:

Cultural Constructions of White Identity," in *Whiteness: The Communication of Social Identity*, ed. Thomas K. Nakayama and Judith N. Martin, 129–48 (Thousand Oaks, CA: Sage, 1999); Kate Davy, "Outing Whiteness: A Feminist/Lesbian Project," *Theatre Journal* 47, no. 2 (1995): 189–206.

36 Marilyn Frye, *Willful Virgin: Essays in Feminism* (Freedom, CA: The Crossing Press, 1992).

37 Ibid., 142.

38 Ibid., 140.

39 Linda Martin Alcoff, "What Should White People Do?" *Hypatia* 13, no. 3 (1998): 24.

40 Noel Ignatiev, "How to Be a Race Traitor: Six Ways to Fight Being White," in *Critical White Studies: Looking Behind the Mirror*, ed. Richard Delgado and Jean Stefancic (Philadelphia: Temple University Press, 1997), 613.

41 Margaret Andersen, "Whitewashing Race: A Critical Perspective on Whiteness," in *White Out: The Continuing Significance of Racism*, ed. Ashley W. Doane and Eduardo Bonilla-Silva, 21–34 (New York: Routledge, 2003).

42 Henry A. Giroux, "White Squall: Resistance and the Pedagogy of Whiteness," *Cultural Studies* 11, no. 3 (1997): 376–89.

43 Andersen, "Whitewashing Race"; Ruth Frankenberg, "The Mirage of an Unmarked Whiteness," in *The Making and Unmaking of Whiteness*, ed. Brigit Brander Rasmussen, Eric Klinenberg, Irene J. Nexica, and Matt Wray, 72–96 (Durham and London: Duke University Press, 2001); Ann Bishop, *Becoming an Ally: Breaking the Cycle of Oppression* (Halifax: Firewood, 1994); Davies, "Concept of Agency," 42–53.

44 Michel Foucault, *The History of Sexuality: Volume 1: An Introduction*, trans. Robert Hurley (New York: Vintage Books, 1980), 98.

45 Davies, "Concept of Agency."

46 Kath Woodward, *Understanding Identity* (London: Arnold, 2002).

47 Foucault, *History of Sexuality*, 99.

48 Woodward, *Understanding Identity*.

49 Ruth Frankenberg, *White Women, Race Matters: The Social Construction of Whiteness* (Minneapolis: University of Minnesota Press, 1993), 148.

50 John Comaroff and Jean Comaroff, *Of Revelation and Revolution: Christianity, Colonialism, and Consciousness in South Africa, Volume 1* (Chicago: University of Chicago Press, 1991), 62.

51 Margaret Wetherell and Jonathan Potter, *Mapping the Language of Racism: Discourse and the Legitimation of Exploitation* (London: Harvester Wheatsheaf, 1992).

52 Camilla Stivers, "Reflections on the Role of Personal Narrative in Social Science," *Signs: Journal of Women in Culture and Society* 18, no. 2 (1993): 408–25.

53 Edward M. Bruner, *Culture on Tour: Ethnographies of Travel* (Chicago: University of Chicago Press, 2005).

54 Robert J.C. Young, *Postcolonialism: An Historical Introduction* (Oxford: Blackwell, 2001), 52–53.

55 Chandra Talpade Mohanty, "Under Western Eyes: Feminist Scholarship and Colonial Discourses," in *Third World Women and the Politics of Feminism*, ed. Chandra Talpade Mohanty, Ann Russo, and Lourdes Torres, 51–80 (Bloomington: Indiana University Press, 1991).

56 Arturo Escobar, "Imagining a Post-Development Era," in *Power of Development*, ed. Jonathan Crush, 211–27 (London: Routledge, 1995).

57 Ziauddin Sardar, "Development and the Locations of Eurocentrism," in *Critical Development Theory: Contributions to a New Paradigm*, ed. Ronaldo Munck and Denis O'Hearn (London: Zed Books, 1999), 44.

58 Arturo Escobar, "The Making and Unmaking of the Third World through Development," in *The Post-Development Reader*, ed. Majid Rahnema and Victoria Bawtree, 85–93 (London and New Jersey: Zed Books, 1997).

59 George J. Sefa Dei, "Towards an African View of Development," *Focus Africa* (November 1992–March 1993): 18.

60 Julius Nyerere, *Man and Development* (Dar-es-Salaam: Oxford University Press, 1974), 28 (emphasis mine).

61 This report was funded by CIDA (Canadian International Development Agency). As such, the study is not entirely free of Northern influence, although it appears that CIDA was concerned to keep at arm's length from the research and the resulting conclusions, which appear to be very much "owned" by AFREDA.

62 D.A.K. Muchunguzi and S.D. Milne, *Perspectives from the South: A Study on Partnership* (Dar-es-Salaam: AFREDA, 1995), 17.

63 Jane L. Parpart and Henry Veltmeyer, "The Development Project in Theory and Practice: A Review of Its Shifting Dynamics," *Canadian Journal of Development Studies* 25, no. 1 (2004): 39–59.

64 Majid Rahnema, "Towards Post-Development: Searching for Signposts, as New Language and New Paradigms," in *The Post-Development Reader*, ed. Majid Rahnema and Victoria Bawtree (London: Zed Books, 1997), 392.

65 Patience Elabor-Idemudia, "Participatory Research: A Tool in the Production of Knowledge in Development Discourse," in *Feminist Post-Development Thought: Rethinking Modernity, Post-Colonialism, and Representation*, ed. Kriemild Saunders, 227–42 (London: Zed Books, 2002); Marilyn Porter, "Introduction," in *Feminists Doing Development: A Practical Critique*, ed. Marilyn Porter and Ellen Judd, 1–14 (London: Zed Books, 1999).

66 Paul Wangoola, *Ten Steps Backward, a Great Leap Forward: A Call for a New African People's Resurgence* (an address on the occasion of the tenth anniversary of ORAP, Bulawayo, September 7, 1991), 4.

67 R.L. Stirrat, "Cultures of Consultancy," *Critique of Anthropology* 20, no. 1 (2000): 31–46.

68 Nancy E. Cook, "Stayin' Alive: The Constitution of Subjectivity among Western Women in Gilgit, Pakistan" (PhD diss., Toronto: York University, 2003).

69 Maria Eriksson Baaz, *The Paternalism of Partnership: A Postcolonial Reading of Identity in Development Aid* (London: Zed Books, 2005); Goudge, *Whiteness of Power*.

70 Uma Kothari, "Critiquing 'Race' and Racism in Development Discourse and Practice," *Progress in Development Studies* 6, no. 1 (2006): 1–7; S. White, "Thinking Race, Thinking Development," *Third World Quarterly* 23 (2002): 407–19; K. Simpson, "'Doing Development': The Gap Year, Volunteer-Tourists and a Popular Practice of Development," *Journal of International Development* 16 (2004): 681–92.

71 Nancy E. Cook, "What to Wear? Western Women and Imperialism in Gilgit, Pakistan," *Journal of Qualitative Sociology* 28, no. 4 (2005): 351–69; Nancy E. Cook, *Gender, Identity and Development in Pakistan* (London: Palgrave Macmillan, forthcoming).

72 Michael Watts, "Should They Be Committed? Motivating Volunteers in Phnom Penh, Cambodia," *Development in Practice* 12, no. 1 (2000): 59–70.

73 Deborah Mindry, "Nongovernmental Organizations, 'Grassroots,' and the Politics of Virtue," *Signs: Journal of Women in Culture and Society* 26, no. 4 (2001): 1187–311.

74 Louise H. Kidder, "Colonial Remnants: Assumptions of Privilege," in *Off White: Readings on Race, Power, and Society*, ed. Michelle Fine, Lois Weis, Linda C. Powell, and L. Mun Wong, 158–66 (New York: Routledge, 1997); Louise H. Kidder, "The Inadvertent Creation of a Neocolonial Culture," *International Journal of Intercultural Relations* 1, no. 1 (1997): 48–60.

75 Narda Razack, "Perils and Possibilities: Racism, Imperialism and Nationalism in International Social Work" (PhD diss., Adelaide, Australia: Flinders University, 2003); Barbara A. Parfitt, *Working across Cultures: A Study of Expatriate Nurses Working in Developing Countries in Primary Health Care* (Aldershot, UK: Ashgate, 1998); S. Razack, *Dark Threats*.

76 Heron, "Desire for Development."

77 Amina Mama, "Sheroes and Villains: Conceptualizing Colonial and Contemporary Violence against Women in Africa," in *Feminist Genealogies, Colonial Legacies, Democratic Futures*, ed. M. Jacqui Alexander and Chandra Talpade Mohanty (New York: Routledge, 1997), 47.

78 Kenneth Cameron, *Africa on Film* (New York: Continuum, 1994).

79 Baaz, *Paternalism of Partnership*.

80 Siba N. Grovogui, "Come to Africa: A Hermeneutic of Race in International Theory," *Alternatives* 26, no. 4 (2001): 425–48.

81 Young, *Postcolonialism*.

82 It is estimated that some 17 million people have died of AIDS in Africa, and another 25 million are HIV positive, of whom 1.9 million are children. Data, *The Issues: AIDS, Debt, Trade, Development Assistance*, 2005. Available: http://www.data.org/whyafrica.

83 The term "NGO" refers to a non-governmental organization. NGO is used here to encompass church-affiliated agencies as well as those not-for-profit organizations that are more usually called NGOs.

84 The same recruitment method was followed with both groups of interviewees, except that in respect to the initial group, a notice about the study was included in the Ontario Coalition for International Cooperation newsletter and I directly approached more development organizations. For the second group of interviewees I contacted mainstream development-worker sending organizations only because, in view of the smaller sample, I was seeking participants who would really be "typical" development workers. Potential interviewees were forwarded an "Invitation to Participate in a Study" that explained the research question and the selection criteria: middle-class white women who have been on long-term (two years of more) contracts in sub-Saharan Africa. If interested, they got in touch with me directly. With the more recent group I specified from the year 2000 onward, but accepted three participants who had returned that year. Interviews were done in person in a location of the participant's choosing, and were recorded for transcription later on.

85 Baaz, *Paternalism of Partnership*.

86 Despite one notable exception among the second group of interviewees, it can be fairly said that in general neither group of participants focused on the effects of the HIV/AIDS epidemic in Africa. This seemed particularly remarkable with those who had more recently been development workers. Perhaps the quality of

relationships with African peoples was a factor here, but it seems that the lack of awareness of the personal impact of HIV/AIDS in co-workers' lives, even in countries where prevalence rates are high, may be a reflection of the focus on ourselves/our selves that is evident in the Keating quote at the beginning of this book.

87 Among the original group of interviewees, whose stories are quoted from here, one-third were married at the time they were overseas, and of these, two families had young children. Three participants had had more than one overseas posting. The majority of participants were in their late twenties to early thirties at the time they went overseas. Two would have been in their early twenties, two were in their mid-thirties, and one was in her late fifties. One-third, or six, of the participants were teachers overseas, four were directors of Canadian NGO programs, and one person's posting was in relief work, that is, working with refugees. The others were in what might loosely be termed community placements, in positions such as Women-in-Development resource person, journalist, agricultural extension worker, and so on. One participant was a doctor. With one exception, everyone had at least one post-secondary degree prior to going overseas, and many had professional qualifications. Three participants had overseas stays of approximately eighteen months: two of these because of early termination of their original two-year contracts and one because that was the contract's length. All the other participants remained overseas as development workers for two to four years, with the exception of two, who stayed for eleven years.

88 Here I draw on Britzman, who states that "ethnography is the study of lived experience and hence examines how we come to construct and organize what has already been experienced." Deborah P. Britzman, *Practice Makes Practice: A Critical Study of Learning to Teach* (Albany: State University of New York Press, 1991), 9.

89 Ware and Back, *Out of Whiteness*, 8.

90 Ann Ferguson, "Resisting the Veil of Privilege: Building Bridge Identities as an Ethico-Politics of Global Feminism," in *Decentering the Center: Philosophy for a Multicultural, Postcolonial, and Feminist World*, ed. Uma Narayan and Sandra Harding (Bloomington: Indiana University Press, 2000), 189.

91. Goulet, for example, described "underdevelopment" in 1971 as follows: "Underdevelopment is shocking: the squalor, disease, unnecessary deaths, and hopelessness of it all!... The most empathetic observer can speak objectively about underdevelopment only after undergoing, personally or vicariously, the 'shock of underdevelopment.' This unique culture shock comes to one as he is initiated to the emotions which prevail in the 'culture of poverty' ... a sense of personal and societal impotence in the face of disease and death, of confusion and ignorance as one gropes to understand change, of servility toward men whose decisions govern the course of events, of hopelessness before hunger and natural catastrophe." Denis Goulet, *The Cruel Choice: A New Concept in the Theory of Development* (New York: Atheneum, 1971), 23; Denis Goulet and Charles K. Wilber, "The Human Dilemma of Development," in *The Political Economy of Development and Underdevelopment*, ed. Charles K. Wilber, 459–67 (New York: Random House, 1988).

92 Cook, "Stayin' Alive"; Baaz, *Paternalism of Partnership*.

93 Michael Edwards, "How Relevant Is Development Studies?" in *Beyond the Impasse: New Directions in Development Theory*, ed. F.J. Schuurman, 77–92 (London: Zed

Books, 1993); Caroline Moser, *Gender Planning and Development: Theory, Practice, and Training* (London: Routledge, 1993).

94 James Ferguson, *The Anti-Politics Machine: "Development," Depoliticization and Bureaucratic Power in Lesotho* (Minneapolis: University of Minnesota Press, 1990).

95 John T. Warren, *Performing Purity: Whiteness, Pedagogy, and the Reconstitution of Power* (New York: Peter Lang Publishing, 2003), 34.

96 Kamala Visweswaran, "Betrayal: An Analysis in Three Acts," in *Scattered Hegemonies: Postmodernity and Feminist Practices*, ed. I. Grewal and C. Kaplan, 90–109 (Minneapolis: University of Minnesota Press, 1994).

97 Frankenberg uses the term "discursive repertoires" to refer to "a set of discourses"; specifically, she states that white women "perceive our environments by means of a set of discourses on race, culture, and society whose history spans this century and, beyond it, the broader sweep of Western expansion and colonialism." Frankenberg, *White Women, Race Matters*, 2.

Chapter 2

1 Stoler, *Race and the Education of Desire*; McClintock, *Imperial Leather* (see chap. 1, n. 31).

2 Michel Beaud, *A History of Capitalism: 1500–2000*, trans. Tom Dickman and Anny Lefebvre (New York: Monthly Review Press, 2001).

3 Catherine Hall, *White, Male and Middle-Class: Explorations in Feminism and History* (New York: Routledge, 1992).

4 Peter Gay, *Schnitzler's Century: The Making of Middle-Class Culture, 1815–1914* (New York and London: W.W. Norton, 2002).

5 As Said notes, the "age of empire" is usually considered to have its formal beginning around 1878, with the "scramble for Africa." Hence Stoler's and McClintock's focus on the era of high empire. Edward Said, *Culture and Imperialism* (New York: Alfred A. Knopf, 1993).

6 Stoler, *Race and the Education of Desire*; McClintock, *Imperial Leather* (see chap. 1, n. 31).

7 Pratt, *Imperial Eyes* (see chap. 1, n. 9).

8 Ibid.

9 Ibid., 7.

10 C. McEwan, "Encounters with West African Women: Textual Representations of Difference by White Women Abroad," in *Writing Women and Space: Colonial and Postcolonial Geographies*, ed. A. Blunt and G. Rose, 73–100 (New York: The Guilford Press, 1994).

11 Woodward, *Understanding Identity* (see chap. 1, n. 46).

12 Said, *Culture and Imperialism*, 58.

13 McClintock, *Imperial Leather* (see chap. 1, n. 31).

14 Stoler, *Race and the Education of Desire*, 151 (see chap. 1, n. 31).

15 McClintock, *Imperial Leather*, 5 (see chap. 1, n. 31).

16 Stoler, *Race and the Education of Desire*, 30 (see chap. 1, n. 31).

17 Pieterse, *White on Black* (see chap. 1, n. 4).

18 Young, *Colonial Desire* (see chap. 1, n. 23).

19 Stoler, *Race and the Education of Desire*, 45–47 (see chap. 1, n. 31).

20 Stoler, *Race and the Education of Desire* (see chap. 1, n. 31).

21 McClintock, *Imperial Leather* (see chap. 1, n. 31).

22 Dorice Williams Elliott, *The Angel out of the House: Philanthropy and Gender in Nineteenth-Century England* (Charlottesville and London: University of Virginia Press, 2002).

23 McClintock, *Imperial Leather* (see chap. 1, n. 31).

24 Beaud, *A History of Capitalism.*

25 Stoler and Cooper's point is that the putative rigidity of "difference" underlying the supposedly fixed characteristics ascribed to the colonized Other was neither inherent nor stable; it revealed more about the imagination of the colonizer than the colonized. Ann Laura Stoler and Frederick Cooper, "Between Metropole and Colony: Rethinking a Research Agenda," in *Tensions of Empire: Colonial Cultures in a Bourgeois World*, ed. Ann Laura Stoler and Frederick Cooper, 1–56 (Berkeley: University of California Press, 1997).

26 McClintock, *Imperial Leather*, 62 (see chap. 1, n. 31).

27 Ibid., *Imperial Leather*, 15.

28 Stoler and Cooper, "Between Metropole and Colony," 34.

29 Himani Bannerji, Shahrzad Mojab, and Judith Whitehead, "Introduction," in *Of Property and Propriety: The Role of Gender and Class in Imperialism and Nationalism*, ed. Himani Bannerji, Shahrzad Mojab, and Judith Whitehead, 3–33 (Toronto: University of Toronto Press, 2001).

30 Stoler, *Race and the Education of Desire*; McClintock, *Imperial Leather* (see chap. 1, n. 31).

31 Davy, "Outing Whiteness" (see chap. 1. n. 35).

32 McClintock, *Imperial Leather*, 6 (see chap. 1, n. 31).

33 Stoler, *Race and the Education of Desire*, 135 (see chap. 1, n. 31).

34 Hall traces this recurring theme to the clash of church and aristocracy in medieval times: "The Church ... saw women as the creation of the Devil and as both inferior and evil.... The aristocracy, on the other hand, developed the counter-doctrine of the superiority of women.... This split between the wicked and the divine, the prostitute and the saint, represents an ideological split and projection by men which has recurred in many forms." Hall, *White, Male and Middle-Class*, 45.

35 McClintock, *Imperial Leather*, 30 (see chap. 1, n. 31).

36 McClintock, *Imperial Leather* (see chap. 1, n. 31).

37 Stoler, *Race and the Education of Desire*, 135 (see chap. 1, n. 31).

38 Richard Dyer, *White* (London: Routledge, 1997).

39 McClintock, *Imperial Leather*, 36 (see chap. 1, n. 31).

40 Hall, *White, Male and Middle-Class.*

41 Leonore Davidoff and Catherine Hall, *Family Fortunes: Men and Women of the English Middle Class, 1780–1850* (London: Hutchinson, 1987), 28.

42 Leonore Davidoff, *Worlds Between: Historical Perspectives on Gender and Class* (Cambridge: Polity Press, 1995); Clare Midgley, "Anti-slavery and the Roots of 'Imperial Feminism,'" in *Gender and Imperialism*, ed. Clare Midgley, 161–79 (Manchester: Manchester University Press, 1998); Antoinette Burton, *Burdens of History: British Feminists, Indian Women, and Imperial Culture, 1865–1915* (Chapel Hill: University of North Carolina Press, 1994).

43 Davidoff and Hall, *Family Fortunes.*

44 Ware, *Beyond the Pale* (see chap. 1, n. 35); Elliott, *The Angel out of the House.*

45 Kari Dehli, "They Rule by Sympathy: The Feminization of Pedagogy," *Canadian Journal of Sociology* 19, no. 3 (1994): 195–216.

46 Mariana Valverde, *The Age of Light, Soap, and Water: Moral Reform in English Canada, 1885–1925* (Toronto: McClelland and Stewart, 1991).

47 McClintock, *Imperial Leather* (see chap. 1, n. 31); Alison Blunt and Gillian Rose, "Introduction: Women's Colonial and Postcolonial Geographies," in *Writing Women and Space: Colonial and Postcolonial Geographies*, ed. Alison Blunt and Gillian Rose, 1–25 (New York: The Guilford Press, 1994); Toni Morrison, *Playing in the Dark: Whiteness and the Literary Imagination* (Cambridge: Harvard University Press, 1992); Ella Shohat, "Imaging Terra Incognita: The Disciplinary Gaze of Empire," *Cultural Dynamics* 2, no. 2 (1991): 41–70.

48 The trope of rape was invoked so as to manage rebellions during the Indian mutiny of 1857. Jenny Sharpe, *Allegories of Empire: The Figure of Woman in the Colonial Text* (Minneapolis: University of Minnesota Press, 1994).

49 Stoler, *Race and the Education of Desire* (see chap. 1, n. 31).

50 McEwan actually quotes this expression in relation to West Africa, but I propose that this epithet is applicable to white Northern perceptions of all of Africa, and many other parts of the world as well. McEwan, "Encounters with West African Women," 74.

51 Jane Haggis, "White Women and Colonialism: Towards a Non-recuperative History," in *Gender and Imperialism*, ed. Clare Midgley, 45–75 (Manchester: Manchester University Press, 1998).

52 Allan Greer, "The Queen Is a Whore," in *Rethinking Canada: The Promise of Women's History*, ed. Veronica Strong-Boag, Mona Gleason, and Adele Perry, 59–74 (Don Mills, ON: Oxford University Press, 2002).

53 Valverde, *The Age of Light, Soap, and Water*.

54 Dehli, "They Rule by Sympathy."

55 Rusty Bittermann, "Women and the Escheat Movement: The Politics of Everyday Life on Prince Edward Island," in *Rethinking Canada: The Promise of Women's History*, ed. Veronica Strong-Boag, Mona Gleason, and Adele Perry, 47–58 (Don Mills, ON: Oxford University Press, 2002).

56 Adele Perry, *On the Edge of Empire: Gender, Race, and the Making of British Columbia, 1849–1871* (Toronto: University of Toronto Press, 2001).

57 The Escheat Movement was a popular land claims movement by settlers against the Crown. Organizing efforts resulted in securing control of the Island House of Assembly in the late 1830s, although the land question was not resolved until 1875. Bittermann, "Women and the Escheat Movement."

58 Perry, *On the Edge of Empire*, 61.

59 Daniel Coleman, *White Civility: The Literary Project of English Canada* (Toronto: University of Toronto Press, 2006).

60 Mary Louise Fellows and Sherene Razack, "The Race to Innocence: Confronting Hierarchical Relations among Women," *Iowa Journal of Gender, Race and Justice* 1, no. 2 (1998): 344.

61 Here I am referencing Rabinow's commentary on Foucault. Rabinow suggests that this organization, one of the disciplinary technologies that preceded and enabled capitalism, requires a "specific enclosure of space" such as a factory or school. Paul Rabinow, "Introduction," in *The Foucault Reader*, ed. Paul Rabinow, 3–29 (New York: Pantheon Books, 1984), 16. I am proposing, however, as Goldberg also argues, that such an "enclosure" can, and is, achieved discursively through the use of terms in the North/South, "First World"/"Third World" binaries. Goldberg, *Racist Culture* (see chap. 1, n. 9).

62 Jane M. Jacobs, *The Edge of Empire: Postcolonialism and the City* (London: Routledge, 1996), 19.

63 Lott's work explores the function of blackface minstrelsy in white *working-class* self-definition as separate from, and superior to, Blacks in nineteenth-century America. As he points out in respect to "the affective origins of racist pleasure ... the scarifying vision of human regression implicit, for whites, in "blackness" was somewhat uneasily converted through laughter and humor into a beloved and reassuring fetish." Eric Lott, *Love and Theft: Blackface Minstrelsy and the American Working Class* (London: Oxford University Press, 1993), 142.

64 Leslie Roman, "Denying White Racial Privilege: Redemption Discourses and the Uses of Fantasy," in *Off White: Readings on Race, Power, and Society*, ed. Michelle Fine, Lois Weiss, Linda C. Powell, and L. Mun Wong (New York: Routledge, 1997), 275.

65 Roman, "Denying White Racial Privilege"; bell hooks, *Black Looks: Race and Representation* (Toronto: Between the Lines, 1992).

66 Dyer, *White*.

67 Goldberg, *Racist Culture* (see chap. 1, n. 9).

68 For example, Hage demonstrates how this operates in respect to white middle-class Australian women as national subjects. Hage, *White Nation* (see chap. 1, n. 17).

69 Britzman, *Practice Makes Practice* (see chap. 1, n. 88).

70 Kirsten Roger, "'Fairy Fictions': White Women as Helping Professionals" (PhD diss., Toronto: University of Toronto, 1998), 115.

71 Sharpe, *Allegories of Empire*; McEwan, "Encounters with West African Women."

72 Julie Stephens, "Feminist Fictions: A Critique of the Category 'Non-Western Woman' in Feminist Writings on India," in *Subaltern Studies 1–6*, ed. R. Guha (Delhi: Oxford University Press, 1986), 118.

73 Yegenoglu astutely argues that the question of sexuality cannot be considered apart from anything else, since sexuality shapes and pervades social relations. Yegenoglu, *Colonial Fantasies* (see chap. 1, n. 14). What meaning is attached to the sexuality is contingent on the fantasies and desires of the gazing subject, so that, for example, in the Middle East "Oriental" women have been positioned as objects of Western desire. In respect to Africa, Fanon's words still reverberate: "whoever says *rape* says *Negro*." Frantz Fanon, *Black Skin, White Masks* (New York: Grove Press, 1967), 166.

74 Lewis, "New Hope for Africa" (see chap. 1, n. 20).

75 Said, *Culture and Imperialism*; van Dijk, *Elite Discourse and Racism* (see chap. 1, n. 18); Sherene Razack, "Domestic Violence as Gender Persecution: Policing the Borders of Nation, Race, and Gender," *Canadian Journal of Women and the Law* 8 (1995): 45–88.

76 Goudge, *The Whiteness of Power* (see chap. 1, n. 2); Vincent Tucker, "The Myth of Development: A Critique of Eurocentric Discourse," in *Critical Development Theory: Contributions to a New Paradigm*, ed. Ronaldo Munck and Denis O'Hearn, 1–26 (London: Zed Books, 1999).

77 Sherene Razack, "Domestic Violence as Gender Persecution."

78 Here I am referring to the desire of individual Canadians to be involved in development work, rather than to Canada's foreign aid policy. As D. Morrison shows, there is a political-economic impetus underlying Canada's approach to aid, dating back to the history of the Cold War. Spending on the voluntary sector that utilizes development workers rose from a meagre 0.02 per cent of the ever-escalating ODA (Overseas Development Assistance) budget in 1955–56,

to approximately 0.4 per cent through the mid-1970s, and then rose to almost 10 per cent in the mid-1980s, where it remains. David Morrison, *Aid and Ebb Tide: A History of CIDA and Canadian Development Assistance* (Waterloo: Wilfrid Laurier University Press in association with the North-South Institute/L'Institut Nord-Sud, 1998), 8. However, while this level of expenditure serves to explain the plenitude of opportunities for Canadians to participate in development work, it does not in and of itself elucidate why it is that we embrace these opportunities as we do. From modest beginnings in 1960, when Canadian Volunteers Overseas was founded at the University of Toronto, the idea of "volunteering" for development work spread immediately to other Canadian campuses, resulting in the creation of the Canadian University Service Overseas (now CUSO) in the following year. There are currently over a dozen Canadian volunteer-sending NGOs, and they have collectively sent some 65,000 Canadians to developing countries. Sean Kelly and Robert Case, *The Overseas Experience: A Passport to Improved Volunteerism (A Report on the Volunteering Patterns of Canadians Who Have Volunteered Abroad in the Development World)* (Ottawa: CUSO, 2006).

79 Frankenberg explains that "'epistemic violence' captures the idea that associated with West European colonial expansion is the production of modes of knowing that enabled and rationalized colonial domination from the standpoint of the West, and produced ways of conceiving "Other" societies and cultures whose legacies endure into the present." Frankenberg, *White Women, Race Matters*, 16 (see chap. 1, n. 49). I am using this term in respect to development's perpetuation of the process she identifies.

80 The racism inhabiting the assumption of "their" unchangeable culture is evocative of Sartre when he says: "On the other side of the ocean there was a race of less-than humans who, thanks to us, might reach our status a thousand years hence" (quoted in preface to Fanon). Fanon, *Black Skin, White Masks*, 26.

81 Rather than referring to the actual countries where participants were posted, which might inadvertently compromise their anonymity, the terms "Southern Africa," "Eastern Africa," "Central Africa," and "Western Africa" are used. These terms appear in brackets where the participant names the particular country: e.g., [Southern Africa]. Similarly, people from that country would be referred to as [Southern Africans].

82 Hooks argues that in the "commodification of Otherness ... there is pleasure to be found in the acknowledgment and enjoyment of racial difference ... [and that] within commodity culture, ethnicity becomes spice, seasoning that can liven up the dull dish that is mainstream white culture." hooks, *Black Looks*, 21.

83 Goldberg, *Racist Culture*, 18 (see chap. 1, n. 9).

84 Visweswaran, "Betrayal" (see chap. 1, n. 96).

Chapter 3

1 Dyer, *White*, 24 (see chap. 2, n. 38).

2 Carol Schick, "Keeping the Ivory Tower White: Discourses of Racial Domination," in *Race, Space, and the Law: Unmapping a White Settler Society*, ed. Sherene H. Razack, 99–119 (Toronto: Between the Lines, 2002).

3 Gregory, *The Colonial Present* (see chap. 1, n. 26).

4 Hage, *White Nation* (see chap. 1, n. 17); Michel-Rolph Trouillot, "Anthropology and the Savage Slot: The Poetics and Politics of Otherness," in *Recapturing Anthro-*

pology: Working in the Present, ed. Richard G. Fox, 17–44 (Santa Fe, NM: School of American Research Press, 1991).

5 Robert D. Wilton, "The Constitution of Difference: Space and Psyche in Landscapes of Exclusion," *Geoforum* 29, no. 2 (1998): 173–85.

6 McClintock, *Imperial Leather* (see chap. 1, n. 31).

7 Wilton, "The Constitution of Difference."

8 Sherene H. Razack, *Looking White People in the Eye: Gender, Race, and Culture in Courtrooms and Classrooms* (Toronto: University of Toronto Press, 1998).

9 Achille Mbembe, *On the Postcolony* (Berkeley: University of California Press, 2001), 3.

10 Said, *Orientalism* (see chap. 1, n. 8).

11 Pieterse, *White on Black* (see chap. 1, n. 4).

12 Richard Phillips, *Mapping Men and Empire: A Geography of Adventure* (London: Routledge, 1997), 13.

13 Mike Featherstone, "Postmodernism and the Aestheticization of Everyday Life," in *Modernity and Identity*, ed. Scott Lash and Jonathan Friedman (Oxford: Blackwell, 1992), 284.

14 Goldberg, *Racist Culture* (see chap. 1, n. 9).

15 Peter Stallybrass and Allon White, *The Politics and Poetics of Transgression* (Ithaca: Cornell University Press, 1986), 8.

16 Mikhail Bakhtin, *Rabelais and His World*, trans. Helene Iswolsky (Bloomington: Indiana University Press, 1984), 10.

17 Stallybrass and White, *Politics and Poetics of Transgression*.

18 Ibid., 41.

19 Ibid., 201.

20 Edward Soja, "The Spatiality of Social Life: Towards a Transformative Retheorization," in *Social Relations and Spatial Structures*, ed. Derek Gregory and John Urry, 90–127 (London: Macmillan, 1985).

21 Ross Chambers, "The Unexamined," in *Whiteness: A Critical Reader*, ed. Mike Hill, 187–203 (New York: New York University Press, 1997).

22 Quoted in Leonore Davidoff, *Worlds Between*, 21 (emphasis in the original) (see chap. 2, n. 42).

23 Goudge, *The Whiteness of Power*, 189 (see chap. 1, n. 2).

24 Mikhail Bakhtin, *Problems of Dostoevsky's Poetics*, ed. and trans. Caryl Emerson (Minneapolis: University of Minnesota Press, 1984), 292.

25 There are supposedly three phases of culture shock: the euphoric honeymoon stage in which culture shock is incubating; a dissatisfied phase where there may be some difficult times and experiences of crisis in everyday life; and, lastly, the regaining of psychological balance, pleasure, and a sense of humour, at which point one becomes interested in belonging in the new environment. Carmen Guanipa, *Culture Shock*, 2002. Available: http://edweb.sdsu.edu/people/CGuanipa/cultshok.htm.

26 The implied "unreality" of the spaces of the "Other" is further underlined by the concomitant use of the term "reverse culture shock"—also known as "re-entry"—that tends to accompany the introduction of the concept of culture shock in predeparture preparation processes.

27 Chambers, "The Unexamined."

28 Julia Watson and Sidonie Smith, "Introduction: De/Colonization and the Politics of Discourse in Women's Autobiographical Practices," in *De/Colonizing the Subject:*

The Politics of Gender in Women's Autobiography, ed. Sidonie Smith and Julia Watson (Minneapolis: University of Minnesota Press, 1992), xvii.

29   Kaplan, *Questions of Travel* (see chap. 1, n. 11).

30   "Expatriate" is a designation that in this book includes other Northerners in a "developing" country. These could be development workers, bilateral aid personnel, and diplomats, as well as individuals working in the private sector. Participants sometimes differentiate between "expatriates" and development workers "like themselves," the distinction being based on personal motivation, the kind of organization an individual works for, and resulting income levels. An "expatriate" in this latter sense would not work for an NGO, and can be assumed to be comparatively highly paid. However, it seems to me that these differences are more apparent than real from the perspectives of African peoples, which is why I do not draw distinctions between categories of Northern or "expatriate" personnel.

31   hooks, *Black Looks* (see chap. 2, n. 65).

32   Grewal, *Home and Harem*, 6 (see chap. 1, n. 12).

33   My questions were not about amorous relationships or sexual experiences, but were framed more generally in terms of developing relationships with people "there." Only one participant per group of interviewees described the most important such relationship for her as a love affair. In light of the exceptional part that such relationships play in participants' narratives, love affairs with the Other are not held up for examination here.

34   Frankenberg, *White Women, Race Matters*, 156–57 (see chap. 1, n. 49).

35   Bakhtin, *Problems of Dostoevsky's Poetics*.

36   Bakhtin, *Rabelais and His World*, 10.

37   Roman, "Denying White Racial Privilege," 273 (see chap. 2, n. 64).

38   Said, *Culture and Imperialism* (see chap. 2, n. 5).

39   Pratt, *Imperial Eyes*, 7 (see chap. 1, n. 9).

40   Stoler and Cooper, "Between Metropole and Colony" (see chap. 2, n. 25).

41   Gender and Development (GAD) is an approach to development that recognizes the centrality of gender relations as a locus of social change. GAD followed after the Women and Development (WAD) approach, which focused on women as economic actors in their own right and their relationship to development. WAD, in turn, took over from Women in Development (WID), where the emphasis was on including women in development projects. Although each of these conceptualizations has had its ascendancy through the 1980s and 1990s, they continue to coexist to varying degrees in development work today. However, GAD remains predominant, which is not to say that there are no other conceptual approaches in use. Marilyn Porter, "Introduction" (see chap. 1, n. 55).

42   S. Razack, *Looking White People in the Eye*, 6.

43   This quite accurately echoes late-nineteenth-century "maternal feminism's" views of non-white men "who were seen as having an almost innate propensity to treat women badly." Midgley, "Anti-slavery and the Roots of 'Imperial Feminism,'" 165 (see chap. 2, n. 42).

44   Yegenoglu, *Colonial Fantasies* (see chap. 1, n. 14).

45   Pratt, *Imperial Eyes* (see chap. 1, n. 9).

46   Alice McIntyre, *Making Meaning of Whiteness: Exploring Racial Identity with White Teachers* (Albany: State University of New York Press, 1997), 45.

47   Michael Keith and Steve Pile, "Introduction Part 2: The Place of Politics," in *Place and the Politics of Identity*, ed. Michael Keith and Steve Pile, 22–40 (London: Routledge, 1993).

48 Homi Bhabha, "Of Mimicry and Men: The Ambivalence of Colonial Discourse," in *Tensions of Empire: Colonial Cultures in a Bourgeois World*, ed. Ann Laura Stoler and Frederick Cooper, 152–60 (Berkeley: University of California Press, 1997).

49 McIntyre, *Making Meaning of Whiteness*, 95.

50 S. Razack, *Looking White People in the Eye*.

51 Stallybrass and White borrow this term from Said, whom they quote as saying: "[Orientalism] depends for its strategy on [a] flexible *positional* superiority, which puts the Western in a whole series of possible relationships with the Orient without ever losing him the upper hand." Stallybrass and White, *Politics and Poetics of Transgression*, 5 (emphasis mine).

52 Stephens, "Feminist Fictions," 53 (see chap. 2, n. 72).

53 hooks, *Black Looks*, 26 (see chap. 2, n. 65).

Chapter 4

1 Stoler, *Race and the Education of Desire*; McClintock, *Imperial Leather* (see chap. 1, n. 31).

2 Hall, *White, Male and Middle-Class*, 1 (emphasis mine) (see chap. 2, n. 3).

3 Dyer, *White* (see chap. 2, n. 38).

4 Davy argues that white women are located on a continuum/world order between the poles of embodied savagery/degeneracy and disembodied enlightenment, the latter being reserved for white men. While a woman cannot attain to this end, she can move closer to it by virtue of being white, heterosexual, and middle-to-upper class. Davy, "Outing Whiteness" (see chap. 1, n. 35).

5 Sharpe, *Allegories of Empire*, 12 (see chap. 2, n. 48).

6 Grewal, *Home and Harem* (see chap. 1, n. 12).

7 McEwan, "Encounters with West African Women" (see chap. 2, n. 10).

8 Bakhtin, *Rabelais and His World*, 10 (see chap. 3, n. 16).

9 Paul Antze and Michael Lambek, "Introduction," in *Tense Past: Cultural Essays in Trauma and Memory*, ed. Paul Antze and Michael Lambek, xi–xxxviii (New York: Routledge, 1996).

10 Richard L. Ochberg, "Life Stories and Storied Lives," in *Exploring Identity and Gender: The Narrative Study of Lives*, ed. Amia Lieblich and Ruthellen Josselson (Thousand Oaks, CA: Sage, 1994), 143.

11 Albert Memmi, *The Colonizer and the Colonized* (Boston: Beacon Press, 1965), 2.

12 In contrast to such a conceptualization, this study follows Foucault's thinking on relations of power. Here is a more precise definition: "Power is not something that is acquired, seized, or shared, something that one holds on to or allows to slip away; power is exercised from innumerable points, in the interplay of nonegalitarian and mobile relations." Foucault, *History of Sexuality*, 94 (see chap. 1, n. 44).

13 Britzman, *Practice Makes Practice*, 5 (see chap. 1, n. 88).

14 Pratt, *Imperial Eyes*, 215 (see chap. 1, n. 9).

15 Said, *Culture and Imperialism*, xxviii (see chap. 2, n. 5).

16 Sharpe, *Allegories of Empire* (see chap. 2, n. 48).

17 One such circumstance has to do with personal safety. As Erica points out: "If I was a Black woman, I don't think I would have felt so safe in some of the situations that I was in." There are likewise narratives that suggest the opposite.

18 This is a term I use advisedly, since it harkens to the notion of power as something that one can "acquire." Nevertheless, empowerment seems to be the only

word that speaks to the effects of our shifting positions toward dominance in relations of power in the Southern development context.

19 Donna Haraway, *Simians, Cyborgs, and Women* (New York: Routledge, 1991).

20 Ochberg, "Life Stories and Storied Lives."

21 This Afrikaner term seems particular apt. A *laager* refers to the circling of wagons for protection in a temporary encampment. This is a symbol of the historical process of white (Afrikaner) settlement of South Africa, a technique repeated in the American "West" during the era of westward expansion in which wagon trains played a crucial role.

22 McEwan, "Encounters with West African Women" (see chap. 2, n. 10).

23 Davidoff, *Worlds Between*, 22 (see chap. 2, n. 42).

24 Hall, *White, Male and Middle-Class*, 1 (see chap. 2, n. 3).

25 Memmi, *The Colonizer and the Colonized.*

26 Seshadri-Crooks, *Desiring Whiteness*, 75 (see chap. 1, n. 23). This is different, as well, from Baaz's more limited conclusion. She suggests that, among her interviewees, perceptions circulate regarding the comparative superiority of Europe, which is evidenced by cultural stereotypes of backwardness on the part of Tanzanians and a general lack of technological advancement and consumer products. The impact on the identities of Northern development workers in Tanzania is that they are transformed into "omniscient being[s] able to provide advice on a wider range of issues" outside their development worker roles. Baaz, *The Paternalism of Partnership*, 111 (see chap. 1, n. 69).

27 Memmi, *The Colonizer and the Colonized*, 12.

28 Ochberg, "Life Stories and Storied Lives."

Chapter 5

1 Alastair Bonnett, "Constructions of Whiteness in European and American Anti-Racism," in *Race, Identity, and Citizenship: A Reader*, ed. Rodolfo C. Torres, Louis F. Miron, and Jonathan Xavier Inda, 201–18 (Malden, MA: Blackwell, 1999).

2 Alasdair MacIntyre, *A Short History of Ethics* (New York: Macmillan, 1966).

3 Rabinow explains: "Disciplinary technologies ... preceded capitalism. In Foucault's argument, they are among its preconditions. Without the availability of techniques for subjecting individuals to discipline, including the spatial arrangements necessary and appropriate to the task, the new demands of capitalism would have been stymied. In a parallel manner, without the fixation, control and rational distribution of populations built on a statistical knowledge of them, capitalism would have been impossible. The growth and spread of disciplinary mechanisms of knowledge and power preceded the growth of capitalism in both the logical and temporal sense. Although these technologies did not cause capitalism, they were the prerequisites for its success." Rabinow, "Introduction," 18 (see chap. 2, n. 61).

4 Kari Dehli, "Women and Early Kindergartens in North America: Uses and Limitations of Post-structuralism for Feminist History," *Curriculum Studies* 1, no. 1 (1993): 18.

5 Michel Foucault, "On the Genealogy of Ethics: An Overview of Work in Progress," in *The Foucault Reader*, ed. Paul Rabinow (New York: Pantheon Books, 1982), 352 (emphasis mine).

6 John Comaroff, "Images of Empire, Contests of Conscience: Models of Colonial Domination in South Africa," in *Tensions of Empire: Colonial Cultures in a Bourgeois*

World, ed. Ann Laura Stoler and Frederick Cooper (Berkeley: University of California Press, 1997), 170.

7 Goldberg, *Racist Culture* (see chap. 1, n. 9).

8 MacIntyre, *A Short History of Ethics*, 194.

9 Foucault, *History of Sexuality* (see chap. 1, n. 44).

10 Hall, *White, Male and Middle-Class* (see chap. 2, n. 3).

11 Hall, *White, Male and Middle-Class* (see chap. 2, n. 3); Lott, *Love and Theft* (see chap. 2, n. 63).

12 Goldberg, *Racist Culture*, 14 (see chap. 1, n. 9).

13 Susan E. Babbitt, "Moral Risk and Dark Waters," in *Racism and Philosophy*, ed. Susan E. Babbitt and Sue Campbell (Ithaca and London: Cornell University Press, 1999).

14 Kathleen Rockhill, "Home Cries," *Tessera* (1993): 41.

15 Jane Flax, "The End of Innocence," in *Feminists Theorize the Political*, ed. J. Butler and J. Scott (New York: Routledge, 1992), 447 (emphasis in the original).

16 Ann Laura Stoler, "Racial Histories and Their Regimes of Truth," in *Race Critical Theories*, ed. Philomena Essed and David Theo Goldberg, 169–391 (Malden, MA: Blackwell, 2002); Howard Winant, "White Racial Projects," in *The Making and Unmaking of Whiteness*, ed. Brigit Brander Rasmussen, Eric Klinenberg, Irene J. Nexica, and Matt Wray, 97–112 (Durham and London: Duke University Press, 2001).

17 Robert Miles, *Racism* (London: Routledge, 1989).

18 Himani Bannerji, *Thinking Through: Essays on Feminism, Marxism, and Anti-Racism* (Toronto: Women's Press, 1995).

19 Robert Jensen, *The Heart of Whiteness: Confronting Race, Racism, and White Privilege* (San Francisco: City Lights Books, 2005).

20 Goudge, *The Whiteness of Power*, 8 (see chap. 1, n. 2).

21 Roman, "Denying White Racial Privilege" (see chap. 2, n. 64).

22 Patti is referring to the lengths of patterned cloth that she describes being worn by many women in the West African town where she was a development worker. When she was living there, dressing in this fashion was one of Patti's adaptation strategies, and elsewhere in her interview she expresses the hope that her "wearing wrappers" was seen as respectful.

23 Chinua Achebe, *Things Fall Apart* (Greenwich, CT: Fawcett, 1959).

24 Carol's letter is reproduced here with her express permission.

25 Kris goes on to actually mention a number of people by name at this point; it is clear that she is primarily referring to African friends and colleagues.

26 Frye, *Willful Virgin*, 139–40 (see chap. 1, n. 36).

27 See note 25 above.

28 Bannerji, *Thinking Through*.

29 This is a limit that is reminiscent of Seshadri-Crooks's notion of suturing. Seshadri-Crooks, *Desiring Whiteness* (see chap. 1, n. 23).

30 Most participants in the second group of interviewees were not retrospectively troubled by questions about the rightness of their involvement in development work. I attribute this to the fact that most of these participants have been on more than one contract as a development worker and so have come to a place of affirmation about it. However, it must be noted that this view was not shared by everyone; indeed, one of the most critical analyses offered about development work comes from a participant in the second group. This person, however,

has reached a conclusion that would enable her to engage in work overseas in future on different terms (i.e., at her own expense).

31 Frankenberg, "The Mirage of an Unmarked Whiteness," 77 (see chap. 1, n. 43).

32 Razack, *Looking White People in the Eye*, 159 (see chap. 3, n. 8).

Chapter 6

1 Cook, "Stayin' Alive," 118–19 (see chap. 1, n. 68).

2 Ibid., 156.

3 Ibid., 188.

4 Baaz, *The Paternalism of Partnership* (see chap. 1, n. 69); Goudge, *The Whiteness of Power* (see chap. 1, n. 2).

5 Hugh Ridley, *Images of Imperial Rule* (London: Croom Helm, 1983), 5.

6 Ferguson, *The Anti-Politics Machine* (see chap. 1, n. 94).

7 Uma Narayan, "Working Together across Differences: Some Considerations of Emotions and Political Practice," *Hypatia* 3 (1988): 43.

8 Philomena Essed, *Understanding Everyday Racism: An Interdisciplinary Theory* (London: Sage, 1991), 2.

BIBLIOGRAPHY

Achebe, Chinua. *Things Fall Apart*. Greenwich, CT: Fawcett, 1959.

Alcoff, Linda Martin. "What Should White People Do?" *Hypatia* 13, no. 3 (1998): 6–26.

Andersen, Margaret. "Whitewashing Race: A Critical Perspective on Whiteness." In *White Out: The Continuing Significance of Racism*, edited by Ashley W. Doane and Eduardo Bonilla-Silva, 21–34. New York: Routledge, 2003.

Antze, Paul, and Michael Lambek. "Introduction." In *Tense Past: Cultural Essays in Trauma and Memory*, edited by Paul Antze and Michael Lambek, xi–xxxviii. New York: Routledge, 1996.

Ashcroft, Bill, Gareth Griffiths, and Helen Tiffin. "Preface." In *The Post-Colonial Studies Reader*, edited by Bill Ashcroft, Gareth Griffiths, and Helen Tiffin, xv–xvi. New York: Routledge, 1995.

Baaz, Maria Eriksson. *The Paternalism of Partnership: A Postcolonial Reading of Identity in Development Aid*. London: Zed Books, 2005.

Babbitt, Susan E. "Moral Risk and Dark Waters." In *Racism and Philosophy*, edited by Susan E. Babbitt and Sue Campbell. Ithaca and London: Cornell University Press, 1999.

Bailey, Alison, and Jacquelyn Zita. "The Reproduction of Whiteness: Race and the Regulation of the Gendered Body." *Hypatia* 22, no. 2 (2007): 7–16.

Bakhtin, Mikhail. *Problems of Dostoevsky's Poetics*. Edited and Translated by Caryl Emerson. Minneapolos: University of Minnesota Press, 1984.

———. *Rabelais and His World*. Translated by Helene Iswolsky. Bloomington: Indiana University Press, 1984.

Bannerji, Himani. *Thinking Through: Essays on Feminism, Marxism, and Anti-Racism*. Toronto: Women's Press, 1995.

———, Shahrzad Mojab, and Judith Whitehead. "Introduction." In *Of Property and Propriety: The Role of Gender and Class in Imperialism and Nationalism*, edited by Himani Bannerji, Shahrzad Mojab, and Judith Whitehead, 3–33. Toronto: University of Toronto Press, 2001.

Beaud, Michel. *A History of Capitalism: 1500–2000.* Translated By Tom Dickman and Anny Lefebvre. New York: Monthly Review Press, 2001.

Bhabha, Homi. "Of Mimicry and Men: The Ambivalence of Colonial Discourse." In *Tensions of Empire: Colonial Cultures in a Bourgeois World*, edited by Ann Laura Stoler and Frederick Cooper, 152–160. Berkeley: University of California Press, 1997.

———. "Unpacking My Library ... Again." In *The Post-Colonial Question: Common Skies, Divided Horizons*, edited by Iain Chambers and Lidia Curti, 210. London: Routledge, 1996.

Bittermann, Rusty. "Women and the Escheat Movement: The Politics of Everyday Life on Prince Edward Island." In *Rethinking Canada: The Promise of Women's History*, edited by Veronica Strong-Boag, Mona Gleason, and Adele Perry, 47–58. Don Mills, ON: Oxford University Press, 2002.

Bishop, Ann. *Becoming an Ally: Breaking the Cycle of Oppression.* Halifax: Firewood, 1994.

Blanton, Casey. *Travel Writing: The Self and the World.* New York: Simon & Schuster Macmillan, 1997.

Blunt, Alison, and Gillian Rose. "Introduction: Women's Colonial and Postcolonial Geographies." In *Writing Women and Space: Colonial and Postcolonial Geographies*, edited by Alison Blunt and Gillian Rose, 1–25. New York: Guilford Press, 1994.

Bonnett, Alastair. "Constructions of Whiteness in European and American Anti-Racism." In *Race, Identity, and Citizenship: A Reader*, edited by Rodolfo C. Torres, Louis F. Miron, and Jonathan Xavier Inda, 201–218. Malden, MA: Blackwell, 1999.

Bourke, Eloise. *Hold the Ridim,' Ride the Ridim.'* Toronto: Ontario Council for International Cooperation, 1993.

Britzman, Deborah P. *Practice Makes Practice: A Critical Study of Learning to Teach.* Albany: State University of New York Press, 1991.

Bruner, Edward M. *Culture on Tour: Ethnographies of Travel.* Chicago: University of Chicago Press, 2005.

Burton, Antoinette. *Burdens of History: British Feminists, Indian Women, and Imperial Culture, 1865–1915.* Chapel Hill: University of North Carolina Press, 1994.

Cahoone, Lawrence. "Introduction." In *From Modernism to Postmodernism: An Anthology*, edited by Lawrence Cahoone, 1–23. Oxford: Blackwell, 1996.

Cameron, Kenneth. *Africa on Film.* New York: Continuum, 1994.

Chambers, Ross. "The Unexamined." In *Whiteness: A Critical Reader*, edited by Mike Hill, 187–203. New York: New York University Press, 1997.

Coleman, Daniel. *White Civility: The Literary Project of English Canada.* Toronto: University of Toronto Press, 2006.

Comaroff, John. "Images of Empire, Contests of Conscience: Models of Colonial Domination in South Africa." In *Tensions of Empire: Colonial Cultures in a Bourgeois World*, edited by Ann Laura Stoler and Frederick Cooper, 163–197. Berkeley: University of California Press, 1997.

————, and Jean Comaroff. *Of Revelation and Revolution: Christianity, Colonialism, and Consciousness in South Africa, Vol. 1.* Chicago: University of Chicago Press, 1991.

Cook, Nancy E. *Gender, Identity and Development in Pakistan.* London: Palgrave Macmillan, forthcoming.

————. "Stayin' Alive: The Constitution of Subjectivity among Western Women in Gilgit, Pakistan." PhD diss. Toronto: York University, 2003.

————. *Gender, Identity and Development in Pakistan.* London: Palgrave Macmillan, forthcoming.

data. 2005. *The Issues: AIDS, Debt, Trade, Development Assistance.* Available: http://www.data.org/whyafrica.

Davidoff, Leonore. *Worlds Between: Historical Perspectives on Gender and Class.* Cambridge: Polity Press, 1995.

————, and Catherine Hall. *Family Fortunes: Men and Women of the English Middle Class, 1780–1850.* London: Hutchinson, 1987.

Davies, Bronwyn. "The Concept of Agency: A Feminist Poststructuralist Analysis." *Journal of Social Analysis* 30 (1991): 42–53.

Davy, Kate. "Outing Whiteness: A Feminist/Lesbian Project." *Theatre Journal* 47, no. 2 (1995): 189–206.

de Wolfe, Alice. "Private Funding Programs: The Gendered Division of Labour in Charitable Development Assistance." Master's thesis. Toronto: Department of Education, University of Toronto, 1988.

Dehli, Kari. "They Rule by Sympathy: The Feminization of Pedagogy." *Canadian Journal of Sociology* 19, no. 2 (1994): 195–216.

————. "Women and Early Kindergartens in North America: Uses and Limitations of Post-structuralism for Feminist History." *Curriculum Studies* 1, no. 1 (1993): 11–33.

Dei, George J. Sefa. "Towards an African View of Development." *Focus Africa* (Nov. 1992–March 1993): 17–19.

Dyer, Richard. *White.* London: Routledge, 1997.

Edwards, Michael. "How Relevant Is Development Studies?" In *Beyond the Impasse: New Directions in Development Theory*, edited by F.J. Schuurman , 77–92. London: Zed Books, 1993.

Elabor-Idemudia, Patience. "Participatory Research: A Tool in the Production of Knowledge in Development Discourse." In *Feminist Post-Development Thought: Rethinking Modernity, Post-Colonialism, and Representation*, edited by Kriemild Saunders, 227–242. London: Zed Books, 2002.

Elliott, Dorice Williams. *The Angel out of the House: Philanthropy and Gender in Nineteenth-Century England.* Charlottesville and London: University of Virginia Press, 2002.

Escobar, Arturo. "Imagining a Post-Development Era." In *Power of Development*, edited by Jonathan Crush, 211–227. London: Routledge, 1995.

————. "The Making and Unmaking of the Third World through Development." In *The Post-development Reader*, edited by Majid Rahnema and Victoria Bawtree, 85–93. London and New Jersey: Zed Books, 1997.

Essed, Philomena. *Understanding Everyday Racism: An Interdisciplinary Theory.* London: Sage Publications, 1991.

Fanon, Frantz. *Black Skin, White Masks.* New York: Grove Press, 1967.

Featherstone, Mike. "Postmodernism and the Aestheticization of Everyday Life." In *Modernity & Identity*, edited by Scott Lash and Jonathan Friedman, 265–290. Oxford: Blackwell, 1992.

Fellows, Mary Louise, and Sherene Razack. "The Race to Innocence: Confronting Hierarchical Relations among Women." *Iowa Journal of Gender, Race and Justice* 1, no. 2 (1998): 335–352.

Ferguson, Ann. "Resisting the Veil of Privilege: Building Bridge Identities as an Ethico-Politics of Global Feminism." In *Decentering the Center: Philosophy for a Multicultural, Postcolonial, and Feminist World*, edited by Uma Narayan and Sandra Harding, 189–207. Bloomington and Indiana: Indiana State University Press, 2000.

Ferguson, James. *The Anti-Politics Machine: "Development," Depoliticization and Bureaucratic Power in Lesotho.* Minneapolis: University of Minnesota Press, 1990.

Flax, Jane. "The End of Innocence." In *Feminists Theorize the Political*, edited by Judith Butler and Joan W. Scott, 445–463. New York: Routledge, 1992.

Foucault, Michel. "On the Genealogy of Ethics: An Overview of Work in Progress." In *The Foucault Reader*, edited by Paul Rabinow, 340–372. New York: Pantheon Books, 1982.

———. *The History of Sexuality: Volume 1: An Introduction.* Translated by Robert Hurley. New York: Vintage Books, 1980.

Frankenberg, Ruth. "The Mirage of an Unmarked Whiteness." In *The Making and Unmaking of Whiteness*, edited by Brigit Brander Rasmussen, Eric Klinenberg, Irene J. Nexica, and Matt Wray, 72–96. Durham & London: Duke University Press, 2001.

———. *White Women, Race Matters: The Social Construction of Whiteness.* Minneapolis: University of Minnesota, 1993.

Frye, Marilyn. *Willful Virgin: Essays in Feminism.* Freedom, CA: Crossing Press, 1992.

Gay, Peter. *Schnitzler's Century: The Making of Middle-Class Culture 1815–1914.* New York & London: W.W. Norton, 2002.

Giroux, Henry A. "White Squall: Resistance and the Pedagogy of Whiteness." *Cultural Studies* 11, no. 3 (1997): 376–389.

Goldberg, David Theo. *Racist Culture: Philosophy and the Politics of Meaning.* Cambridge: Blackwell, 1993.

Goudge, Paulette. *The Whiteness of Power: Racism in Third World Development and Aid.* London: Lawrence and Wishart, 2003.

Goulet, Denis. *The Cruel Choice: A New Concept in the Theory of Development.* New York: Atheneum, 1971.

———, and Charles K. Wilber. "The Human Dilemma of Development." In *The Political Economy of Development and Underdevelopment*, edited by Charles K. Wilber, 459–467. New York: Random House, 1988.

Greer, Allan. "The Queen Is a Whore." In *Rethinking Canada: The Promise of Women's History*, edited by Veronica Strong-Boag, Mona Gleason, and Adele Perry, 59–74. Don Mills, ON: Oxford University Press, 2002.

Gregory, Derek. *The Colonial Present: Afghanistan—Palestine—Iraq*. Oxford: Blackwell, 2004.

Grewal, Inderpal. *Home and Harem: Nation, Gender, Empire and the Cultures of Travel*. Durham: Duke University Press, 1996.

Grovogui, Siba N. "Come to Africa: A Hermeneutic of Race in International Theory." *Alternatives*, 26, no. 4 (2001): 425–448.

Guanipa, Carmen. *Culture Shock*, 2002. Available: http://edweb.sdsu.edu/people/CGuanipa/cultshok.htm.

Hage, Ghassan. *White Nation: Fantasies of White Supremacy in a Multicultural Society*. Annandale NSW, Australia: Pluto Press, 1998.

Haggis, Jane. "White Women and Colonialism: Towards a Non-recuperative History." In *Gender and Imperialism*, edited by Clare Midgley, 45–75. Manchester: Manchester University Press, 1998.

Hall, Catherine. *White, Male and Middle-Class: Explorations in Feminism and History*. New York: Routledge, 1992.

Haraway, Donna. *Simians, Cyborgs, and Women*. New York: Routledge, 1991.

Heron, Barbara. "Desire for Development: The Education of White Women as Development Workers." PhD diss. Toronto: University of Toronto, 1999.

hooks, bell. *Black Looks: Race and Representation*. Toronto: Between the Lines, 1992.

Ignatiev, Noel. "How to Be a Race Traitor: Six Ways to Fight Being White." In *Critical White Studies: Looking Behind the Mirror*, edited by Richard Delgado and Jean Stefancic, 613. Philadelphia: Temple University Press, 1997.

Jacobs, Jane M. *The Edge of Empire: Postcolonialism and the City*. London: Routledge, 1996.

Jensen, Robert. *The Heart of Whiteness: Confronting Race, Racism, and White Privilege*. San Francisco: City Lights Books, 2005.

Kaplan, Caren. *Questions of Travel: Postmodern Discourses of Displacement*. Durham and London: Duke University Press, 1996.

Keating, Lulu. *The Midday Sun*. Don Haig, Producer. Canada: Missing Piece Productions, 1989. Women's Television Network, Toronto, 30 September 1995. [Film].

Keith, Michael, and Steve Pile. "Introduction Part 2: The Place of Politics." In *Place and the Politics of Identity*, edited by Michael Keith and Steve Pile, 22–40. London: Routledge, 1993.

Kelly, Sean, and Robert Case. *The Overseas Experience: A Passport to Improved Volunteerism (A Report on the Volunteering Patterns of Canadians Who Have Volunteered Abroad in the Development World)*. Ottawa: CUSO, 2006.

Khanna, Ranjana. *Dark Continents: Pychoanalysis and Colonialism*. Durham and London: Duke University Press, 2003.

Kidder, Louise H. "Colonial Remnants: Assumptions of Privilege." In *Off White: Readings on Race, Power, and Society*, edited by Michelle Fine, Lois Weis, Linda C. Powell, and L. Mun Wong, 158–166. New York: Routledge, 1997.

————. "The Inadvertent Creation of a Neocolonial Culture: A Study of Western Sojourners in India." *International Journal of Intercultural Relations* 1, no. 1 (1977): 48–60.

Kothari, Uma. "Critiquing 'Race' and Racism in Development Discourse and Practice." *Progress in Development Studies* 6, no. 1 (2006): 1–7.

Lewis, Stephen. "New Hope for Africa." *Globe and Mail*, May 25, 2000, A15.

Longreen, Hannah. "The Development Gaze: Visual Representation of Development in Information Material from Danida." In *Encounter Images in the Meetings between Africa and Europe*, edited by Mai Palmberg, 221–232. Uppsala: Nordic Africa Institute, 2001.

Lopez, Alfred J. "Introduction: Whiteness after Empire." In *Postcolonial Whiteness: A Critical Reader on Race and Empire*, edited by Alfred J. Lopez, 1–30. Albany: State University of New York Press, 2005.

Lott, Eric. *Love and Theft: Blackface Minstrelsy and the American Working Class*. London: Oxford University Press, 1993.

MacIntyre, Alasdair. *A Short History of Ethics*. New York: Macmillan, 1966.

Mama, Amina. "Sheroes and Villains: Conceptualizing Colonial and Contemporary Violence against Women in Africa." In *Feminist Genealogies, Colonial Legacies, Democratic Futures*, edited by M. Jacqui Alexander and Chandra Talpade Mohanty, 46–62. New York: Routledge, 1997.

Mbembe, Achille. *On the Postcolony*. Berkeley: University of California Press, 2001.

McClintock, Anne. *Imperial Leather: Race, Gender and Sexuality in the Colonial Contest*. New York: Routledge, 1995.

McEwan, Cheryl. "Encounters with West African Women: Textual Representations of Difference by White Women Abroad." In *Writing Women and Space: Colonial and Postcolonial Geographies*, edited by Alison Blunt and Gillian Rose, 73–100. New York: Guilford Press, 1994.

McIntyre, Alice. *Making Meaning of Whiteness Exploring Racial Identity with White Teachers*. Albany: State University of New York Press, 1997.

Memmi, Albert. *The Colonizer and the Colonized*. Boston: Beacon Press, 1965.

Midgley, Clare. "Anti-slavery and the Roots of 'Imperial Feminism.'" In *Gender and Imperialism*, edited by Clare Midgley, 161–179. Manchester: Manchester University Press, 1998.

Miles, Robert. *Racism*. London: Routledge, 1989.

Mindry, Deborah. "Nongovernmental Organizations, 'Grassroots,' and the Politics of Virtue." *Signs: Journal of Women in Culture and Society* 26, no. 4 (2001): 1187–1311.

Mohanty, Chandra Talpade. "Under Western Eyes: Feminist Scholarship and Colonial Discourses." In *Third World Women and the Politics of Feminism*, edited by Chandra Talpade Mohanty, Ann Russo, and Lourdes Torres, 51–80. Bloomington: Indiana University Press, 1991.

Morrison, David. *Aid and Ebb Tide: A History of CIDA and Canadian Development Assistance*. Waterloo: Wilfrid Laurier University Press in association with the North-South Institute/L'Institut Nord-Sud, 1998.

Morrison, Toni. *Playing in the Dark: Whiteness and the Literary Imagination*. Cambridge, MA: Harvard University Press, 1992.

Moser, Caroline. *Gender Planning and Development: Theory, Practice, and Training*. London: Routledge, 1993.

Muchunguzi, Dennis A., and Scott D. Milne. *Perspectives from the South: A Study on Partnership*. Dar es Salaam: AFREDA, 1995.

Narayan, Uma. "Working Together across Differences: Some Considerations of Emotions and Political Practice." *Hypatia* 3 (1988): 32–47.

Nyerere, Julius. *Man and Development*. Dar-es-Salaam: Oxford University Press, 1974.

Ochberg, Richard L. "Life Stories and Storied Lives." In *Exploring Identity and Gender: The Narrative Study of Lives*, edited by Amia Lieblich and Ruthellen Josselson, 113–144. Thousand Oaks, CA: Sage, 1994.

Parfitt, Barbara A. *Working across Cultures: A Study of Expatriate Nurses Working in Developing Countries in Primary Health Care*. Aldershot, UK: Ashgate, 1998.

Parpart, Jane L., and Henry Veltmeyer. "The Development Project in Theory and Practice: A Review of Its Shifting Dynamics." *Canadian Journal of Development Studies* 25, no. 1 (2004): 39–59.

Perry, Adele. *On the Edge of Empire: Gender, Race, and the Making of British Columbia, 1849–1871*. Toronto: University of Toronto Press, 2001.

Phillips, Richard. *Mapping Men and Empire: A Geography of Adventure*. London: Routledge, 1997.

Pieterse, Jan Nederveen. *White on Black: Images of Africa and Blacks in Western Popular Culture*. New Haven, CT: Yale University Press, 1992.

Porter, Marilyn. "Introduction." In *Feminists Doing Development: A Practical Critique*, edited by Marilyn Porter and Ellen Judd, 1–14. London: Zed Books, 1999.

Pratt, Mary Louise. *Imperial Eyes: Travel Writing and Transculturation*. London: Routledge, 1992.

Rabinow, Paul. "Introduction." In *The Foucault Reader*, edited by Paul Rabinow, 3–29. New York: Pantheon Books, 1984.

Rahnema, Majid. "Towards Post-Development: Searching for Signposts, as New Language and New Paradigms." In *The Post-Development Reader*, edited by Majid Rahnema and Victoria Bawtree, 377–403. London: Zed Books, 1997.

Razack, Narda. "Perils and Possibilities: Racism, Imperialism and Nationalism in International Social Work." PhD diss. Adelaide, Australia: Flinders University, 2003.

Razack, Sherene H. *Dark Threats & White Knights: The Somalia Affair, Peacekeeping, and the New Imperialism*. Toronto: University of Toronto Press, 2004.

———. "Domestic Violence as Gender Persecution: Policing the Borders of Nation, Race, and Gender." *Canadian Journal of Women and the Law* 8 (1995): 45–88.

———. *Looking White People in the Eye: Gender, Race, and Culture in Courtrooms and Classrooms*. Toronto: University of Toronto Press, 1998.

Ridley, Hugh. *Images of Imperial Rule*. London: Croom Helm, 1983.

Rockhill, Kathleen. "Home Cries." *Tessera* (1993): 37–44.

Roger, Kirsten. "'Fairy Fictions': White Women as Helping Professionals." PhD diss. Toronto: University of Toronto, 1998.

Roman, Leslie. "Denying White Racial Privilege: Redemption Discourses and the Uses of Fantasy." In *Off White: Readings on Race, Power, and Society*, edited by Michelle Fine, Lois Weiss, Linda C. Powell, and L. Mun Wong, 270–282. New York: Routledge, 1997.

Said, Edward. *Culture and Imperialism*. New York: Alfred A. Knopf, 1993.

———. *Orientalism*. New York: Pantheon, 1978.

Sardar, Ziauddin. "Development and the Locations of Eurocentrism." In *Critical Development Theory: Contributions to a New Paradigm*, edited by Ronaldo Munck and Denis O'Hearn, 44–62. London: Zed Books, 1999.

Schick, Carol. "Keeping the Ivory Tower White: Discourses of Racial Domination." In *Race, Space, and the Law: Unmapping a White Settler Society*, edited by Sherene H. Razack, 99–119. Toronto: Between the Lines, 2002.

Seshadri-Crooks, Kalpana. *Desiring Whiteness: A Lacanian Analysis of Race*. London: Routledge, 2000.

Sharpe, Jenny. *Allegories of Empire: The Figure of Woman in the Colonial Text*. Minneapolis: University of Minnesota Press, 1994.

Shohat, Ella. "Imaging Terra Incognita: The Disciplinary Gaze of Empire." *Cultural Dynamics* 2, no. 2 (1991): 41–70.

Simpson, Kate. "'Doing Development': The Gap Year, Volunteer-Tourists and a Popular Practice of Development." *Journal of International Development* 16 (2004): 681–692.

Soja, Edward. "The Spatiality of Social Life: Towards a Transformative Retheorization." In *Social Relations and Spatial Structures*, edited by Derek Gregory and John Urry, 90–127. London: Macmillan, 1985.

Stallybrass, Peter, and Allon White. *The Politics and Poetics of Transgression*. Ithaca, NY: Cornell University Press, 1986.

Stephens, Julie. "Feminist Fictions: A Critique of the Category 'Non-Western Woman' in Feminist Writings on India." In *Subaltern Studies 1–6*, edited by Ranajit Guha, 92–125. Delhi: Oxford University Press, 1986.

Stirrat, R.L. "Cultures of Consultancy." *Critique of Anthropology* 20, no. 1 (2000): 31–46.

Stivers, Camilla. "Reflections on the Role of Personal Narrative in Social Science." *Signs: Journal of Women in Culture and Society* 18, no. 2 (1993): 408–425.

Stoler, Ann Laura. *Race and the Education of Desire: Foucault's History of Sexuality and the Colonial Order of Things*. Durham and London: Duke University Press, 1995.

———. "Racial Histories and Their Regimes of Truth." In *Race Critical Theories*, edited by Philomena Essed and David Theo Goldberg, 169–391. Malden, MA: Blackwell, 2002.

———, and Frederick Cooper. "Between Metropole and Colony: Rethinking a Research Agenda." In *Tensions of Empire: Colonial Cultures in a Bourgeois World*, edited by Ann Laura Stoler and Frederick Cooper, 1–56. Berkeley: University of California Press, 1997.

Supriya, K.E. "White Difference: Cultural Constructions of White Identity." In *Whiteness: The Communication of Social Identity*, edited by Thomas K. Nakayama and Judith N. Martin, 129–148. Thousand Oaks, CA: Sage, 1999.

Trouillot, Michel-Rolph. "Anthropology and the Savage Slot: The Poetics and Politics of Otherness." In *Recapturing Anthropology: Working in the Present*, edited by Richard G. Fox, 17–44. Santa Fe, NM: School of American Research Press, 1991.

Tucker, Vincent. "The Myth of Development: A Critique of Eurocentric Discourse." In *Critical Development Theory: Contributions to a New Paradigm*, edited by Ronaldo Munck and Denis O'Hearn, 1–26. London: Zed Books, 1999.

Valverde, Mariana. *The Age of Light, Soap, and Water: Moral Reform in English Canada, 1885–1925*. Toronto: McClelland & Stewart, 1991.

van Dijk, Teun. *Elite Discourse and Racism*. Newbury Park, CA: Sage, 1993.

Visweswaran, Kamala. "Betrayal: An Analysis in Three Acts." In *Scattered Hegemonies: Postmodernity and Feminist Practices*, edited by I. Grewal and C. Kaplan, 90–109. Minneapolis: University of Minnesota Press, 1994.

Wangoola, Paul. *Ten Steps Backward, a Great Leap Forward: A Call for a New African People's Resurgence*. An Address on the Occasion of the 10th Anniversary of ORAP, Bulawayo, 7 September 1991.

Ware, Vron. *Beyond the Pale: White Women, Racism and History*. London: Verso, 1992.

———, and Les Back. *Out of Whiteness: Color, Politics, and Culture*. Chicago: University of Chicago Press, 2001.

Warren, John T. *Performing Purity: Whiteness, Pedagogy, and the Reconstitution of Power*. New York: Peter Lang Publishing, 2003.

Watson, Julia, and Sidonie Smith. "Introduction: De/Colonization and the Politics of Discourse in Women's Autobiographical Practices." In *De/Colonizing the Subject: The Politics of Gender in Women's Autobiography*, edited by Sidonie Smith and Julia Watson, xiii–xxxi. Minneapolis: University of Minnesota Press, 1992.

Watts, Michael. "Should They Be Committed? Motivating Volunteers in Phnom Penh, Cambodia." *Development in Practice* 12, no. 1 (2000): 59–70.

Wetherell, Margaret, and Jonathan Potter. *Mapping the Language of Racism: Discourse and the Legitimation of Exploitation*. London: Harvester Wheatsheaf, 1992.

White, Sarah. "Thinking Race, Thinking Development." *Third World Quarterly* 23 (2002): 407–419.

Wilton, Robert D. "The Constitution of Difference: Space and Psyche in Landscapes of Exclusion." *Geoforum* 29, no. 2 (1998): 173–185.

Winant, Howard. "White Racial Projects." In *The Making and Unmaking of Whiteness*, edited by Brigit Brander Rasmussen, Eric Klinenberg, Irene J. Nexica, and Matt Wray, 97–112. Durham & London: Duke University Press, 2001.

Woodward, Kath. *Understanding Identity*. London: Arnold, 2002.

Yeats, William Butler. "The Second Coming." Stanza 1 [Poem]. 1921.

Yegenoglu, Meyda. *Colonial Fantasies: Towards a Feminist Reading of Orientalism.* Cambridge, MA: Cambridge University Press, 1998.

Young, Robert J.C. *Colonial Desire: Hybridity in Theory, Culture and Race.* New York: Routledge, 1995.

———. *Postcolonialism: An Historical Introduction.* Oxford: Blackwell, 2001.

INDEX

A

accountability of development workers, 101–2, 140–41, 144, 152–53. *See also* morality of development work; resistance

Achebe, Chinua, 135–36

affluence: discrepancies in, 86–87, 108; power relations and, 75–79, 94–95, 143

AFREDA (African Research, Education and Development Association), 13, 161n61

Africa: Canadian engagement with, 147 (*see also* Canada); as "dark continent," 56; media images of, 38–41 (*see also* media); role in Northern identity, 55–56. *See also* racialized domination; sub-Saharan Africa

AIDS. *See* HIV/AIDS

Alcoff, Linda Martin, 9–10

alternative development: in moral narrative, 111; myth of, 103–4, 128–29, 135, 138–40; seeking, 21, 127, 140–45, 151–56; as sustainable, 14. *See also* resistance

altruism: denial of, 46–48; racialized discourse and, 150; self-consciousness of, 40; with self-interest, 53–54; in view of development worker, 2, 43–45, 88, 157n2. *See also* selfishness

Andersen, Margaret, 10

anti-conquest strategies, 28, 44–45, 81, 154. *See also* containment strategies

anti-racism initiatives, 153

Arabs, 3–4

Ashcroft, Bill, 8

B

Baaz, Maria Eriksson, 14, 18–19, 149, 172n26

Back, Les, 19

Bakhtin, Mikhail, 58

Bannerji, Himani, 127

Bhabha, Homi, 30, 83, 158n16

Bishop, Ann, 10

Blanton, Casey, 3

bourgeois subjects: as entitled to intervene, 36–37, 43–45; formation of, 27–34, 37–38, 55–56, 156; formation of development workers and, 25; imperative for moral goodness in, 125–27, 140, 142, 144–45, 154; as raced, gendered, and superior, 28–29; as shifting positions, 91; use of term, 6, 10–11; women as, 35–36, 91–93, 152, 171n4; women as "honorary men," 112–15, 122. *See also* Other/Othering; women (white) in development work

Bourke, Eloise, 159n21